Quill on Willow

Quill on Willow: Cricket in Literature

Eric Midwinter MA, DPHIL, OBE

Aeneas

First Published 2001
By AENEAS Press

PO Box 200
Chichester PO18 0YX
West Sussex
United Kingdom.

Typeset in AGaramond

Printed and bound by MPG Books
Bodmin
Cornwall
United Kingdom.

ISBN: 1-902115-22-8

British Library Cataloguing in Publication Data.
A catalogue record of this book is available from the British Library
Midwinter, Eric.

CONTENTS

FOREWORD

The publication of a new book by Eric Midwinter is always a cause for celebration whether he is writing about cricket or a wider world beyond the boundary. His enthusiasm for his subject is immediately apparent. This distinguished historian brings many strengths to the matter in hand. Among them are a cogent lucidity, an academic's discipline, a fine command of the language and an engaging sense of humour. He wears his knowledge lightly, never becoming pompous, stuffy or self-important. A sureness of touch secures the reader's attention. His informed appreciation of cricket and cricketers, as well as of books and bookmen/women enables him to demonstrate authoritatively the links between sport and writing. There is no need for him to scrabble around, 'forcing' a spurious connexion where, in reality, none exists.

Dr Midwinter has always had an acute awareness of not only the physical environment of events but also the wider culture in which books are made and games are played. This is coupled with a deep understanding of the value of recreation and the context in which it is found. While maintaining a general overview, his focus is on the details of the particular. Both are rooted in his extensive reading of primary and secondary sources which, from Austen to Amis and from Meredith to Murdoch, is a cornucopia of talents many and varied.

As an aside, it is quite in character for him, when making use of the work (and works) of others, to give full credit to each such 'contributor' in the text itself. This proper professional courtesy is, unfortunately, not always observed by others in the field.

The author himself has an unusual talent, namely the capability of bringing back to life novelists and other writers who have long departed for the Elysian Fields. He does not pass over, however, some of the best of our own time.

Eric Midwinter has always informed and entertained the reader and in *Quill on Willow: Cricket in Literature . . .*, he continues to do so. He modestly describes this volume as "simply a series of essays touching on the subject of cricket and literative fiction." Of course, that is accurate, as far as it goes - but it needs to go further if it is to do him justice. While it may be said that each chapter is an island entire of itself and, therefore, may be enjoyed separately, together they are brought felicitously into a coherent, chronological, seamless whole. He writes with understanding. His perspective is made clear from the start: "cricket, like literature, has woven itself into the social fabric of English life."

The main intention is to demonstrate how famous Victorian novelists avail themselves of cricket in three distinct but complementary ways to enhance their general purpose: to point up characterisation; to strengthen the moral texture of the storyline with cricket as metaphor and/or symbol; as a device to move on the plot. He also finds time and space to glance at poetry, television, radio and the cinema.

Writing in what are troubled times for cricket (June 2001), when its reputation for integrity and sportsmanship has been sadly shaken by the savage body blow of corruption, it comes as a great relief to find here no examples of such chicanery.

The wise words of C L R James echo down the years: "What do they know of cricket who only cricket know?" Never, perhaps, have they been more appropriate than in the context of this study. There remain many, no doubt, who would insist that sport in general and cricket in particular has nothing to do with politics, but the opposite view is inescapable. The game does not exist in isolation. Cricket is a part of, not apart from, society and 'is played accordin.' The sport is influenced and affected by its contemporary setting. That context is constructed from, or, indeed created by such factors as morality, religion, education, economics, the arts. In other words, the physical, spiritual, intellectual environment *et al* create the climate for cricket.

All aspects of cricket (including how, when, where and between whom matches are contested) are affected, both directly by, say, the law of the land, and indirectly, as for example by matters of fashion. This fundamental truth is at the forefront of these relishable and enlightening essays: erudite at one moment; hilarious the next.

Although the tone is invariably affable, when there is plainly a need for straight-talking, trenchant comment is not avoided. The administration of professional cricket in this country is frankly addressed: "an over-constructive institution unhappily harried of late into panic-stricken synthetic and probably damaging repairs, the consequence, in part, of having left the problem too long without making more natural and organic reform."

On a lighter note, the links between Victorian full stops and long stops may be textual or 'relative', so to speak. Some of them are so large in physique and force of personality, that their frame down the years reverberates to such an extent that only their Christian names are required for them to be immediately identified: e.g. Alfred and Lionel. Others are not so firmly banged ino the memory of even the most enthusiastic of cricket devotees' memory. Go on - admit it - you did not know George Eliot had a nephew who played in a first-class match. A question about that fabulous fact should stop a few pub-quiz 'experts' in their tracks, up and down the land.

Authors create characters who loom large in the memory of those experiencing them. As a result of the author's craft, one of the many pleasures of reading is characters who live long in the memory of those encountering them. Anyone who doubts that the cold and redoubtable Mrs Proudie of *Barchester Towers* would have opened the batting for England had she been minded so to do must take the matter up with that lady in person. A word of warning: nominally the Bishop's wife, she is, in truth the bishop's Wife. In *Rachel Ray*, two curates are spoken of in withering terms: "but what are they? They go to cricket matches and among young women with bows and arrows." It would be an indelicate digression to explore the significance of the metaphorical use of these toxophilites. A brief (and necessarily, in the interests of good taste, incomplete) specialist vocabulary requires mention of shaft, quiver, inner, feathers. In any case, their interests are well served by the radio where they have somehow secured a daily advertisement for their practitioners.

There is a sense of fun here, important less we take our sport and ourselves far too seriously. Who was the 19th century storyteller moved to appreciate a friend's cricketing prowess in verse that could not be improved upon by the great William McGonagall himself?

> Great as a bowler, greater as a bat
> But at a 'short slip' greater yet than that.

Eric Midwinter rightly points out there are many different interpretations of the information the authors provide. The data stays the same but the response of each reader differs in as much as his/her understanding is shaped by the world of personal experience as much as is that of the authors.

Perhaps the final word, for the moment, anyway, should be those of the hero's driver in *The Adventure of Harry Richmond* (written by George Meredith and published in 1871). Cricket is a "fine, manly sport; it might kill a man but it never meant mischief: foreigners had a bit of an idea that it was the best game in the world."

Clive Porter
Editor; The Journal of the Cricket Society.

Chapter 1.

CRICKET IN LITERATURE

George Bernard Shaw took 26 first-class wickets for Glamorgan, but, if his obituary be trusted, 'he was not a batsman'. The hundreds, many of them American and Japanese, still hurrying to Shaw's Corner, his shrine at Ayot St.Lawrence in deepest Hertfordshire, may be surprised by these facts.

Yet they are true and, at the same time, untrue, in that this is, of course, an alternative GBS, a Welshman, born at Treharris in what was then Glamorgan, in 1931, who played sixteen times for the Welsh county between 1951 and 1956, and who, aged 52, was sadly killed in a car accident in South Australia in 1984. This is a coincidence, as much an accident as the intriguing truth that William Shakespeare played for Worcestershire, whereas many believed he had a cast-iron Warwickshire birth qualification. However, this was Wing-Commander William Harold Nelson Shakespeare, OBE, MC, AFC, President of Worcestershire County Cricket Club at the time of his death in 1976. He was 83, having been born in Worcester in 1893. He played 26 matches for the county of his birth in an intermittent pattern from 1919 to 1931, scoring, in toto, 789 runs; it is thought William Shakespeare 'would have been valuable if he could have played regularly.'

These two cases may be just a little more than accidents. In the depression years in South Wales, leftish and/or serious play-going parents may have found comfort in choosing for their new-born babe the names 'George Bernard' after the Fabian socialist and playwright, while the temptation to Christen a Shakespeare 'William' must be alluring, especially if one is resolved to add the names of two other Anglo-Saxon heroes, Harold and Nelson. On the same tack, it is difficult to believe that Mr and Mrs Widdowson, when naming their infant 'Sam Weller' in 1851, did not have in mind some reference to the droll original of that label in *The Pickwick Papers*, first published in 1836/37 but always popular thereafter. Sam Weller Widdowson played one match for Nottinghamshire in 1878, many matches as a centre forward for Notts Forest and one soccer match for England against Scotland in 1880, as well as being noted as a hurdler and sprinter.

These oddities do, at least, demonstrate the manner in which literature may be embedded in the normality of everyday existence. Cricket, like literature, has woven itself into the social fabric of English life. It is, then, hardly surprising to find these two great cultural elements, cricket and literature, meeting in mutual celebration and enforcement. Even the somewhat ascetic George Bernard Shaw was not free from such connections. Benny Green tells us that, in 1894, when attempting to underline the popular appeal of England's most well-known singer, a man called Santley, he wrote 'to the Briton with a turn for music he is just what Dr Grace is to the Briton with a turn for cricket.'

This is an attempt to discover some, by no means all, of those interstices. To do full justice to the place of cricket in literature would require a complete reading of all prose, verse and drama since the early 18th century, so frequently is the game mentioned. So this is advisedly a discrete selection. As Sam Weller, if not Sam Weller Widdowson, asked, 'vich wanity do you like the flavour on, sir?' The chief flavour tasted here is the novel, particularly the novel in the 19th and early 20th centuries when cricket was at its pinnacle as both pastime and cult. That said, there are cuts into the poetic field and glances at the theatre and the cinema, all the while seeking the linkages between the literary and the cricketing.

Probably no sport has so much fictional prose and poetry based upon it as does cricket. The number of novels, short stories and poems directly dealing with cricket is legion. These might be generically grouped together as cricket fiction, writings, that is, where cricket is the be-all and end-all. These are not the main subject for this undertaking, except where - Hugh de Selincourt's *The Cricket Match* is a fine example - the quality of style and treatment transcends the actual cricket and rightly aspires to a different, even a superior, form of assessment. The same applies to a handful of cricket poems, both serious and comic.

This study is more about the interplay of cricket and literature, the fashion in which cricket is used by often justly famous writers to improve their fictional scene and message. There appear to be three main ways in which this occurs. One is where cricket is deployed to point up characterisation - George Meredith's *Evan Harrington* may serve as an illustration of this. Another is where cricket is employed as metaphor or symbol - a polished example of this may be found in John Galsworthy's *The Man of Property*. A third theme is where cricket is utilised as the mover, the analogue or the counter-point of plot development - and L.P.Hartley's *The Go-between* is an elegant instance of that tendency.

Another and possibly overarching element is less direct but, for an understanding of the growth of cricket, perhaps more relevant. The intelligently observed writings of, among others, Jane Austen or Anthony Trollope, may tell us incisively more about the conditions in which cricket took root than a dozen learned works chronicling the history of the game. The way cricket is deployed by humourous or by crime or by rurally-oriented writers, in a scene or a conversational exchange, also tells us much about the circumstances in which cricket was and is played and how it became and was retained as part of the national life-style.

Furthermore, there is the component of authors being themselves involved in cricket, either as players, with all that might tell us about their literary endeavours, or because of their family connections. Some of these, too, may have played a role in, depending on the cases, the cricket or the writing of the given party, although several of these are included as little more than intriguing curios, but none the less interesting, one hopes, for that.

In a sentence, therefore, the following pages try to outline and analyse the interface between cricket on the one hand and both writings and writers on the other, in general acknowledgement of the wondrous part played by both cricket and literature in the cultural life of our society. The intellectual excitement of a grand plan is eluded in these chapters. There is no intricate interplay of plot and argument. This is, simply, a series of essays touching on the subject of cricket and fiction. They are intended for those with a general interest in either or, as often seems to be the case, both. That has led to what Yul Brynner, in his dashing role as the King of Siam, might have called a 'puzzlement.' It has been hard to decide on the likely levels of pre-knowledge among readers either in cricket or literary information. On balance, most items of data are explained or defined, in the hope that the cricket buff will not be contemptuous of simple cricketing facts and figures, nor the book-worm irritated by, to him or her, obvious detail.

Because of the hope that the book has this mixed but ordinary appeal, the apparatus of academic referencing has been avoided, except for the occasional footnote at the end of chapters, usually in respect of previous articles by the author on the given subject. Otherwise, and in a study heavily reliant on the much-appreciated labours of others, with secondary authorities as important as primary sources, it has been judged less obtrusive to embrace such references and ever-appreciative acknowledgments, without too much interruption, within the text. One recalls Noel Coward's counsel that the note at the foot of a page is like a knock at the door when you are upstairs in the bedroom making love.

In many senses, this book amounts to a drawing together of the researches and writings of previous tillers in the field. That proper and very sincere recognition of colleagues, both past and present, gives rise to the thought that the literature of cricket might be deemed a mini-subject in its own right. In what might be called the university of cricket scholarship the leading faculties are obviously mathematics, that is, statistics, and history, including an excellent biography department, whilst the visual arts and the memorabilia sections are also extremely active. Possibly there is, then, a small place for those of us with a special interest in the relationship of cricket and literature and, in this regard, one finds particularly inspiriting the splendid, if different, work of Andrew Hignell, Head of Geography at Wells Cathedral School and the Glamorgan CCC honorary statistician, who has, almost single-handedly, constructed a school of geography on the cricketing campus. His pioneering exploits, ebulliently undertaken, in both the human and physical fields of cricketing geography encourage one in the faith that other themes, such as literature, might be open to further scrutiny.

One cricketing commentator who has long believed in and practised the creed of cricket as a feeder into and out of other social and cultural topics is Clive Porter, the highly-regarded Editor of *The Journal of the Cricket Society*. His infectious encouragement of those of us, like myself, who have tried to find common ground between cricket and other walks of life has been exemplary. I am, in general, indebted to him for his enthusiastic friendliness and, in particular, for his generosity in agreeing to write a foreword to this book. Moreover, he drew my attention to numerous infelicities in the text and, in general, has been energetically supportive.

Charles Lamb, the fluent essayist, Elia, affected to despair at too much reading of literature. In his 1825 paper, *Readers against the Grain*, he pretended that the nation was doomed to ruination: 'Young men who thirty years ago would have been play-goers, punch-drinkers, cricketers, etc., with one accord are now - Readers! - a change in some respects, perhaps salutary, but I liked the old way best.'

This book is predicated on the fond belief that sufficient cricket-lovers are also book-lovers, as well as punch-drinkers and play-goers. Some may think it heretical to despoil the grandeur of Eng. Lit. with scraps of sporting lore. However, as was said by George Bernard Shaw - though not the one whose best analysis for Glamorgan was 5 for 38 - 'how can what an Englishman believes be heresy? It is a contradiction in terms.'

Chapter 2

FICTION TAKES GUARD

Let us clear the decks of cricket fiction before examining cricket in fiction. In 1950 Gerald Brodribb published an exhaustive list under the title *Cricket in Fiction* and this was updated in 1988. His long roster includes 47 novels; 96 novels which embrace 'elements or episodes of cricket'; 25 collections of stories by individual authors; 37 other short stories; 21 novels for adult readers with school settings and incidental cricket; 47 such novels for younger readers, as well as advice on a host of boys' stories, magazines and serials. It is a collection that leaves one gasping, a breathlessness intensified by inspection of the indefatigable nature of the research involved in its assemblage. Writing in 1964, John Arlott estimated that some 8000 cricket books had been published; one imagines that it is now well over the 10,000 mark, with cricket fiction making a goodly contribution.

Fortunately for those of us who have neither the time nor stamina to peruse all the works cited by the diligent Gerald Brodribb, there are anthologies that provide what adult educators call 'tasters'. For example, *The Cricketer's Companion* (1960, with a second edition in 1979 and then updated as *The Kingswood Book of Cricket* in 1992) edited by Alan Ross, one of the most sublime of cricket writers, includes some excellent samples of cricket fiction, as well as a fine review of the topic by Gerald Brodribb, a revised version of his article from *All Round the Wicket* (1951). 'Most of these fictional accounts of cricket', he writes, 'have been introduced incidentally, but there are a few novels in which the playing of cricket has been the central theme.' He makes it clear that the vast majority of the former instances fall into the categories of school stories, detective stories and village green stories. Some place will be found for a closer look at those examples later in this study.

Probably the best anthology dedicated to cricket fiction is *Lord's & Commons; cricket in novels and stories* (1988). From Jeffrey Archer to Billy Bunter, but also from George Meredith to P.G. Wodehouse, we are supplied with some two scores of excerpts, exquisitely collated and introduced by the distinguished editor, John Bright-Holmes. Be they fiction or non-fiction, most cricket anthologies, indeed anthologies on most subjects, often suffer from one of the two extremes *apropos* their editor. Some are miserly in their scant linkages, providing the interested reader with but sparse data or comment. Others are over-indulgent, intruding inconveniently and getting in the way of the substantive content. One is pleased to make an exception in the case of Benny Green and, for instance, his several aggregations of *Wisden* material: such is the sparkling fascination of his polymathic and chirpy commentary that we yield to the truth that he is usually more stimulating than the matter he recommends to our attention.

Such genius apart, one looks for the happy medium in the work of the genuine anthologist and here John Bright-Holmes - *The Joy of Cricket* (1984), a most comprehensive collection of cricket writing, is another example of his charming approach - shines. Always pithily informative yet wearing his considerable learning lightly, he greets each writer, presents him or her to us and then, when we have enjoyed his chosen extract, sometimes to the point where we are moved to find and read the whole work, we are as delicately moved forward to the next. Sufficient, never too weighty nor too lean, rather like the ideal master of ceremonies or compere, timing his intercessions to a nicety: anthologising, at this level, amounts to a miniature art-form.

Lord's & Commons includes the most updated Gerald Brodribb table of cricket fiction and both John Arlott and he have picked out two or three novels that they believe to be outstanding as specimens of this *genre*. Both of these astute and erudite critics mention *The Son of Grief* (1936), a sombre tale by Dudley Carew, the title taken from the lines of A.E.Housman. Allen Peveril is an amateur who turns professional as a competent all-rounder for Downshire, but the outcome is sobering: Peveril is described as 'at once craving and frightened of the society of other men.' Gerald Brodribb also draws attention to *Pro; an English Tragedy* (1926) by Bruce Hamilton. Teddy Lamb, the son of a famous cricketer, plays for Midhamptonshire and he, too, suffers many vicissitudes throughout a career that ultimately leads to his suicide. It is sad and strange that the two chief novels on professional cricketers should be so harrowing and so convincing. John Arlott speaks highly of two novels by William Godfrey, *The Friendly Game* (1957) and *Malleson at Melbourne* (1956), advising that the writing is mature and experienced, while he also recommends *The Devil in Woodford Wells* (1946). This is a fictional account, by Harold Hobson, much more well-known as an incisive dramatic critic, based on the life and times of Lord Frederick Beauclerk, that resolute, if somewhat remiss cleric, a descendant of Charles II and Sweet Nell of Old Drury, an inveterate gambler, who irascibly played for 35 seasons and who, according to G.D.Martineau, 'introduced sawdust for use on wet grounds, as a cleaner expedient for white stockings than the coal slack favoured by Sheffield.'

For his part, Gerald Brodribb picks for special mention *A Mother's Son* (1907) co-authored by C.B.Fry and his formidable wife, Beatrice. C.B.Fry must be the most famous all-round sportsman to have written a novel, even if in concert with the lady with whom he enjoyed so peculiar a marital relationship. The story concerns the exploits of one Mark Lovell whose talents are rewarded with Test cricket. His career illustrates a distinct trend in cricketing fiction: in Gerald Brodribb's phrases, where there are 'gilded amateurs', the tales of professionals are 'rather melancholy.' He also cites three early novels, two of them by Horace G.Hutchenson, himself a sportsman of some weight, to wit, *Creatures of Circumstance* (1891) and *Peter Steel, the Cricketer* (1895).

The third is J.C.Snaith's *Willow the King* (1899), possibly the finest of the pre-1914 cricket novels. John Collis Snaith wrote other novels, such as *Fierceheart, the Soldier and Mistress Dorothy Marvin*, and, in his day, he was a popular writer. He was born in Nottingham in 1876 and died in Hampstead in 1936, aged 80. An able left-hander, he played one first-class match for Nottinghamshire in 1900, scoring 21 at Lord's for the county against MCC. In the same year he played for Notts versus the West Indies at Trent Bridge and took four wickets in that non-first-class game. He played for Notts Amateurs and the county second string, while he once took all ten wickets for the Authors' XI - 10 for 32 against the Rev. E.Stogden's XI at Elstree - and, aged 40 in 1914, he shared in a second wicket stand of 340 for Skegness against Cossall Colliery, of which his contribution was 156, not out.

The pleasingly drafted story of this useful cricketer is dedicated 'to my colleagues of the Nottingham Forest Amateur Cricket Club' and the cricket components, from 'Rectory rules' to first-class, are most convincing. They include some detailed descriptions of balls bowled and strokes attempted. The novel is cleverly sub-titled 'the story of a cricket match', for it is a none too deeply etched romance, with the story-teller-cricketer, Richard Cranford 'Dimmy' Dimsdale finding his life's bliss riding on a vicarage garden game in which he must do better than his loved one, Grace Trentham. The assured, cricket-oriented daughter of the local rector, she is a heroine after the style of Wilkie Collins' tough-minded Marian Halcombe in *The Woman in White* (1860) or even the wilful Bathsheba Everdene in Hardy's *Far from the Madding Crowd* (1874). Such confident and active young women are far removed from the insipid and passive portrayals of much Victorian literature and they reveal a far greater shift toward the acceptance of a less confined typology of womanhood.

There is an ambivalence about this, upon which J.C.Snaith's story perhaps unconsciously touches. Things were changing. The youthful Charlotte Dod had, from 1886, terrorised her hitherto rather static tennis opponents with vigorous smashes and what was explicitly referred to as 'man-like' athleticism, yet Eleanora Sears was, in 1909, dispatched from the polo field by her captain for wearing trousers. The Victorian sportsman-knight wished to treat womankind as chivalrously as he did the vanquished foe, and yet, so close was sport, especially cricket, to religion, that to deprive women of its succour left him decidedly uneasy. Thus the door was left ajar for womanly participation, provided the Madonna-like image was preserved and gracefulness was not abandoned in favour of unsavoury competitiveness. The ambiguity is well summarised by the Gilbert and Sullivan song 'a Bright and Beautiful English Girl', from the comic opera, *Utopia Limited*, first performed in 1893. 'Her magnificent comeliness' is sustained through a set of energetic but never unfeminine activities:

> With a ten mile spin she stretches her limbs,
> She golfs, she punts, she rows, she swims...

to the point where even the most knowing Savoyards are undecided whether the lyric is affectionately satiric or sentimentally straight.

The handsome Miss Trentham represented this convention with admirable poise and self-possession. At the point where it seemed she would score more runs than 'Dimmy', she boldly struck down her wickets and the 'match' is settled to their mutual satisfaction.

Amiably pleasing as is *Willow the King*, it must give place to the novel widely regarded as the only case where a piece of fiction devoted solely to cricket actually transcends the subject to become acknowledged as a minor classic in its own right. This is Hugh de Selincourt's *The Cricket Match*. J.M.Barrie said quite simply that it was 'the best book written about cricket or any other game' and other critics echo this generous sentiment. In 1951 Gerald Brodribb wrote that the novel 'quite apart from its description of the game, is a magnificent study of village life in Sussex. It is a book of great sensibility, and for this reason it excels the others.' 'One cricket novel stands high above the remainder', wrote John Arlott in 1964, '...cricket at some points seems the theme, at others (it is) incidental, which means that it is the convincing background of a fully realised novel.' John Bright-Holmes, writing in 1988, calls it 'probably still the best single novel written about cricket in general and village cricket in particular.'

Hugh de Selincourt, born in 1878, reached his maturity in the baleful shadow of the Great War, and, if that moulded his sometimes less than optimistic outlook, his style was shaped by the more allusive manner of the 1920s. Not for him the solid grandeur of the huge Victorian novel; rather did he become the master of the briefer, more homogeneous form. He was schooled, like another cricket nut, P.G. Wodehouse, at Dulwich College and he was a student at University College, Oxford. He lived most of adult his life near Pulborough on the Sussex Downs and he chose the critical life, being for three years literary critic for *The Observer* and contributing a chapter to *The Cambridge History of English Literature*. He acted as the theatre and books reviewer of several London newspapers and himself wrote a dozen plays. Not all his score of novels are about cricket, although he achieved most present and future prestige with these. As well as *The Cricket Match*, he wrote a collection of short stories under the title of *The Game of the Season* (1931) and *The Saturday Match* (1937). He died in 1951, aged 72, and, with just a hint of disdain, his *Wisden* obituary speaks of 'his love of cricket of the village-green variety' and avers 'there is no evidence that he was a specially accomplished player himself.'

Country Life called his most famous novel 'a classic...beautifully distils the essence of a lasting aspect of village life' and the *Times* judged it a 'miniature masterpiece...about more than cricket. It strikes a perfect length about class, and age, and the English character.' *The Cricket Match* was published in 1924 and has been re-published frequently, with a lovingly and freshly illustrated version particularly catching the eye in 1990. For seven years Hugh de Selincourt captained the West Sussex village side of Storrington, the reality behind the fictional setting of Tillingfold. The book presents a total recall of the events in the village from dawn to dusk on Saturday 24 August 1921, with the fixture against old rivals Raveley as the centre-piece.

The cricket provides both the framework and the kernel of the novel. It does for the story what the Church of England does for the *Barchester Chronicles* of Anthony Trollope, that is, it is sometimes intensely important in itself and sometimes the stage for an interplay of character. The Grecian unities are impeccably observed. The novel covers the daylight hours of that summer Saturday and never deviates from its village location. Tillingfold beat Raveley by two runs in a thrilling but not overtly dramatic nor uncommon game.

The cricketers are drawn from all classes. There is privileged Edgar Trine, scion of the squirearchy, son of the big house, mixing for sporting, but hardly for social, reasons, with Sid Smith, the impoverished brick-layer and quick bowler. They come from all age-groups. There is John McLeod, persevering as warm-hearted secretary and prudent opening bat, despite reaching his fifties and finding the modern world a little testing, and there is Francis Allen, the dry-humoured, sagacious old scorer. At the other extreme is the excitable middle-class teenager, Horace Cairie, desperately seeking his early opportunities. Over against the mechanics and shopkeepers of the village, there is intellectual Dick Fanshawe, all 'brooding intensity', while his friend, Paul Gauvinier, artist and enlightened captain, is the aesthetic Hugh de Selincourt in flimsy disguise.

The eleven, with their friends and families and servants, represent the gamut of temperaments from the depressive to the ebullient. There are the niggling conflicts, shaming jealousies and wearisome dislikes, as well as the *camaraderie* and pleasures, which attend any group of people gathered together for any collective endeavour. It is skilfully accomplished. They may be prototypes but they never deteriorate into stereotypes. There are no grotesques. Indeed, for any recreational cricketer, past or present, there is ample scope for rueful identification. The characterisation is never forced and always persuasive.

The same is true of the village. Tillingfold is no romantic hamlet, like Agatha Christie's St Mary's Mead of Miss Marple fame. There is no duck pond, no single village shop, spilling over with lots of wares, and no gnarled oldest inhabitant, sitting, foaming tankard in hand, outside the local tavern. This is no setting for the average detective story or children's adventure tale. Tillingfold is more of a township, stirring its stumps after the bestiality of the 1914-1918 war and looking to its less parochial future. There are seven pubs and umpteen shops and the cricket match is played on the recreation ground, not on the village green. Motor buses and football encroach. Some of the old ways have been restored, but there are hurtful signs of imminent change. The mix is accurate and well-observed. This is Storrington in fictional guise and the stance of the novel, especially as seen through the perceptive eyes of the de Selincourt/Gauvinier figure, is exactly that of the then 42-year old author, just past the mid-point of his life and the most crucial historical episode of that life-span.

It is this simple cohesion of themes and of people, engagingly, but never sentimentally, treated, that makes *The Cricket Match* a minor classic. Of course, it is possible to read the book as a pleasing yarn about inferior cricket or to enjoy its period pastiche. However, beyond that, and without pretension, it accomplishes what a good novel should. It offers a sense of microcosm, of a cross-section of society under sympathetic scrutiny.

Nonetheless, the cricket is the indispensable dimension of *The Cricket Match*. It is both a good novel and a cricket novel in the same way that *Kidnapped* is both a good novel and an adventure novel. *The Cricket Match* certainly comes closer than any other book to fulfilling that kind of dual criteria. Much of the rest of this study deals with fiction where the cricket is less directly involved and where it is clearly incidental, used tactically in support of other themes or efforts at characterisation, as in detective or school stories wherein, clearly, the murder mystery or the educative ambience takes precedence. Although the lens will swing from Charles Dickens and Jane Austen to James Joyce and Iris Murdoch, Hugh de Selincourt, given his masterpiece, *The Cricket Match*, has no need to be embarrassed by the company he is invited to keep.

Footnote: some of these thoughts on Hugh de Selincourt's work were included in an article, 'No Stranger to Fiction; cricket's use in literature' in *Cricket Lore*, vol.1 no.4, May 1992.

Chapter 3

THE CRICKET ON THE HEARTH

In July 1845 Charles Dickens' customary exuberance turned enthusiastically to the planning of a cheap weekly periodical to be entitled *The Cricket*. Alas for the cricketing buff, the name and content was inspired by the chirruping of the cicadas, constantly heard by him on his recent Italian tour. He told his friend and biographer, the rather pompous and Podsnapian John Forster, that it would contain 'much of the 'Carol' philosophy, cheerful views, sharp anatomization of humbug, jolly good temper...and a vein of glowing, hearty, generous, mirthful, beaming reference...' indeed, the converse recipe, unluckily, of some cricket journals over the generations. The idea came to nothing of itself, but Charles Dickens poured some of the envisaged sentiment into his next Christmas story, *The Cricket on the Hearth*, in the tradition of *A Christmas Carol* and *The Chimes*. This was a charming tale of the blind girl, whose father had created for her an imaginary ambience of bright luxury, published the same year - any comparisons are coincidental - that Surrey County Cricket Club was formed and the Oval opened for business.

Given the exhilaration and energy of his adult life, it is sad to recall that Dickens, as a child, had little opportunity or verve for sport, otherwise cricket might have played a greater part in the immortal canon. 'He was never', wrote John Forster, 'a good little cricket-player'. Dickens spoke of this to George Dolby, his 'readings' manager, in 1866, remarks transformed into direct speech by the historian, Peter Rowland: '...I was always a puny, weak youngster and never used to join in games with the same zest that other boys seemed to have. I never was remarkable, during my younger days, for anything but violent, spasmodic attacks, which used to utterly prostrate me, and for indomitable energy in reading. Cricket, 'chevy', top, marbles, 'peg in the ring', 'tor', 'three holes', or any of a thousand and one boys' games, had no charm for me, save such as lay in watching others play.' His loss was, care of that perceptive reading and watching, our gain, but it does seem that, although David Copperfield was his chosen autobiographical model, there was more of little Paul Dombey about 'the queer small boy' who was familiar with all the classic English novels by the age of ten.

Dickens was the quintessential Londoner and the unique narrator of the lives of the genteel lower middle classes, and, whilst an indefatigable walker of prodigious length (up to thirty miles a day, along with other such unflagging Victorians, like Gladstone) he was no athlete. However, when living at Gad's Hill Place, near Rochester, in the later phase of his life, during the 1850s and 1860s, Charles Dickens, the urban self-made professional man, decided to play the squire. There were other literary figures - W.S.Gilbert, for instance, with his near-menagerie and swimming pool at Grim's Dyke, Stanmore, near Harrow - who aspired to this status. They were, of course, copying the customary step taken by up-and-coming industrial families, so to proceed upwardly. Among cricketing instances, one might mention A.N.Hornby, 'the squire of Lancashire', as Neville Cardus perspicaciously nicknamed him, a child of the Blackburn cotton trade, his elders the upholders of the dogmas of Manchesterism, who, polished by Harrow, made his home amid the plush greenery of the Cheshire plain at Parkfield, near Nantwich, with his guns, his stable of magnificent hunters, his country house cricket ground and his rural Tory values.

However, Dickens, as countrified gent, never eschewed his humane beliefs and delight in his broader public, ever hopeful 'of a more intimate union than exists at present between the different classes in the state'. What many landowners might have done once a year or on special occasions, there were 'scenes, not infrequent there' when Charles Dickens, putting the action to the word, organised at Gad's Hill gala days for huge crowds, up to three thousand in number, all carried off, to his great pleasure, in manifestly decent order. G.K.Chesterton famously said of Dickens, as he might easily have said of some well-known cricketers, 'the critics blustered but the people wept and cheered'. Here was the author, who consciously wrote to draw within his pale of influence and interest all sections of society, committed to the same dimension of 'integrated culture' in other sides of his public and private life.

Happily, he recognised that cricket was a key instrument in that regard and Forster records how these *fetes* 'took generally the form of cricket matches', sometimes even, apparently, in wintry months. Dickens himself wrote that 'encouraged by the cricket matches experience, I allowed the landlord of the Falstaff to have a drinking booth on the ground...there was not a dispute, and there was no drunkenness whatever.' According to his biographer, Fred Kaplan, 'he had neighbourhood working people onto his back meadow for cricket matches and foot races for which he sponsored prizes', while he entertained 'regular guests from the Higham Cricket Club'. The family cricket, billiards and other games were competitive, 'each participant having a reputation and handicap. At cricket matches, he tended to be an umpire, in the billiards rooms an observer, in croquet an occasional participant, and in the theatricals a regular performer'. It is said that he ceremoniously bowled the first ball of a game on occasion. Sir Jeremiah Colman wrote to *The Cricketer* in 1941 to announce that, not only were 'cricket pictures prominently displayed on the walls' of Gad's Hill Place, but that he had two oil paintings, one of Charles Dickens bowling the first ball in a charity match, and one of him scoring. The (disputed) date for the former depiction was 1868 and Sir Jeremiah loaned it to the National Gallery in the 1930s.

Sir Henry Dickens, the author's son, recalled his father as scorer, 'sustained in the arduous job by the cooling drinks'. There is another account elsewhere of him scoring when a Gad's Hill team played the locals in a kind of 'Hall' and 'Village' annual fixture, very typical of the times, almost akin to a kind of 'Gentlemen and Players' match at a parochial level. He was remembered by a contemporary 'in his white jean coat, and his grey hat set a little on one side, his double glasses on, going conscientiously through his work: scoring down 'byes', and 'overs', and 'runs'; at times encouraging an indifferent hit with an encouraging 'Well run! Well run!' There is even the suggestion that Hans Christian Andersen, on a visit to Gad's Hill in 1857, played some cricket with the family - although 'the bony bore', as that same family rather unkindly nicknamed him, very much over-stayed his welcome and was more interested in manufacturing daisy-chains and cutting paper patterns and generally being rather tedious.

A *Wisden* obituary records an exciting incident that occurred during one of these games. George Henry Remnant died in 1941 at the good age of 92. He was born in Rochester in 1848 and played 42 times for Kent as a professional. As a young man, he played for the Gad's Hill team and became a friend of Dickens. Perhaps that friendship originated in the anxious moments when, playing in a match on Dickens' meadow, he drove a ball into a trap from where the novelist's children and their governess were watching. The frightened pony bolted. Remnant cast aside his bat, raced after the runaway trap and checked the pony's headlong flight before anything more damaging had been done than a bump or two and a scare. How close life sometimes comes to schoolboy fiction. Who knows, without this act of gallantry, Charles Dickens' last surviving grandson, Henry Charles Dickens, who died in 1966 aged 83, might never have existed to become, according to *Wisden*, 'a keen cricketer' and a long-time member of MCC.

We know that the young Kent colt scored 78 on his Gad's Hill debut, much to his patron's delight, and that, in 1869, he was invited to wear an armlet of lavender and represent Dickens at a Gad's Hill sports meeting. 'I hope', said Charles Dickens, encouragingly, 'as my colour-bearer, you will carry off the prize.' George Remnant readied himself at scratch in the mile handicap race; Dickens climbed on to an ancient wheel barrow and, as starter, fired an ageing muzzle-loading pistol. The young cricketer raced home the winner - his apt prize was a cricket bat and a pair of pads. His county record - 564 runs at an average just below eight and but 19 wickets - was not spectacular, but he went on to be coach at Eton, where the formidable Lord Harris, then a mere Hon George Robert Canning was one of his trainees: it may have been the last time that opinionated peer listened to anyone's advice. Remnant later became a first-class umpire and his son, Ernest Richard (1881-1969) played 121 games for Hampshire.

Dickens was ever the protagonist of good fellowship and good cheer. We are indebted to the elegant researches of the historian and cricket biographer, Gerald Howat, for information about the early pamphlet, *Sunday under Three heads*, printed in 1836, in which the socially conscious novelist bewailed the narrow-mindedness of the clergy and their pious allies who forbade sports on the Sabbath. He recounts the tale of a Sunday evening of 'very animated cricket'. The old clergyman, whose morning service the writer had attended, approaches but, just as Dickens 'was almost on the point of crying out' a warning, he happily realises that the cleric is the benevolent soul who has organised the activity and all is well. The cleric 'had been a wonderful cricketer himself...it was his field they played in...it was he who had purchased stumps, bat, and all!'

The legendary chronicler, H.P-T (P.F.Thomas) devoted a page of *The Cricketer Winter Annual* of 1929/30 to this polemic. The 24-year old Charles Dickens, under the pen-name of Timothy Sparks, used the pamphlet, a year before his presentation of *The Pickwick Papers*, in the wake of the defeat of a strict Sabbath observance bill in the House of Commons that would have stopped all passenger traffic and closed all places of amusement on that sacred day. He was anxious lest the puritans might revive their stern project and his 'three heads' were 'as it is; as Sabbath Bills would make it and as it might be made'. Patently, Dickens approves of , to use a modern coinage, 'a third way', whereby Sunday might become 'a recognised day of relaxation', with hearty worship matched, without impiety, with 'needful recreation', including 'the sharp stroke of the bat as it sent the ball skimming along the ground.' Charles Dickens clearly identified himself with those protagonists of 'rational recreation' who, in the coming Victorian age, argued that wholesome sports would attract working men from the idleness of the tavern and, in fact, properly temper the 'sour austerity' of grim religiosity.

However, this rural idyll scarcely penetrated his work; indeed, his later novels conveyed more and more of the sombre melancholy of metropolitan life, as well as, for he remained a restless and cheerful fighter, its bustling, gladdening aspect. Some twenty years before moving into Gad's Hill, in 1837, Dickens had, in *The Posthumous Papers of the Pickwick Club*, presented his comic account of Dingley Dell being heavily defeated by All-Muggleton, although it should be recalled that he set the novel in the early 1820s. Dumkins and Podder, 'two of the most renowned members of that most distinguished club', opened and 'remained unconquered' while 'the scouts were hot and tired; the bowlers were changed and bowled till their arms ached.' Dickens is amusing about that constant in the game, the earnest endeavours of mediocre performers: the ball 'bounded far away over the heads of the scouts, who had just stooped low enough to let it fly over them'...Did a slim gentleman attempt to catch it, it struck him on the nose, and bounded pleasantly off with redoubled violence, while the slim gentleman's eyes filled with water, and his form writhed with anguish.' All is lost when 'All-Muggleton had notched some fifty-four, while the score of Dingley Dell was as blank as their faces' and, shortly afterwards, Dingley Dell capitulate.

The episode is enlivened by our - and Samuel Pickwick's encounter with Alfred Jingle, recalling, in his characteristic irregular and monosyllabic style, the single wicket contest in which he had tussled with the tireless endurance of Colonel Sir Thomas Blazo in the West Indies: '- wouldn't give in - faithful attendant - Quanko Samba - last man left - sun so hot, bat in blisters - ball scorched brown - five hundred and seventy runs - rather exhausted - Quanko mustered up last remaining strength - bowled me out - had a bath, and went out to dinner.' In answer to anxious inquiry about the loyal Quanko, Jingle explained, 'never recovered it - bowled on, on my account - bowled off, on his own - died, sir.'

In the anxious early months of 1941, with a winter of debilitating blitzing barely finished, the cricket buffs of the day found the energy to debate the Dingley Dell fixture in *The Cricketer Spring Annual* and subsequent Cricketers of that eventful war-time year. Bernard Darwin, the sports' writer who wrote a fine biography of W.G.Grace in 1934 and who had a *penchant* for golf as well as cricket, expressed astonishment that 'the most widely read account of cricket in prose' was penned by someone 'who palpably did not understand' the game. 'What does it mean?' asks Bernard Darwin rhetorically...'Nobody has ever known. I am inclined to believe that he thought the two batsmen remained firmly at his own wicket...In fact he wrote an immortal and heavenly account of something that he knew nothing whatever about.'

Now Bernard Darwin may ever so slightly have been gently pressing his tongue into his cheek, for he also castigates Henry Newbolt's school captain in that his advice to the last man in when there was a deathly hush in the close and ten to make - 'play the game' - 'in this context has no meaning at all.' No matter: the Dickens-lovers, including Sir Jeremiah Colman, rose in some force. James D.Coldham wrote a lengthy letter explaining that Charles Dickens never intended for his account to be taken seriously: 'It was meant to be a farce!', and he cites the critic, E.B.V.Christian, who describes it as 'farce rather than history'. Coldham reminds that the Pickwickians were supposed to report their activities for the benefit of their fellow-members of the Pickwick Club and that they often did so after hearty libations. Mr Snodgrass would, on this occasion, 'have afforded most useful and valuable information, had not the burning eloquence of the words or the feverish influence of the wine made that gentleman's hand so extremely unsteady as to render his writing nearly unintelligible and his style wholly so.' In support of his case that Dickens had a genuine knowledge of the game, James Coldham adds a helpful quotation from a little-known Dickensian work, *Athletes at Ease*, in which Dickens claimed that cricket 'acts as the social cement of classes...The cricketer's life is certainly the most purely enjoyable which any young man could lead. Is there any week in England, or in the world, like the Canterbury Week?'

One last comment on the match which H.P-T termed an 'extravagantly impossible encounter.' Dickens placed *The Pickwick Papers* well before the 1830s in which they were published, writing of a time when the stage-coach was pre-eminent and the railways unknown. We tend to assume that the format of cricket was ordained and unchanging from an early era, but, until widespread travel was more feasible and cricket had become a more nationally acknowledged sport, it is likely there were manifold variations on its basic theme. Charles Dickens, gifted, among myriad talents, with a superb memory, may, in part, have recalled a variant or maverick formula from his youth and presented us with the delectable picture of Luffey bowling perpetually and vainly to Dumkins and Struggles in hopelessly eternal battle with Podder.

We may have been lucky to enjoy the Dingley Dell piece at all, for *The Pickwick Papers*, originally the base for the illustrator, Robert Seymour, to produce amusing sporting prints with prose attached, was captured and transformed by the young Dickens, especially after the unfortunate artist's suicide. In his exuberant hands, it became, of course, something of a spoof picaresque novel, with a dashing if roguish hero on his adventurous travels, after the manner, say, of Henry Fielding's *Tom Jones*. The humour arises from the dichotomy of just such a youthful *élan* being embodied within the failing carcass of a stout, breathless older gentleman. The shooting and skating and cricket are soon left behind as Dickens seeks comedy in more romantic situations. All in all, there is not much sport thereafter in Dickens' work.

Three cricketing hints provide tiny exceptions. In *The Old Curiosity Shop* (1841) Nell and her grandfather, during their prolonged and indeterminate wandering away from the machinations of the malicious dwarf, Daniel Quilp, arrive where 'the clustered houses of the village peeped out from the woody hollow below. It was a very small place. The men and boys were playing at cricket on the green.' At once cricket is used, as so often, to help indicate a calmer, stiller quality of life, over against the tiring, fear-stricken perambulation of Nell Trent and the hapless old man. It is also acts as a small preface to the scene where Little Nell, having sought lodgings at the village school-house, watches as the dying scholar, the beloved favourite of the 'poor schoolmaster', glances at 'his idle bat, that lay with slate and book and other boyish property', with the last sounds he hears being those of 'The boys at play upon the green'. It is a grim foreshadowing of Little Nell's own premature death and, a consistent theme of the book, the inability of adults to protect children.

Next, in *Martin Chuzzlewit* (1844) the guileless Tom Pinch, eventually disillusioned with the hypocrisy of Mr Pecksniff, is rapidly whisked off by coach from modest Salisbury to rakish London. It is a swaggering, hectic sort of journey, with 'Yoho' the preface to every stage. 'Yoho, among the gathering shades; making of no account the deep reflections of the trees, but scampering on through light and darkness, all the same, as if the light of London fifty miles away, were quite enough to travel by, and some to spare. Yoho, beside the village-green, where cricket players linger yet, and every little indentation made in the fresh grass by bat or wicket, ball or player's boot, sheds out its perfume on the night...' Here again that pastoral cameo indicates the tranquil existence Tom Pinch is so precipitately casting aside, as he is swept away to the faster, darker habits of the metropolis.

In *Little Dorrit* (1857), one of Charles Dickens' later and more mature novels, he strenuously attacks the debilitating strangulation of that petty, lazy and inefficient bureaucracy which had caused so much suffering in the then recent Crimean War. In a private letter of 1855, Dickens, with reference to his writing of Little Dorrit, asserted that he wished to explore how 'we have got ourselves involved in meshes of aristocratic red tape to our unspeakable confusion, loss and sorrow.' Thus, in passages as telling as other classic attacks on corrupt officialdom, such as Gogol's *The Inspector General*, he sardonically assails the dilatory and complacent ineptness of the Circumlocution Office, so much so that George Bernard Shaw believed *Little Dorrit* to be Dickens' most seditious novel. There was a wider perspective, for the keynote of the book is, simply, imprisonment and the critic, Professor Lionel Trilling, has termed the Circumlocution Office 'the prison of the creative mind of England.'

Toward the end of the novel the diffident hero, Arthur Clennam, is once more trying to unlock the secrets of the Circumlocution Office and glean some slight piece of information or energise some small piece of action. Ferdinand Barnacle, a younger representative of this deeply entrenched and smug administration, excuses its defensiveness in cricketing terms. ' 'Look at it from the right point of view, and there you have us - official and effectual. It's like a limited game of cricket. A field of outsiders are always going to bowl at the public service, and we block the balls.' Clennam asked what became of the bowlers? The airy young Barnacle replied that they grew tired, got dead beat, got lamed, got their backs broken, died off, gave it up, went in for other games.' Despite the crucial reforms in the civil service, dating from this time and perhaps influenced by the keenness of Charles Dickens' onslaught, there may be many, a hundred and fifty years on, prepared to echo his frustrated sentiments.

Other than these incidentals, Charles Dickens remained more or less faithful to his fascinating gallery of impoverished tradesmen, unctuous but devious lawyers, unbending businessmen, down-at-heel paupers and the rest, all inhabiting a chaotic, chiefly urban arena, with little leisure, save his generous allowance of hearty fare and substantial drink, and with little place for the clean, tidy, pastoral formalism of cricket.

However, there is another allusion to cricket. Another of his modern biographers, Peter Ackroyd, records a three-page letter Dickens sent from America to his son, Harry. It was in 1868, two years before Charles Dickens died. It concerned the organisation of the Gad Hill's Cricket Club, of which Dickens offered to be chairman, to donate £5 a year and 'to overlook its business affairs.' It was to be made up of 'gentlemen' and 'working men', itself a gloss on his own political stance. He instructed Harry thus: 'The first thing to be avoided is, the slightest appearance of patronage...The second thing to be avoided is, the deprival of the men of their just right to manage their own affairs'. His solution was Harry's self-nomination as captain that he might deal the more effectively with the 'gentlemen'. Dickens proposed that they should pay twice the subscription of the 'working men' but that all should have an equal vote. 'Draw up the club's rules...' but 'Whatever you do, let the men ratify; and let them feel their little importance, and at once perceive how much better the business begins to be done'. Peter Ackroyd comments, 'Here we have Dickens' dream of society in miniature, an harmonious arrangement of all classes in which the paternalism of the gentleman captain is linked with the due recognition of the 'little importance' of the workers...' And we had been led to believe that Walter Scott was Tony Blair's favourite author...

Then there is the might-have-been tale of Dickens' proposed visit to Australia. Several historians - for instance, Jack Pollard in his *Australian Cricket*, 1803-1893, published in 1987, and D.J.Mulvaney, in his *Cricket Walkabout*, published in 1967 - have urged that Charles Dickens was indirectly responsible for the first visit of an English cricket team to Australia. The Melbourne hoteliers and restauranteurs, Felix Spiers and Christopher Pond, had hoped to book the author for a reading tour, but the deal fell through. Their agent in Britain, Mr Mallam, negotiated a substitute proposal whereby a team, with six Surrey professionals as the core, travelled on the *SS Great Britain* and arrived at Melbourne on Christmas Eve, 1861. They played fourteen matches, the first of them on New Year's Day, 1862, against XVIII of Victoria. The players picked up a fee of £150, plus £100 bonus and all expenses met, an arrangement lavish enough to encourage a whole series of such trips.

But stay the torrent of ifs and buts along the lines of would there have been no Test cricket had Charles Dickens accepted that tempting offer. There is an alternative version, a kind of reversal of fortunes. In his *Seasons in the Sun; the History of the Victorian Cricket Association* (1993) Robert Coleman argues that the sponsors made a massive £11,000 from the tour and 'Encouraged by their first entrepreneurial venture, the following year they offered Charles Dickens £10,000 for a lecture and reading tour, but he declined.'

If one seeks through the voluminous pages of Dickens' various biographies, some sort of answer may be found. Fred Kaplan has Dickens embarked on a series of provincial readings over the autumn and winter of 1861/62, including an abbreviated version of *David Copperfield* in Rochester. According to Fred Kaplan, it was during the summer and autumn of 1862 that he was tempted to take up the Spiers and Pond offer of £10,000 for an eight months' tour of readings. Charles Dickens was sorely attracted by the riches proffered, calculating that he might, in fact, make £12,000 in six months, given the right circumstances, but all manner of professional and personal - such as abandoning his mistress, Ellen Ternan, for a lengthy spell - reasons caused him to pause and reflect. 'The indecision went on for months': eventually, it was Christmas 1862 before Dickens finally determined not to visit the antipodes. On balance, it does seem that the Coleman story is the more accurate, and there is no immediate biographical evidence that he received two invitations.

One final thought. Charles Dickens editorial advice to W.H.Wills, of *Household Words,* might be of use to the cricketing authorities: 'brighten it', he urged, 'brighten it, brighten it'.

Chapter 4

AUSTEN J. (HANTS) AND
MR A. TROLLOPE (BARSETSHIRE AND ENGLAND)

The whimsical humorist, Paul Jennings, once wrote a poem which began 'I often get lost in the works of Jane Austen.' His anxiety arose from some confusion over her several heroines and his worry that he constantly attached them, in his remembrance, to the wrong hero or, worse, the right villain. He would, however, have had less trouble with references to cricket, for, in the entire, admittedly not huge, Janeite canon, there seems to be only one chief mention. It occurs in *Northanger Abbey*, published posthumously in 1818, a year after her untimely death, but actually written in 1798, as *Susan*, and then revised and completed in 1803.

The cricketing allusion is in respect of one of Paul Jennings' perplexing heroines, Catherine Morland. Prior to what Jane Austen ironically termed her 'training for a heroine' from the age of fifteen, she had worried her mama by dint of her tomboyish proclivity. Her mother, distracted by domestic and maternal cares, had been forced to leave an elder daughter to shift for herself. Thus 'it was not wonderful that Catherine, who had by nature nothing heroic about her, should prefer cricket, base ball, riding on horseback and running about the countryside at the age of fourteen to books.' Thereafter she becomes the most romanticised of young ladies, for *Northanger Abbey* is an amusing parody on the Gothic novel, with its melodramatic and supernatural entrapment of disadvantaged heroines within sinister surroundings, after the manner of William Beckford's *Vathek* (1786) or Ann Radcliffe's *The Mysteries of Udolpho* (1794). Catherine Morland, then, was not destined to be the predecessor of Rachael Heyhoe-Flint or Jane Britten in English women's Test colours.

That link of cricket and 'base ball' has been pooh-poohed by some as female ignorance of the true nature of English reality, with its patent concentration on cricket. Riper judgement might suggest that it may be further evidence of the general intermingling of folk-games, especially in rural areas, such as Jane Austen's home county of Hampshire, which existed until the turn of the 19th century and perhaps beyond. There was no need for rational formulae and widely accepted laws when a few servants or, in Catherine's case, children played locally together. Cricket and 'base ball' - which, in some early forms, was played, like cricket, with only two 'bases' - could easily have been compounded. One recalls the fuss, described in the previous chapter, over Charles Dickens' purported lack of comprehension of cricket, given, by modern assessment, the peculiar Dingley Dell rules.

Equally, the rather fragile Horace Walpole has been called to task for suggesting that Frederick Louis, Prince of Wales, died in 1751 from an 'abscess' caused not by a cricket ball at practice, but by a tennis ball, that is for the missile used in the 'gallery' type of Real Tennis. Again, one must ponder whether, 250 years ago, the same sort of ball might have been used for species of two closely related sub-games. Incidentally, it was Horace Walpole who, with his publication in 1765 of *The Castle of Otranto*, started the craze for the Gothic novel so coolly satirised in *Northanger Abbey*. As for the fatal cricket or tennis ball, it has led some inquiring minds to wonder that, if Frederick Louis had ascended the throne rather than George III, Britain might not have lost the American colonies. Presumably, had that happened, civilisation would have been denied the delights of, *inter alia*, the Americanised version of 'base ball', for which Jane Austen defiantly keeps the two words separated.

All that aside, it is plain that Jane Austen is more celebrated, cricket-wise, for her descendants. Her oldest brother, James, had a son, James Edward, who, for family reasons, adopted the surname Austen-Leigh. He lived from 1798 to 1874 and, in 1870, he wrote a memoir of his famed aunt. His marriage in 1828 to Emma Smith was blessed by a burgeoning family of seven cricketing brothers. The *Wisden* obituaries of five of this clan appeared variously under Leigh and Austen-Leigh. Spencer (1834-1913) was the only one to indulge in first-class cricket, making thirteen appearances in all, ten of them for Sussex in the early 1860s, with his first-class debut being for the Gentlemen of England in 1857. 'A splendid and free hitter' was how the immortal Haygarth described him. He played many matches for the Gentlemen of Sussex and for the Gentlemen of Berkshire, a fitting political balance in that he was born in the second county and died in the first.

The Rev. Augustus (1840-1913) was perhaps the most successful professionally of Jane Austen's great-nephews. He was Vice-Chancellor of the University of Cambridge from 1893 to 1895 and, at the time of his death, both Provost of King's College, Cambridge and President of the University cricket club. The Rev. Arthur Henry (1836-1917) captained the Cheltenham College XI in 1855 and played for St John's College, Oxford and also for the Gentlemen of England. Edward Compton (1839-1916) died at Eton where he had been a master from 1861 to 1905. He played for Eton and for the Gentlemen of Berkshire, for whom he scored 190 in 1860 against the Gentlemen of Sussex. The last surviving son was Charles Edward (1832-1924) who lived to be 92. He played for Harrow, MCC and, like several of the brothers, Berkshire. A sixth brother, William (1843-1921) co-wrote a life of his great-aunt Jane in 1913 with his nephew Richard Arthur Austen-Leigh. The seventh played for MCC: this was Cholmeley (1829-1890). He was Christened after the maiden name of the cantankerous and trouble-stirring Mrs Leigh Perrot, whence came the 'Leigh' and whence came to the Austen-Leighs, in grim gratitude for their adoption of the other family's escutcheon, the Perrot fortune, including their Berkshire house, 'Scarlets', at Speen, near Newbury.

And that was that...except that Jane Austen, in the subtle way of great novelists, submits a footnote to the saga of cricket's development. She offers an insight into the abiding strength of 'county' cricket which has been sustained to the present day, in spite of the huge urban predominance and incidence of the first-class game from as early as her own life-time. London was its major centre from the latter half of the 18th century, while the railways ensured that, in the Victorian period, the great provincial and industrialised foci would also provide the venues for important cricket occasions. English cricket has never, at its higher levels, been a pastoral sport, but it has ever been an essential aspect of the game's ideology to preserve that Arcadian myth. In the 18th century, before county clubs, as such, were formally established, it was the custom for grand landowners, who, at least, had the excuse that they owned massive swathes of the apposite shire, attached the county label to the teams they fielded. In the 19th century this pastoral tone was sustained. When, for example, professional and business men, principally living in the Manchester area, wished to collect together to play at a higher grade than with their respective clubs, they described themselves as the Gentlemen of Lancashire.

The Austen-Leighs, playing for the Gentlemen of Berkshire - most counties had a 'Gentlemen's XI' during the Victorian decades - personify the convention. In part, of course, the emphasis on the social distinction of their 'gentle' quality is significant, but the decision to adhere to the shire classification is very important. It is, for instance, in marked contrast to the slightly later development of nationally identified football teams which invariably - although the 'County' addition for Notts, Stockport, Newport and Derby makes for interesting contemplation - took the tag of the town or city where they were resident. When it comes to a summer and winter twinning, one thinks of Warwickshire and Aston Villa, Lancashire and Manchester United or Yorkshire and Leeds United. Particularly after football became professionalised, the county associations played an increasingly smaller part in the organisation of the game.

The county had had a long history, especially in terms of conserving the regional focus of the gentry and their families. That perceptive and deep-seeking historian of the 18th century, Lewis Namier, called them the 'county commonwealths' of England. Even as late as the close of the 19th century, they remained, in the words of the local history expert, A.M.Everitt, 'the matrix of local society in which political opinion in the provinces was formed.' Throughout the 17th and 18th centuries well-educated ladies and gentlemen would speak of their 'country' in reference to their 'county', while the habit of stressing the second syllable - coun-*tree*, as we sometimes still hear it in folk-songs - emphasised this closeness. Needless to say, the double meaning of 'country', as both nation and rurality, contributed to this lexicographic motley.

In *Mansfield Park,* published in 1814, Jane Austen presents us with something close to this interpretation on several occasions. She speaks of 'one of the largest estates and finest places in the country', when the reference seems to be to the county; there is talk of 'ladies residing in the country', in this case, in regard of Northamptonshire; and there is mention of 'an establishment being formed in another country', when, self-evidently, the referral is to another shire, not to another nation. By and by, Jane Austen, with exemplary exactitude, also in *Mansfield Park* (in which, sufferers from the Paul Jennings' syndrome may wish to be reminded, Fanny Price is the somewhat priggish and unusually self-effacing heroine) refers to our homeland as 'the United Kingdoms'.

In those choices of phrases may be seen an inkling of why our erstwhile lords and masters stuck so rigidly to the 'county' terminology. It was excessively important to them and to the ambit of their immediate society at a time when many treated their 'county', socially and politically, not least given the transport problems, as we nowadays think of our 'country'. After all, Jane Austen never visited London. Even today, in some ranks of society, there is a tendency to speak loftily and snobbishly of being born in Loamshire or of visiting Stableshire, when it is clear that the speaker was actually born at or heading towards just one spot within the county in question.

Thus does the work of great-aunt Jane, and the keen performances of her great-nephews for the Gentlemen of Berkshire, unite to tell us something about why and how the notion of 'county' cricket became so persistent. Jane Austen, rather like Snow White with her seven great-nephews, also informs us exactly about the status of the 'gentleman' who was to play so significant a role in the evolution of top-class cricket, but a worthy successor of Jane Austen in the rich lineage of English novelists was, at a more crucial juncture, to define this phenomenon with acute and kindly observation.

In one of his last novels, *The Fixed Period*, published in 1882 shortly after his death that same year, Anthony Trollope includes a prescient fantasy of cricket in the spring of 1980. A Test match between England and Britannula at Gladstonopolis in the South Pacific is described, with some reference to the likely mechanisation of the game, including 'a machine upon the head by which brain and features are protected.' It is a totally uncharacteristic novel, being a lampoon on colonial expansion and, with Sir Kennington Oval and Sir Lords Longstop opening the batting and runs amassed by the thousand, it is far from Anthony Trollope's normal even-tempered pace and grip on reality. Curiously enough, England contrived to play a couple of Tests against Australia in the January and February of 1980, after a first Test of a three-match mini-rubber in the December of 1979, thereby fulfilling some element of Trollope's prophecy.

That apart, Anthony Trollope has curiously little to say about cricket, despite the fact that many of his stories are based among the very social echelons that made Lord's and other arenas their second home. An enthusiastic twice-a-week huntsman, he peppered his writing with actual or metaphoric chases, but there is little or no cricket. A reasonable sample of a third, that is, sixteen out of the 47 novels, reveals but a couple of other mentions. For example, in *The Warden* (1855), complaining of the dullness of Archdeacon Grantly's rectory at Plumstead Episcopi, he finds that worthy's sons uncompanionable: one of them 'told me once that he considered cricket, on the whole, to be a gentleman-like game for boys, provided they would play without running about...' Such effeteness scarcely appealed to the energetic Trollope. For all that paucity of direct reference, Anthony Trollope manages to convey more of the <u>social</u> character of Victorian cricket than any other contemporary author. This is because his chosen ground, outlined with loving elaboration, encompasses the two chief sociological factors that influenced the kernel of 19th century cricket. One of these is the infinitely complex relationships of the English social classes in the post-1830 period. The other is the ecclesiastical aspect of Victorian life and its profound effect on everyday existence.

Older readers may recollect Billy Bennett, most trenchantly expansive of the 'cod' monologists from the fine old days of the variety theatre. His bill matter was 'Almost a Gentleman'. Anthony Trollope might have recognised the false delicacy of such discrimination. Almost was as bad as far distant. One could not be a bit gentlemanly, anymore than one could be a bit pregnant. It was an unqualified condition. It exactly controlled the spot where one attached oneself to the social fabric. The church pew ('paid' not 'free'); the theatre seat (stalls not gallery); the pub bar (saloon not public); the 'class' - emphatic word - of railway carriage; the shop entrance or counter; even the 'select' or 'common' end of the seaside resort - gentlemen and their families went one way and non-gentlemen the other. In daily practice, as three 'classes' of railway carriage reminds, it was ever more complicated than that, and Anthony Trollope was outstanding among English novelists of the era in assessing the tiny gradations of class distinction and usage.

At Miss Thorne's *fete champetre* at the Ullathorne estate in *Barchester Towers* (1857) there are problems in deciding who should be seated where and with whom: 'It is in such definitions that the whole difficulty of society consists'. Mrs Greenacre grows incensed because Mrs Lookaloft, whom she regards as a co-eval, has contrived to be 'sitting as grand as fivepence in madam's drawing-room', although the prudent doctrine of Farmer Greenacre - 'if so be that we cannot enjoy the dinner that madam gives us because Mother Lookaloft is sitting up there on a grand sofa, I think we ought all to go home' - might be attractive to more modern demotic values.

Elsewhere Trollope placidly concluded that 'the one great line of demarcation in the world was that which separated gentlemen from non-gentlemen'. The term derives from the older division of 'gentle' and 'simple', for the pieman, Simon, was not, as one suspects most of us believed as, in child-like lisp, we chanted the nursery rhyme, stupid, merely inferior. Echoing the novelist's preoccupations, Victoria Glendinning, in her felicitous biography of Anthony Trollope, wrote that 'gentlemen recognised one another by complex codes of dress, gesture, taste, use of language and shrewd references.' In *The Last Chronicle of Barset* (1867) the well-endowed Archdeacon Theophilus Grantly receives the new but relatively impoverished (only one servant) vicar of St Ewold's, Josiah Crawley. Their children are about to marry, and the latter is embarrassed that his daughter has no money. The Archdeacon consoles him: 'We stand', said he, 'on the only level ground on which such men can meet each other. We are both gentlemen'.

Such passages inform us more readily about the nature of the organisation of Victorian cricket than a host of dense academic texts. From the consolidation of county cricket from around the middle of the century, and for another hundred years, cricket strove to maintain an integrated construct of Gentlemen and Players, just as, in other fields, including the army, the great households and many business companies, something of the same cross-class unity prevailed. It is, of course, over-simplistic to use Gentleman and Player as synonyms of amateur and professional, paid and unpaid. In cricket, as in society at large, and as the Trollopean opus constantly makes lucidly apparent, 'gentleman' is a social not an economic category. The game was rather given away by the 1879 MCC enquiry into 'the definition and qualification of amateur cricketers'. This decreed that £50 should be the maximum expenses for an amateur's season, at a time when some run-of-the-mill professionals, in those days of 'no-play, no-pay' and with top match fees of £4 or £5, inclusive of expenses, would have happily settled for such a sum.

W.G.Grace is the classic instance of the man who could not afford economically to play as an amateur and could not afford socially to play as a professional. Another colourful dichotomy is that of A.C.MacLaren and Nottinghamshire's William Gunn. The majestic amateur was, vocationally speaking, a disaster, with a series of madcap and bungled schemes to his discredit. The professional was co-founder of the prosperous Gunn and Moore sports goods' firm and died a wealthy man in 1921, leaving a small fortune of £57,392. Of course, there were amateurs who lived in luxury and professionals who died in penury; the point is that money was not necessarily the defining marker. As for Anthony Trollope, always the champion of gentlemanly behaviour himself, he fulmigated against the profiteering Exhibition teams of professionals in his preface to *British Sports and Pastimes*, branding their itinerant displays in mid-19th century as 'the monster nuisance of the day.'

From the myriad anecdotes about the class divisions in cricket one brief but picturesque sample makes the point succinctly. It is recalled by John Ede in a cogent article on this whole subject, published in the Journal of *The Cricket Society*, vol.14, no.1, Autumn 1988, and entitled 'It's Not Cricket'.

The Warwickshire and England wicket-keeper, 'Tiger' Smith, met his captain as they emerged from their separate gates to take the field. 'Good morning, Tiger', said the skipper; 'Good morning, my Lord', answered E.J.Smith, and, emboldened by his leader's apparent good cheer, added, 'just right for cricket.' His Lordship immediately snapped back, 'twice a day - good morning and good night - that's enough for me.'

An interesting analogue may be found in the world of track and field athletics, which, like many other sports, was formally developed from public school and varsity origins. In 1866 the Amateur Athletic Club of England was founded to 'supply the want of an established ground upon which competitions in amateur athletics sports might take place between gentlemen amateurs'. The phrase 'gentlemen amateurs' was perhaps more exact than cricket's looser usage of 'gentlemen' and 'amateurs' as alternatives. Indeed, the Club went on to define an amateur as 'any gentleman', not only who did not seek financial gain from his sport, but who was not 'a mechanic, artisan or labourer'. Even when tradesmen and clerks attempted to join such circles, there were, initially, ructions: they had the brass but not the polish. Moreover, it was arguments in 1893 about the reimbursement of bona fide losses of working time that led to the formation of the Northern Union, known as the Rugby League from the 1920s, leaving Rugby Union to the gentlemen.

The fascination, in cricketing and other circles, lay in that fact that, although being a 'gentleman', like being a 'lady', admitted of no modifying qualification, it was an extremely subtle differentiation. It was not a rigid caste system with a wide 'no gentleman's land' between the groupings. The borderlands were close and touching, with the decisions more instinctive than formal. Describing Samuel Prong in *Rachel Ray* (1863), Anthony Trollope praises him for his devoutness, sincerity, intelligence and hard work, continuing, '...true in most things to the instincts of his calling - but deficient in one vital qualification for a clergyman of the Church of England; he was not a gentleman'. Interestingly, Trollope denies that Mr Prong is a liar or a thief or ill-mannered: 'I am by no means prepared to define what I do mean, - thinking, however, that most men and most women will understand me.'

Trollope's condemnation of that errant clergyman acts as a link between the two aspects now being considered. The clergy of the Church of England played a major role in the extension of cricket among the populace in

Victorian times. For instance, Jack Williams, that very thorough and at the same time very astute historian, has calculated that, as late as 1900, 97 out of 111 cricket clubs in the Bolton area and 59 out of 81 in the environs of Burnley had church affiliations. Possibly a third of Oxbridge blues in the Victorian period became clergymen and, in this bright age for the Anglican communion, they and hundreds of others, equal in enthusiasm if not in competence, ensured that cricket was a vital part of community and church life. We are at once reminded of Charles Dickens' promotion of Sunday church-going and cricket as complementary facets of the good life.

The 'Muscular Christianity' of men like Charles Kingsley, Thomas Hughes and H.H.Montgomery saw in cricket a wholesome and sinless (particularly in its avoidance of the lure of alcohol) recreation for their parishioners and a way of, to employ a modern term, bonding them together in an activity that was healthy in mind and in body. It was of a piece with that extraordinary transformation of English society during the Victorian age by which a seriousness of attitude, a strictness of behaviour and a decency of approach enabled, to use Jeffrey Richards' terms from his cultural analysis of the period, the 'smooth' to dominate, by and large, over the 'rough' elements in day-by-day life.

Anthony Trollope, and not only in his most popular *Chronicles of Barchester* (1855-67), paid affectionate attention to the values and trials of the Anglican clergy. As with his scrutiny of class attitudes, however, his was a perspicacious eye and pen, and it did not suit his purpose to lump all clergymen together into one theological basket. Just as he exhibited a usually kindly bias toward gentlemen, he also showed a genial prejudice in favour of what he, like other contemporary writers, referred to as the 'high and dry' wing of the Church of England. He found uncongenial the Evangelical or 'low church' element whose leaders set a strict example of serious piety. He was a trifle unfair to them, for, although they often lacked intellectual depth and understood little of the church as a social institution, they were a substantial influence and the work of reformers like Lord Shaftesbury or of organisations like the British and Foreign Bible Society or the Church Missionary Society owed much to their 'enthusiasm', as it was not always courteously called.

The high church party was more easy-going and conservative by inclination, which suited Trollope. It was keen to encourage education through the National Society, if only to prevent the dreaded Dissenters, as the non-conforming sects were then generally known, from taking undue advantage and, all in all, its clergy adopted a more tolerant and worldly-wise approach to the problems of its parishioners. Thus Trollope, although always a balanced drawer of character with a conscious eschewal of the 'sensational', leans towards the likes of Archdeacon Grantly, of congenial 'high church' opinions, in *Barchester Towers*, as against the 'low church' likes of Bishop and Mrs Proudie and Reverend Mr Slope, with their dogmatic and sometimes insidious traits, to say nothing of the ungentlemanly Mr Prong.

It must be stressed that there was little argument over doctrine and ceremony: this was a broad church, with differing pools of emphasis. Again, one should not confuse the specific Evangelical C.of E. grouping with the overall evangelical character of society. The historian, Sir Robert Ensor, has wisely concluded that 'No one will ever understand Victorian England who does not appreciate' that, among civilised communities, Victorian England 'was one of the most religious the world has known. Moreover its particular type of Christianity laid a peculiarly direct emphasis upon conduct...very largely a doctrine of salvation by works.' He goes on to suggest that the Victorians 'made other-worldliness an everyday conviction and, so to say, a business proposition.' This insistence that duty should come before pleasure was at its height about 1870, just as cricket was flourishing everywhere. On the whole, historians have not unreasonably proposed that, at this time and after, if the Church of England was the Conservative Party at prayer, cricket was the Church of England at play.

Now just as Anthony Trollope makes us think twice about the nature of amateurism and the gentleman cricketer, he also prompts us to accept a rider to that general proposition about Anglican clergy at the wicket. In one of his very few actual mentions of the game he makes it clear that there was some controversy within the church on this matter. While the Dissenting ministers tended yet to regard sport as a distraction from religious observance and habit and the Roman Catholic priesthood, often born in Ireland and educated on the continent, tended to be uncomprehending of cricket, the Anglican cloth also had its patches of anti-sporting notions, chiefly among the low churchmen.

In *Rachel Ray*, Mrs Prime, an adherent of the sanctimonious Mr Prong, refers contemptuously to two 'high and dry' curates in the following derogatory terms: '...but what are they? They go to cricket-matches, and among young women with bows and arrows'. In the latter case, part of the objection was possibly to the tightly-fitting, masculine-styled, hence provocatively unseemly, dress of the young women, while, in the former, a pertinent objection was to playing cricket on the Sabbath. This was, certainly until half-way through the 19th century when the Saturday half-day came on song, the only decent opportunity for a game of cricket. Some parsons, like Charles Kingsley or those of the Grantly ilk, were wont to encourage the young men of their congregation to play cricket. They might bring their equipment to morning service and then play cricket afterwards and before evensong, an excellent example of the attempt to match social and divine obligations and to find some degree of harmony as between the social classes.

The esteemed church historian, Owen Chadwick, in his 1966 study, *The Victorian Church*, states that the Proudies, Slopes, Prongs and their like 'disapproved of fox-hunting parsons, cricketing parsons, ballroom parsons.' No wonder the affable Anthony Trollope - even if his heartiness was sometimes a mask for a more sensitive spirit - did not appreciate such restraint. It does seem, then, that cricket did not enjoy a monopoly of support from within the Church of England during the reign of Queen Victoria. For some, almost certainly the majority, for the group embraced both the country Tory parsons and the Christian Socialists of the Thomas Hughes brand, cricket was as close to a Christian ritual as one could relish in recreational terms, whilst for others it remained a token, like hunting or dancing, of forgetfulness of holiness and pious ways.

Anthony Trollope, therefore, sharpens our understanding of Victorian cricket at two seminal points in its structure. The persistence in cricket, for good or ill, of both its amateur ethic and of its pseudo-religious gloss long outlasted the Victorian origins and cultural aptness of both. Cricket was, for much of the 20th century, an over-conservative institution, unhappily harried of late into panic-stricken, synthetic and probably damaging repairs, the consequence, in part, of having left the problems too long without making more natural and organic reforms. Anthony Trollope, a lover of tradition, would have sympathised. What he had to say about politics, in *Phineas Redux* (1874), one of his series of shrewd political 'Palliser' novels, may be also apposite to cricket - as well as, maybe unfortunately, still to politics today. 'It is the necessary nature of a political party in this country to avoid, as long as it can be avoided, the consideration of any question which involves a great change...the best carriage horses are those which can most steadily hold back against the coach as it trundles down the hill.'

Footnote: for those interested in these issues I do strongly recommend Gerald Howat's fascinating little book, *Cricket Medley* (Sports History Publishing, 1993, £5.99). Two of its essays, 'Cricket and the Victorian Church' and 'Cricket and the Victorian Novel' are highly relevant and offered great assistance in the writing of this chapter - and the latter includes a lovely description of the Trollopean mock-Test match of 1980. Some aspects of the Jane Austen analysis were included in a short piece, *For County and Country*, in 'Bodyline Books Catalogue', vol 4, summer 1998, and much of the Trollope commentary was included in an article, *Mr A. Trollope (Barsetshire and England)* in 'Cricket Lore', vol. iv, no 7, 2001.

Chapter 5

CRICKET MATCHINGS; A MATTER OF RELATIVITY

There follows a chapter of accidents. The twisted proverb has it that 'where's there's a will, there's relations' and, certainly, one's kins-folk are not easy to avoid, should, unhappy thought, one wish to do so. Great writers are no more immune than the rest of us to the chance permutations of their descendants and it should cause no surprise that some of these turned out to be cricketers of varying degree. This is a rudimentary account of some of this fortuitous lineage, where, quite incidentally, family members of literary stock have distinguished themselves at cricket. It is a set of curios. No arcane theory is advanced to explain that, because of Snooks' success as a thriller writer, grandson of Snooks became a Berkshire googly bowler. One might just as simply have assembled a list of great writers whose progeny became butchers.

Two excuses - by no means justifications - may be offered. First, there does seem to be an innocent human pleasure in establishing such linkages. No article on the actress, Angela Lansbury, is complete without a mention of her grandfather, George Lansbury. Plainly, her evacuation to Hollywood at the start of World War II had more influence on her long career, culminating in her television portrayal of the author-sleuth, Jessica Fletcher, than her descent from the side-whiskered, serge-suited Christian pacifist and Labour Party leader, belligerently accused in the 1930s by Ernest Bevin of hawking his conscience around the country. Yet we quite like hearing of these oddities of relationship, whether it be Sigmund Freud's grand-son, Clement, being into *cuisine*, or Bobby Charlton's daughter taking to our TV screens to tell us how miserable tomorrow's weather is going to be.

It is the quaintness of the juxtaposition that is mildly diverting. Families all engaged in the same activity are commonplace. Cricket supplies untold examples of that facet of human endeavour: the phalanxes of Graces, Tyldesleys, albeit in separate dispensations, Hearnes, Fosters, Walkers, Gunns, Edriches, Langridges are legion. We have already learned, in chapter 4, of Jane Austen's septet of cricketing great-nephews. Writing also runs in families: there is a dynasty of Waughs in literature, just as there is a brotherhood of them in cricket. There is no cause for amazement. It is the slightly unusual connection that has the *frisson* of an appeal.

Second, the very fact that commentators and obituarists are keen to inform us of relationships between cricket and literature may underpin the claim made in the introductory chapter that these are two aspects of our cultural heritage that do have similarities and ties. In some part, an obituary will make reference to any famous ancestor, but one does feel, and it is no more than an instinctive feeling, that, in a cricketing notice, the famed writer will be more likely to be mentioned than the prestigious engineer or surgeon. Indeed, there have been cases where the justification for the minor printed eulogy of the cricketer may well have been the existence of a literary fore-bear.

Take the case of Sir Alfred Erasmus Dryden, who was born in 1821 and who died in 1912, at the goodly age of 90. He played for Winchester in 1839 and 1840 and for Oxford University against Cambridge University in 1841, 1842 and 1843. In his six varsity innings he made 56 runs, with a highest score of 28. Even allowing for the comparatively low scoring of his epoch, it is not the most impressive of records and it is little wonder that the major fact retailed in *Wisden* about the baronet is that, on the distaff side, he was a direct descendant of the poet and dramatist, John Dryden. John Dryden (1631-1700) was far removed in time and inclination from the cricketing knight. A civilised and moderate figure, the child of a Northamptonshire vicarage, he cultivated the heroic couplet zealously, as in the satirical lines of *Absalom and Achitophel* (1681) and wrote his plays - such as *All for Love* (1678) on the grand theme of Anthony and Cleopatra - his critical essays, his translations of, for instance, Virgil and his many poems, several, for he was our first official Poet Laureate, on political topics, with a remarkably lucid acumen. Possibly his descendant, Alfred Erasmus, savoured his fore-bear's couplet:

How blessed is he, who leads a country life,
Unvex'd with anxious cares, and void of strife.

Then there is Walter Scott Seton-Carr, whose forenames rather give away the game, for he was the god-son of Sir Walter Scott. At least the two men shared some of the same times, ten years, to be exact, for the famous Scottish novelist, who was born in 1771, died in 1832, just those few years after the birth of his god-son. It was the success of his initial novel, *Waverley*, in 1814, that led the energetic Scott, nursed by the astute publisher, Alexander Constable, to transfer his chief attentions from verse to prose. He became perhaps the most popular author of his age, with stories like *Rob Roy* (1817)

The Heart of Midlothian (1818) and, said to be Tony Blair's favourite novel, *Ivanhoe* (1819). Not only did this voracious writer rescue and redeem the image of a Scotland chastened by the collapse of the 1745 Jacobite Rebellion, he consolidated the idea of the historical novel, especially as an adjunct of the Romanticist movement. Moreover, he fed the 19th century's avid appetite for medievalism that, among other aspects, affected cricket antiquarianism into the 20th century, and he also provided, in characters like Ivanhoe, an exemplar of the code of chivalry by which the Victorian gentleman was supposed to live and which, in turn, informed the precepts of good sportsmanship, modesty in victory and graciousness in defeat. Now, perhaps sadly, regarded less favourably, in both popular and critical terms, for what is deemed the turgidity of his daunting output, he surely helped to secure the social atmosphere in which cricket, say, from the 1830s, flourished.

More of that in later chapters, for, apart from those not insignificant general points, there is little evidence that the furiously busy Walter Scott found much time to spend at games with his god-son. W.S.Seton-Carr was very much the contemporary of Sir Alfred Dryden. He was born in 1822 and, true to his roots, died in Auchinskeoch, Dalbeattie, in 1910, aged 88. In between whiles he went to Rugby School in 1836 and played in the very first match between MCC and the school, at Lord's in 1840, a year before the legendary 'Tom Brown's match' at Rugby. He scored 4 and 10 and took a couple of wickets, and that was that.

What is interesting is that these two men, Dryden and Seton-Carr, who both lived to mature ages, are memorialised in cricketing obituaries for, apparently, two reasons only: some youthful cricketing ventures and involvement with a celebrated *litterateur*. It is possible that making 28 for Oxford University or taking two wickets at Lord's was not only the highlight but the only light in their modest lives, although we must recollect that cricket obituaries are notoriously reluctant to permit extramural activities to enter their eulogistic lists. Where, for example, broadsheet obituaries will speak feelingly of grieving widows and bereft orphans, the enormous majority of past *Wisden* notices steer cautiously clear of such domestic encumbrances, as if the sex-act was unworthy of ugly mention and as if, guileless notion, cricketers formed a monastic cloister of submissive celibacy. Either way, it is notable that the one fact chosen, above and beyond these pupil or student cricketing exploits, is the literary link.

Some of the same interpretation applies to Rev. John de Soyres, born in Somerset in 1849. Although, again, *Wisden* is silent on the subject of whether the reverend gentleman was husband and/or father, we do learn that, after education at Brighton College and Cambridge University, he had enjoyed an excellent clerical career. Emigrating to New Brunswick in 1888, he 'had made for himself a reputation as the most distinguished preacher in Eastern Canada.' He died, aged 55, in New Brunswick. In his case, we are offered precious little cricketing data, beyond the statement that he 'was a great lover of cricket.' Then comes the crowning glory. We are solemnly informed that he was the nephew of Edward FitzGerald, the translator of *The Rubaiyat of Omar Khayyam*, who also wrote the slightly chilling Calvinistic stanza:

> The Ball no Question makes of Ayes and Noes,
> But Right or Left as strikes the Player goes;
>   And He that toss'd Thee down into the field,
> *He* knows about it all - HE knows - HE knows!

The variety fan will note in those final phrases a presage of Hylda Baker's admiring judgement on the tall, mute Cynthia - 'she knows, yer know.' Edward FitzGerald (1809-93) unlike his nephew, rarely left his native shire of Suffolk, let alone the nation at large. After his local schooling at Bury St Edmunds and his undergraduate years at Trinity College, Cambridge, as a contemporary of Tennyson and Thackeray, he settled down to an existence of placid evenness. He translated widely from classical and European as well as Oriental literature, of which his 1859 version of *Omar Khayyam*, a 12th century astronomer and poet, retains something of its Victorian popularity today. Its rather escapist, lustrous but morose tones acted as a counterpoise to the humdrum and increasingly secular mood of late Victorian life and thought. It acted as a spur to the Aesthetic movement and to the pessimism of writers such as Matthew Arnold and Thomas Hardy. Various cricket selectors, however, might wryly nod in agreement with his view of life:

> 'Tis all a Chequer-board of nights and days
>   Where Destiny with Men for Pieces plays;

Nothing could have been more alien than FitzGerald's gloomy approach to the hearty, sports-loving attitudes of the ex-public schoolboys and varsity men who were to the fore, as clergymen, like FitzGerald's nephew, teachers, military officers and colonial officials, in bringing cricket and other forms of 'rational recreation' to home and Empire. A colossally disastrous marriage apart, Edward FitzGerald's life in Suffolk remained quiet and uneventful, his chief relaxation from his erudite toil being some coastal yachting. He was a withdrawn and melancholy figure and it is hard to believe he was accepted as a model by his more outgoing, cricket-loving, evangelical nephew.

Canon the Rev. Frederic Rawlins Evans has a much greater claim to cricketing renown than his fellow-clergyman, John de Soyres. Born in 1842, he was coached at Rugby School by Alf Diver, who toured North America with George Parr in 1859, the first-ever overseas trip by an English team, and by Cambridgeshire's Tom Hayward, who also toured with George Parr in 1859 and the member of yet another steadfast cricketing clan. F.R.Evans played for Rugby in 1860 and in 1861 and then for Oxford for three years, 1863-65, under the captaincy of R.A.H.Mitchell. Oxford beat Cambridge in all three years, with F.R.Evans contributing exactly 100 runs at a helpful average of 20. He was not bowled overmuch, partly because, at a time when round-arm remained confused with over-arm, until the latter's legalisation in 1864, there were doubts over his action. He was no-balled in the 1863 varsity match for raising his hand above his shoulder. Once such revolutionary tactics were licit, he blossomed and, in 1865, in his only match for Gentlemen *versus* Players, he had match figures of 7 for 83, assisting the Gentlemen to an eight wickets win, after they had lost the previous nineteen encounters. He then pursued his clerical career, but, like many another, he found time to complement the cloth with the willow. He played regularly for the Free Foresters and also for Warwickshire and Worcestershire. He played some twelve first-class games, making 302 runs and taking a handful of wickets.

He was born at Griff House, Nuneaton, in Warwickshire. He was for many years Rural Dean of Monk's Kirby and Honorary Canon of Worcester and he also became Rector of Bedworth. He died, aged 88, at Bedworth Rectory, Warwickshire, in 1927. His birth and death in the Nuneaton area of Warwickshire gives a clue as to his literary connection. He was the nephew of the novelist George Eliot, born Mary Ann Evans, who shared with him a Warwickshire birth qualification, and it is with this fact, if parenthetically, that *Wisden* saw fit to begin his obituary.

As with the others authors cited, it is difficult to visualise Frederic's Aunt Mary trying him out on the Griff House lawn, *a la* Martha Grace, with a few good-length lobs. Indeed, as a serious and intense doubter in supernatural matters, Mary Ann Evans might not have been over-pleased to have a nephew in the church. Intellectually formidable and unrelentingly earnest, George Eliot (1819-1880) stands pre-eminent among English women novelists, with works, many of them with a Warwickshire regional base, such as *Adam Bede* (1859) *The Mill on the Floss* (1860) *Silas Marner* (1861) and *Middlemarch* (1871-72). *Middlemarch,* a profound and many-faceted study of society in the years around 1830, with Coventry serving as the locus for that highly dispassionate scrutiny, is hailed by many commentators as the best of all English novels. Her biographer, Frederick Karl, has written that, along with Queen Victoria and Florence Nightingale, 'she was one of the three most famous women in England...(and) gave the era its intellectual sweep, offered it moral stability.'

After a long and mutually supportive relationship with George Henry Lewes, despite the social and private problems posed by his marital situation, she married late in life the much younger John Walter Cross, a product of Rugby with some interest, it seems, in sport, but depressed and sexually low-keyed by nature. She was 60 and he was 40, that is, much the same age as F.R.Evans: uncle-in-law and nephew may have been contemporaries at Rugby. There is a biographical hint that it was only when honeymooning in Venice that the groom realised he was expected to fulfil his duties carnally. Faced with this alarming prospect, he jumped through the hotel window into the Grand Canal, conventionally the symbol of romantic ardour, not its quenching. Environmentalists averred that he ran more risk from poisoning than drowning, but, in the event, honest Gondoliers dragged him out and it is suspected that, at least in its functional aspect, that was what Graham Greene might have called the end of the affair.

For all we come to know of its doctors and clerics and farmers and merchants, Middlemarch appears to boast neither a cricket club nor, in fact, much wholesome fun-making at all, outside of a few rural pastimes, whilst the miserly weaver, Silas Marner, seeks no redemption among the cricketers, if there are any, on the village green of Raveloe, if there is one. It is not that George Eliot's work lacks humour, for substantial dry play is made of her no-nonsense country-folk, steeped in parochial custom and usage, the likes, for instance, of Martin Poyser and his wife in *Adam Bede.* But there is nothing of cricket and little of other sports. Of course, that is not a fault; there is no earthly reason why there should be, but it does widen the gap between aunt and nephew.

Sorrowfully, the chasm was a yawning one. Frederic Rawlins Evans was one of the four children of Isaac Pearson Evans, George Eliot's brother who was three years older than his sister, and of Sarah Rawlins. Five months after her birth, George Eliot's family had moved to Griff House, which 'remained', according to her biographer, 'as the quintessential place for her, sacred in its potentialities for human development and happiness.' She spent her early years there, enjoying an affectionate relationship with Isaac, but her rationalist thought and irregular domicile with G.H.Lewes led to an extremely lengthy rift with the somewhat narrow-minded and unbending Isaac. She fictionalised these episodes in the relation of Maggie and Tom Tulliver in *The Mill on the Floss*. It is unlikely that she saw anything of her nephew beyond his infancy, if at all. Isaac took over residence at Griff House and there is some poignancy in the fact that young Frederic was born and bred in the very residence his famous aunt forever regarded as her 'temple' but from which she was barred.

Among these fortuitous alliances, the one that attaches a writer to a cricketer in terms of optimal fame is that of the Tennysons. Alfred, Lord Tennyson's grandson, Lionel, captained England and Hampshire, and, excluding C.B.Fry with his part-authorship of *A Mother's Son*, that is probably the highest reaches scaled by any cricketer with literary connections, whilst, alternately, it would be hard to challenge the pre-eminence of the grand Victorian Poet Laureate. The Hon. Lionel Hallam Tennyson was born in Westminster in 1889 and reared in the poet's monumental home, Farringford, on the Isle of Wight. He spent time in Australia with his father, the high-ranking colonial official, Hallam Tennyson, named after the poet's intimate, A.H.Hallam, on whose tragically premature death he penned *In Memoriam*: Lionel was the name of Tennyson's other son.

The younger Lionel then went to Eton and on to Trinity College, Cambridge. University life was brief; Lionel 'ploughed', as the old-time slang had it, his first year exams and became a subaltern in the Coldstream Guards, later transferring to the Rifle Brigade. He led the life of the playboy, gambling extravagantly beyond his means, but, himself almost like some fictional hero, he demonstrated valour and coolness in the Great War, after which he married Clarissa Tennant of the wealthy brewing family, by whom he had two sons before they were divorced in 1928. He inherited the title, becoming the third Baron Tennyson, in 1928 and in 1934 he married a pretty American woman, Carroll Elting.

In 1919 he took over, and held for fourteen turbulent years, the Hampshire captaincy and, in 1921, with, not uncommonly, English cricket in some turmoil, he led England in three matches, and, all told, played in nine Tests. With his left hand injured, his right-handed forays for 63 and 36 at Leeds in 1921 against the all-victorious Australians were properly acknowledged as courageous. In June 1922 he was involved in probably cricket's greatest and most fabled escape. After Warwickshire had scored 223, Hampshire were brushed aside for 15, and Warwickshire's skipper, Hon. Frederick Calthorpe, suggested golf for the final day. An incensed Tennyson at once bet heavily on a Hampshire victory; inspired his colleagues to mount 521 unlikely runs, among which his valet-chauffeur-wicket-keeper, Walter Livsey, contributed a fine century; then saw his dumbstruck opponents skittled for 158, leaving Hampshire very comfortable victors by the wide margin of 155 runs. He played 477 first-class matches, scoring 16,828 combative runs, with a useful average of just over 23.

Large of body and of heart, this invigorating if erratic and rather *passé* character lived on until 1951 when he died at Bexhill-on-Sea. He wrote a couple of volumes of autobiography, but a recent essay by the eloquent Jeremy Malies, in his stylish compendium, *Great Characters from Cricket's Golden Age*, published in 2000, more exquisitely captures the essence of the man. He reminds us that Lionel Tennyson, although born in the shadow of his august grand-parent, was not too learned on that subject, apparently thinking, if anecdote be believed, that Alfred Tennyson composed *Hiawatha*.

Again one sees something close to an 180 degrees turn, *apropos* personality, over the three generations. Born in 1809, Alfred Tennyson's early years were spent, unhappily and impressionably, in a gloomy Lincolnshire vicarage - it is surprising how frequently the church surfaces in these oddities of cricketing and literary connection. In 1850, after years of emotional instability and social upheaval, he succeeded William Wordsworth as Poet Laureate and found contentment in marriage to Emily Sellwood. Thenceforward he became the prestigious bard of the Victorian epoch, loudly praised on all sides. Some of his poems, like *The Charge of the Light Brigade*, *Maud* ('Come into the garden, Maud, for the black bat night has flown.') *Crossing the Bar*, *Ring Out, Wild Bells*; *Ulysses*; *Break, Break, Break*; *Flower in the Crannied Wall*, still have resonance today, especially for those schooled in the classrooms of the middle decades of the 20th century. The tauter and refined minds of modern criticism tend to find 'Alfred Lawn Tennis-on' mawkish in sentiment and prolix in fashion, but his grandeur was assuredly at one with the pomp of his age.

In terms of family relationships, it is interesting to note the unusual discontinuity between Tennyson's life and work. As the cerebral American novelist and critic, Henry James, put it, 'Tennyson was not Tennysonian.' Over against the awesome and often trumpeting sweep of his verse, he was himself rough-mannered, perennially neurotic and reclusive, remembered by his grandson, as Jeremy Malies wittily reminds us, as 'a beard at the foot of the bed.' Lionel, said to have bought a Rolls Royce from the proceeds of a £7000 wager on the prospective bowel movements of two flies, was scarcely the grandson the old poet would have thought fitting, either as a Tennyson or a Tennysonian.

Is the reverse specimen any more revealing? Our few examples of kindred spirits have so far been one way in transference, that is, the ancestor has been the literary person and the descendant, to deploy E.W.Swanton's modest title, a sort of a cricketing person. There is one promising instance where the father was the cricketer and the son the well-known author. Joseph Wells was born in Kent in 1828 and appeared for Kent rather late in life, playing just seven matches for them in the summers of 1862 and 1863. His moment of glory came in the first of those seasons, when, at Box's Ground, Brighton, he removed four Sussex batsmen in as many balls.

Marvellously, the second of this woeful quartet was no other than Spencer Austen-Leigh, one of Jane Austen's great-nephews. Thus did the father of H.G.Wells oust the great-nephew of Jane Austen: 'Emma Meets the Invisible Man.' This feat gave Joseph Wells 6 for 35, but he barely doubled that total of victims in his brief career and scored but 48 first-class runs. Joseph Wells plied his cricketing trade chiefly away from the county circuit, as player and coach at Bromley Cricket Club, for several years with the West Kent club at Chiselhurst, at Bickley Park CC and at Norwich Grammar School. His Haygarth attribution is not excessively laudatory; 'bowls very fast round-armed...as a bat he does not excel.' He died in Hampshire in 1910.

The nephew of Timothy Duke, a reputable maker of cricket bats and balls, trading in Penshurst, Kent, Joseph Wells, like many of his fellow professionals, adopted the retail trade in cricket wares to augment his coaching and playing income. He added china-ware, lamp-wicks and paraffin to his somewhat indeterminate stock and that distinct lack of commercial focus may have contributed to his failure as a shop-keeper. He broke his leg in 1877 and was not able to play again, a further cause of money difficulties. In 1866 Herbert George Wells was born over the shop at 47 High Street, Bromley. His mother, Sarah Wells, was a ladies' maid and H.G.Wells enjoyed some peripheral access through her to 'big houses.' Broken legs ran - not perhaps the most felicitous verb - in the family. The landlord of the Bell Inn in Bromley, showing scant regard for the elder Wells' expertise, as registered by Haygarth, at short slip, dropped the juvenile H.G. on the pub floor. The landlady, her emotions mingled ones of guilt and pity, spoilt the injured child with delicacies and, importantly, books, while his father, noting this interest, began to borrow books for him from the Bromley Library Institute. His long fascination with literature was thereby engendered.

After a miserable *sortie* into the drapery business, he became a student assistant at Midhurst Grammar School, winning a scholarship to the Normal School of Science (later Imperial College, London) where he came under the seminal influence of T.H.Huxley, the prominent populariser of science, and took a first-class degree in zoology. His outstanding science fiction - *The Time Machine* (1895) *The Invisible Man* (1897) *The War of the Worlds* (1898) - obviously stems from these experiences. During this time he taught, at Holt Academy, Wrexham and at Henley Hall School, Kilburn, where the head was the father of A.A.Milne, another whom we will have cause to meet later in these annals. While at Wrexham he permanently damaged a kidney on the football pitch, and soon decided to make writing his full-time career. He made a short-lived marriage - another unfortunately consistent trait in this series of potted biographies - in 1891 to his cousin, Isabel, before a much lengthier marriage, despite his roving ways (particularly exhibited in his amorous liaison with the progressive novelist, Rebecca West) to Amy 'Jane' Robbins in 1898. Prophet and didact as well as author, H.G.Wells remained a cogent figure in British intellectual and political life until and beyond his death in 1946.

However, whereas his father very much influenced the attitudes of this pert, self-assured and occasionally militant personality, the cricketing aspect does not seem to have been a large part of this. Critics normally judge that, rather than his more politicised novels, like *The New Machiavelli* (1911), his superior work is to be found in his novels of social comment, such as *Love and Mr Lewisham* (1900) *Kipps* (1905) and the then highly progressive, even scandalous, *Ann Veronica* (1909). He latched on to the lower middle class gentility and brave, if sometimes pathetic, pretensions of his parents. It is his father as struggling, bungling, day-dreaming tradesman, not as fast round-arm bowler, that he cast in several fictional guises, notably as the eponymous hero, feckless yet cheery, of *The History of Mr Polly* (1910).

At least one cricket match may be found in the works of H.G.Wells. He left it late. In 1942 he published *You Can't be too Careful*, the phrase running like a mantra through the novel, which he wrote in his Regent's Park dwelling, refusing to leave it despite the hazards of German bombing. By now his insistent optimism about the perfectibility of humanity was taking an understandable pounding and his last work - *Mind at the End of its Tether* in 1945 - strikes a decidedly despairing tone. You Can't be too Careful evinces some of this morose pessimism. Sub-titled 'a Sample of Life; 1901-1951', it is the biography of one Edward Albert Tewler, who, as the dates suggest, is allowed to live a little later than the year of publication. Unlike Kipps or Mr Polly, he is - Wells' own word - 'detestable', a wretched, unpleasant man, with none of the blithe spirits of either his fictitious predecessors or Wells pere.

His furtive and deceitful life is set against an evolutionary background, the *motif* being that humankind is a long chalk from becoming a rational and thoughtful species: '...until *Homo Tewler* has got thus far in the balance and control of his incoherent resistances and egotisms, it is preposterous, it is ridiculous, to call him *Homo Sapiens*. That is simply flattering a disagreeable and suicidally backward animal to its own extermination.' The coupling of the personal narrative, although often, after H.G.Wells' fashion, wryly droll, with the weightier and extremely overt message, has left this novel rather lower than many of his others in present day standings. The actuality of another sixty years of history has also overtaken some of its concerns. The mood-swings between the conceptions of a Millennial perfection and glob-al Armageddon have yielded to a more pragmatic view of human existence, with what might be called a DIY mode of political practice more in vogue, a recognition that the battles for human improvement must be fought and re-fought in each generation.. Even among the most progressively radical minds, the anthem is not so much now 'the Internationale', as 'Pick yourself up, brush yourself down, and start all over again.'

Edward Tewler, this specimen of ignoble manhood, is brought up 'narrer' by an over-protective Strict and Peculiar Baptist mother and finds himself schooled in that convention by Mr Myame. Although that earnest peda-gogue, with his handful of charges, accuses greater schools of being obsessed with 'cram and cricket', he does object to what he calls 'loafing about' and acknowledges that cricket may be played 'in a socially acceptable manner' that is 'conducive to morality.' A game is arranged annually with the equally small Bolter's College, where the blazers have a Union Jack on their pockets, and these patriots, eked out with alleged new boys or suspicious additional staff, always win. Edward Albert's nickname is 'butter-fingers' and he enters the fray 'unwillingly and unhopefully', fielding indeterminately between long stop and third man. 'Then a ball hit him...Edward Albert scrabbled at his feet and secured a ball and with all his soul and strength threw it at the wicket keeper. It missed him by about a yard and a half, and knocked the bails of the wicket.' He has run out one of the suspect opponents, 'a blend of Spofforth and Ranjitsinhji.' In response to the congratulations, he modestly murmurs, 'I fort it best to throw straight at the wicket, Sir.' His captain, Mr Plipp, emboldened by this unusual success, brings Tewler on to bowl. A high lob, which H.G.Wells, ever a little uncomfortable with the jargon, calls 'a perfect Yorker', alights on the leg stump of Bolter's best slogger. Myame's School emerge the victors, with Tewler a triumphant none, not out.

'And that is how he became a cricket fan...He did not play very much himself because you cannot be too careful about corrupting your style by inferior practice.' Furthermore, 'A new confidence appeared in his bearing' and Tewler turns violently on Horry Budd, who had been disposed to bully him mildly. Thus the cricket match serves the task of shifting Edward Albert Tewler a notch or two upward towards manhood and giving him a certain shifty boldness. A little later, when he is about to inherit some property, he fantasises about 'seeing a match at Lord's. Maybe I'll be *in* the match.' Significantly, he has, for his momentous run-out, thrown in the wrong ball; the shot had beaten him easily and he had been struck by a ball from a neighbouring game. He has cheated, and that capacity for re-inventing events becomes a discernible thread in the story. Much later he is awarded the George Cross for an act of seeming heroism. serving with the Home Guard at Brighthampton. Once more, 'He rearranged the facts with the same readiness with which he had accepted his triumph in the annual cricket match.' Perhaps, as so often happens, he came to believe the revised version, as, Wells infers, humans do at ever more important levels of truth .

So, in one eventful chapter, H.G.Wells, possibly thinking occasionally of his father, utilises cricket to outline character and advance plot. Forgive a self-indulgent interpolation: shortly after H.G.Wells' death I received, during the stately proceedings of a northern grammar school speech-day, the fourth form progress prize from the hands of the President of the Board of Trade, Harold Wilson. It was that compassionate and ebullient novel, *The History of Mr Polly*. 'Good choice', said Mr Wilson approvingly, and, forty years on exactly, I found myself in a position to mention the occasion to the now ennobled Lord Wilson, somewhiles into his dotage, and speak of my youthful affection for H.G.Wells' writings. Although Harold Wilson, in spite of substantial and sturdy achievements, could be a trifle spiky in political affairs, he was ever infinitely kind in personal relations with ordinary mortals, and I am pleased to seize a small chance to pay that tribute.

So much for a random half dozen *exempla*. Those intrepid enough to attempt to discern a pattern in this tiny clutch of samples, with their thousand and one variables, might simply point to the utter dissimilarity within each of these pairings, as if both nature and nurture had been on vacation, leaving barely a link, apart from the familial one, between the members of each duo. This, then, was rightly introduced as a chapter of accidents. These are curios which leave little room for thoughts about generational continuities, rather pointing to the indiscriminate turns of life's lottery wheel. Personal futures are sometimes difficult to gauge from family circumstances. As F.R.Rawlins' Auntie Mary sagaciously remarked in *Middlemarch*, 'among all forms of mistake, prophecy is the most gratuitous.'

Chapter 6

THE VICTORIAN NOVELIST AT THE CREASE

The little girl who thought - 'Send Us Victorias' - the National Anthem included an urgent request for plums might be forgiven if the fruit in question had been literary plums plucked from the reign of the Queen who gave them their name. If with cinema, radio, television and their allied offshoots, the 20th century was eventually to witness a primarily audio-visual culture, the 19th century was most definitely a literary one, especially so in Europe and the United States.

The novel, often as luxurious and weighty as a rich plum pudding, certainly became pre-eminent as the chief literary form in Britain, and it did so precisely at that point where popular culture adopted an unprecedentedly national format. Great as had been the flowering, say, of Elizabethan drama or Miltonesque poetry, the sheer mechanics of promoting a truly national cultural output were just not available before the reign of Queen Victoria. There were barriers of language, of transport, of schooling and of social attitudes, so that any overall civilised presentations were usually enjoyed by only a small, often metropolitan *coterie*, while a substantial amount of artistic enjoyment, be it theatre, music, story-telling, remained dauntlessly local in character.

The advent of the railways was one of the crucial changes, with, from its momentous start in the 1820s and 1830s, a total of 20,000 miles of rail in place by the death of Queen Victoria, carrying 2.5 million passengers a day, plus, as significantly, much freight, including books and newspapers. In that regard, what W.E.Gladstone had called 'the tax on knowledge' had, mainly under his ministrations, been banished. Advertising duty was abolished in 1853; stamp duty on periodicals in 1855, and paper duty in 1861. In 1836 there were 40 million newspapers sold; by 1861 it was 160 million, whilst, in 1896, *Lloyd Weekly News* became the first newspaper to touch the magic mark of a million copies' circulation. In turn, the production of books and newspapers was helped by much improved industrial techniques and the general progress of such manufacture may be judged by the remarkable leap in the numbers employed in the paper, printing and stationery trades from 90,000 in 1870 to 200,000 in 1901.

Literacy was possibly rather more advanced than is sometimes thought.

There tends to be a view that, until the 1870 Education Act and the onset of the School Boards, ours was a non-literate society, a view which forgets that there was considerable schooling, much of it state-subsidised since the 1830s, although, admittedly, it was haphazard. There is some argument that the pressure for the 1870 legislation came, in part, from the social problem of listless young people, from what were rather impolitely called 'the dangerous and perishing classes'. In a scenario that had redolence for the 1980s and early 1990s, albeit for a slightly later age-group, these were youngsters for whom there was neither work nor school to occupy them: 'attendance' was the critical issue, not literacy. Many had, in fact, been at school for a few years before this stage and learned the Three R's. Moreover, some commentators - among them teachers with perhaps a professionally vested interest - ignore the capacity for the non-school community to convey necessary skills to the young. For example, about three-quarters of girls in domestic service in 1870 were literate, functionally trained to manage a recipe or a shopping-list, as well as maybe some simple moral tracts.

Of course, such literacy was not of a high level, but in 1865 61% of the Royal Navy could read well and only 11% not at all; 80% of miners could, in the 1850s, read and write reasonably well, while, at about the same time, a survey of East Anglia workhouses showed that 87% of the paupers could read and 53% could write. That last fact reminds us that, at those low levels of education, reading is much more prevalent than writing. All in all, and from a poor figure of about 10% literacy in 1500 and some 50% in 1750, it is argued that, by the 1850s, it was 75%. Optimistic opinion puts the figure for working-class literacy as high as 90% by 1870. The sums appear high and, of course, the yardsticks used are not too exacting. Nonetheless, the Penny Post, launched in 1840, was, within a few decades, dispatching 450 million letters a year; someone had to be writing them and reading them. These are complex calculations, the like of which might cause even the most dedicated cricket statistician to flinch, and, among the devoted compilers of such numbers, W.B.Stephens, for his *Education, Literacy and Society, 1830-1870* (1987) deserves reverent mention.

The rush of books was flood-like. As Queen Victoria ascended the throne, there were approximately 2000 new books a year; by the time she died, it was 10,000. The number of novels grew exponentially from 12% (250) of the former to 25% (2500) of the latter figure. There were no fewer than 42,000 Victorian novels. There were no fewer than 3500 Victorian novelists, a third of them women. They each wrote an average of seventeen books, but the average conceals a wide gamut, for 7% compiled a third of the whole. 2%, that is, a hundred, wrote over a hundred each, a different but magnificent sort of century. We tend to think Charles Dickens, with fifteen or sixteen mainline novels, was a superhuman author and, indeed, he demonstrated daemonic energy, but, against that broader perspective, he seems quite lethargic. The point is he did not need to write more than this to make a plentiful income, whereas most of his fellow-practitioners had to churn out the books by the score to scratch a living. In fact, only about 200 or 300 of the, on average, 1200 authors writing at any one time were completely self-supporting through the revenue from their novels, including Anthony Trollope, weighing in with 47 full-length stories.

As is made clear, for example in Michael Wheeler's expert study, *English Fiction in the Victorian Period*, 1830-1890, an important breakthrough was the shift from the three-decker novels, associated with authors like Sir Walter Scott, to the cheaper prints, many of them emerging first in serial form. It was a far cry from half a guinea (52.5p - £1.57,5p for the three, when a working man's weekly wage was about £1) for each volume to a monthly or weekly shilling, just five new pence, for an episode. Mrs Henry Wood's famous *East Lynne* ('Dead, dead, and never called me mother') was published in 1861 and had sold 430,000 copies by 1898. In the ten years after Dickens' death in 1870, over 4 million copies of his books were sold.

There were public and private supports for this vast outpouring. In 1842 Charles Edward Mudie opened the first of his circulating libraries and W.H.Smith, with both his station sales points - hence the term 'railway novels - and his own brand of library, soon followed suit. Public libraries were introduced in 1850, although, initially, the blunder was allowed of permitting funds for buildings but not for books. This soon became a healthy process. In the mid-1880s there were 107 public libraries, with 1.8 million books; by the Great War, there were 438 libraries, with 9.4 million books.

Nor one should forget the group reading. The middle-class *pater familias* really did read Dickens to the family and perhaps the servants, although it is a moot point whether they all enjoyed it with equal enthusiasm. Then there were the readings in Mechanics' Institutes and similar places for working class folk. It was not unlike the family in a circle around the television set today or the customers gathering in the pub to watch football on the big screen. It all added up to an immense national feast of reading and listening.

After its boisterous Hanoverian existence, cricket, hugely bolstered, indeed, shaped and formalised by, the manic gambling of the metropolitan aristocracy, had slumped over the time of the Revolutionary and Napoleonic Wars, a depressive phase in British history, socially, economically and politically. Arthur Haygarth's fourteen invaluable volumes of cricket matches, 1744 to 1878, demonstrate this. He lists 35 fixtures in 1798, then down to a nadir of but two scores for 1811 and 1812, before a jump to 84 by 1840. The number of county clubs was fifteen in 1840; by 1870 only five counties did not have clubs, and county matches, at first-class and lower levels, trebled between 1838 and 1863. In Keith Sandiford's words, 'The age also witnessed an incredible upsurge of club cricket...By 1900, virtually each town, village and hamlet boasted its local cricket heroes.' In the last quarter of the 19th century there were no less than 214 cricket clubs in Birmingham and 224 in Liverpool.

Cricket matured toward its prime in the years from 1890 to the beginning of the 1914-1918 war, a quarter century when cricket reigned supreme as the major spectator and recreational sport. The first-class programme, built around the nascent county championship, steadily grew, with overseas' cricket, including Test matches, to follow. In 1837, when Queen Victoria came to the throne, there were eighteen first-class matches, all in Britain. In the year she died, 1901, there were 219 such fixtures in the British Isles, including those shared with the visiting South Africans, plus two in North America and, over the 'winter' of 1901-1902, a further 39 in Australia, India, New Zealand and the West Indies, a total of 260 first-class games.

Soon association football made its inroads. The turn of the century witnessed the turn of cricket's fortunes: it was about 1900 when the numbers annually watching first-class cricket - roughly a million - was approached by total Football League gates. Hitherto Charles Alcock, Secretary of Surrey Cricket Club and inventor of the FA Cup and rightly meriting some such label as 'the Father of Modern Sport', was amused at the paucity of the Oval crowds for the football final, compared with the swarms for the cricket. 20,000 would often attend a big cricket match, whereas the early cup finals in the 1870s attracted just a thousand or two; it was 1889 before the 20,000 mark was attained for the Cup Final. Cricket, of course, sustained interest on a global, or rather on an imperial and post-imperial basis, but it never again, in Britain, dominated what in a proper connotation of the word, Ranjitsinjhi (or perhaps his amenuensis, C.B.Fry) called 'spectacular' sport.

The Victorian cascades of novels and of first-class cricket matches reaching flood-tide at much the same time is not entirely coincidental. In the longer term, perhaps the most penetrating connection of literature and cricket is that common elements contributed to the growth of both novel-reading and top-class cricket in the Victorian era. Without the railways it would have been impossible to develop a regular first-class programme, such were the vicissitudes of travel beforehand, while the spread of cricket overseas relied heavily on the steam-ship. As did the novel...one of the most poignant scenes of socio-literary history is the steam-ship sailing into New York harbour in 1841 carrying copies of the latest episode of Charles Dickens' *Old Curiosity Shop*. Crowds waited on the quay, shouting 'is she dead?', so anxious were they to learn of the fate of Little Nell.

Cricket buffs came to await the scores of cricket matches with the same apprehension and, oftentimes, distress. Rail and ship, later the electric telegraph, conveyed such data much more quickly, with the rapidly expanding press very active in this regard. The three days it is said to have taken to carry the official news to England of the victory of the Battle of Waterloo in 1815 abruptly seemed to be an *eon*, as the transmission of news, as well as people, was accelerated. An illustration of this is the manner in which it suddenly became essential to share the same measurement of time. No one beforehand had managed to travel quickly enough or send messages swiftly enough to make it necessary to have such chronological conformity. The time varied from town to town, just as, today, there are variations of lighting-up times. The standard British clock was a novelty: it was 1880, with the Statutes (Definition of Time) Act, before Greenwich Mean Time became legally enforceable.

The influential Exhibition XIs of mid-19th century, touring hither and yon, benefited from both the ability to travel more easily and to publicise more effectively. Culturally, an analogue exists between the likes of that intrepid and formidable cricket entrepreneur, William Clarke, organiser of the All-England eleven from 1846, plying his profitable trade and spreading the gospel of cricket, and similar and contemporary itinerant concerns. There were travelling fit-up theatres or waxworks, for example, featured in Charles Dickens' *Nicholas Nickleby* (1838/39) and *The Old Curiosity Shop* (1840/41), with, respectively, Vincent Crummles and Mrs Jarley the *alter egos* for the redoubtable William Clarke.

There was a little more leisure time and a little more money available for buying books or playing cricket. The 'short Saturday' - it was still an eight hour day, with a finish at 2.0 pm; hence the traditional football kick-off of 3.0 pm - was granted textile workers in 1847, the prelude to a general Saturday half-day, while the ritual of the middle class annual holiday was introduced in the 1860s. Railwaymen were the first manual workers to obtain holidays with pay in the 1870s. It is perhaps no coincidence that 1871 saw both the introduction of bank holidays and the first use of turn-stiles on cricket grounds. Wages rose 40% between 1860 and 1875 and by 1900 they were 80% higher than in mid-century.

Let us not go overboard. The portrait of the good people of Victorian England watching county cricket by day and buried in the latest Thackeray novel by night is a beguiling but, in any comprehensive sense, a misleading one. Nevertheless, it constitutes a component of a more complicated whole and there are certainly similarities explaining why some people of all classes were drawn to cricket and to the novel. It is, therefore, scarcely surprising that Victorian novelists sometimes utilised a cricketing scene or metaphor in their work, as we have already remarked in the examples of Dickens and Trollope, confident that it would be readily understood by the vast majori-ty of their readers.

Sometimes the novelist in question proves to be an unexpected employer of cricketing reference and Mrs Gaskell is possibly one who might elicit some surprise. Although Elizabeth Gaskell, the daughter of William Stevenson, a civil servant and occasional preacher, was born in Chelsea in 1810, her life and work were to be strongly associated with Manchester. After a somewhat nomadic girlhood, including spells at school in Stratford-upon-Avon and with relatives in Newcastle upon Tyne, as well as, more influentially, in Knutsford, some miles south of Manchester on the Cheshire plain, she mar-ried the Unitarian parson, William Gaskell. He was minister at Cross Street Unitarian Chapel in the centre of Manchester, where he was noted for his academic pursuits. The publication of her first novel, *Mary Barton*, in 1848, led to an encouraging friendship with Charles Dickens, and she first pub-lished her gentle tale of *Cranford*, a thin disguise for Knutsford, in his *Household Words* between 1851 and 1853. Another of her novels, *North and South* (1855) is possibly the only classical title that constitutes a famous cricket fixture. Her biography of Charlotte Bronte (1857) led to the kind of legal shenanigans we more readily associate with present-day libel courts, principally because of her candid remarks about the   relationship   of Branwell Bronte with Mrs Edward Robinson to whose children he was household tutor.

In 1864, not far from the Queen's Hotel where, that same year, Lancashire County Cricket Club was formed, she began serialisation in *The Cornhill Magazine* of what has been described as 'the most underrated novel in English.' More sadly, in 1865, the year Lancashire beat Middlesex by 62 runs in their initial main county match, Mrs Gaskell died, the last chapter of her greatest novel unwritten but with its outline confided to her publisher. It was *Wives and Daughters*, a fitting conclusion to a career in authorship that touched sympathetic chords with her honourable treatment of industrial deprivation and gladdened hearts with stories set in more genteel pastures. To Wives and Daughters she brought an urbane, almost Austenian balance, replete with steady pace and temperate humour.

The story is set in Hollingford, for which, again, as in *Cranford*, Duncombe in *Mr Harrison's Confessions* and the Eccleston of *Ruth* (1853) read Knutsford, where Mrs Gaskell spent some of her formative years with her aunt, Mrs Lumb, and not too far distant from her grandparents just four miles away at Sandlebridge. Cumnor Towers, the great estate of Lord and Lady Cumnor in the novel, is based on Tatton Park, the seat of the Egerton family and the Assembly Rooms of the George Inn were, in reality, those of the Royal George Inn. Hamley Hall, home of the solidly conservative Squire Hamley and his two sons, one of whom, Roger, a neo-Darwinian scientist, eventually turns out to be the book's hero, is taken from nearby Old Tabley Hall. One or two of the characters are derived from real life. Mr Gibson, the hardworking and mettlesome doctor and father of the winsome heroine, Molly Gibson, is modelled on Mrs Gaskell's much-loved doctor-uncle, Peter Holland, who practised in Knutsford. Mr Gibson re-marries unwisely, and Molly's step-mother, Clare Kirkpatrick is fashioned very tellingly after Elizabeth Gaskell's own step-mother.

The book is set in the mid-1820s, that is, about the time Mrs Gaskell was resident in Knutsford. The characters' journeys from and to London, courtesy of flying coaches and Macadamised roads, had been reduced from three days to one day, but the hints of railways in the book sound like people nowadays talking of passenger space travel. The novel is intricately plotted, but its central line is Molly Gibson's gradual coming to maturity, while, very much to the point, the novel includes a couple of cricketing references.

The first is a minor one. Describing how the land agent, Mr Preston, who has designs on Molly's step-sister, the vivacious Cynthia, has emotional flaws masked by highly competent professional and social skills, Mrs Gaskell lists, among these various talents, that he is 'a capital cricketer'. Did he perhaps play for Hollingford Cricket Club? Herein lies the second reference. One of the doctor's apprentices, Mr Coxe, attempts maladroitly to woo Molly. To sublimate what he terms his 'calf love', Mr Gibson says, 'I might have pre-scribed your joining the Hollingford cricket Club and set you at liberty as often as I could on Saturday afternoons.'

A cold douche of cricket as an anti-inflammatory for the stricken heart is not readily to be found in the conventional pharmacopoeia, but we are left with the intriguing question of whether, forty years later, Elizabeth Gaskell was fondly remembering her days as a teenage cricket spectator in Knutsford. We know from the detailed researches of Tony Percival into Cheshire cricket that, when XXII of Cheshire played the All England Exhibition XI at Macclesfield in 1854, one Thomas Stevenson played and that he represented Knutsford. Curiously, Stevenson was Mrs Gaskell's maiden name. Tony Percival has also kindly drawn my attention to a notice in *Bell's Life*, dated 28 September 1843, of a match on Knutsford Racecourse between Knutsford Royal Albert and Over and the Winsford Club. Knutsford won by three wickets, although the report rather pleasingly devotes five lines to the actual cricket and twenty-two lines to the post-match festivities.

Possibly there was cricket on the Knutsford Racecourse prior to that. It is a cheerful thought that Elizabeth, then a pretty and amiable Unitarian ado-lescent, might have spent her Saturday afternoons watching the real-life Prestons and Coxes at play.

However, the Victorian novelist who utilised cricket quite frequently was the now little-read George Meredith. He was born in Portsmouth in 1828 and, after a faltering start as a solicitor, he settled for what was eventually a prosperous life as a journalist, as a poet well esteemed in his day, and, his stolid bread and butter, thirty years as a reader for Chapman and Hall, the publishers, as well as a novelist. In 1849 he married Mary Ellen Nicholls, the widowed daughter of the outlandish satirical writer, Thomas Love Peacock, author of books like *Nightmare Abbey*, and some of his father-in-law's 'urbane ridicule' was invested into his own writing. Mary Ellen soon decamped to Capri with the artist, Henry Wallis, but George Meredith found contentment in his second marriage, to Marie Vulliamy, and in cordial life at Box Hill. He had three children, two by his second wife, and one of these, William Maxse Meredith, also a reader for Chapman and Hall, played cricket for J.M.Barrie's Allahakbarries, of which much more anon in chapter 11. George Meredith died in 1909.

As a publisher's reader, George Meredith had his ups and downs: he encouraged Thomas Hardy and George Gissing, but frowned upon Samuel Butler's *Erewhon* and that best of best sellers, *East Lynne*. His own novels might be described shortly as comedy romances. 'The Comic spirit', he wrote, 'is not hostile to the sweetest songfully poetic.' He did not write in realistic mode, scorning what he called 'cobwebs in the putrid corner', rather striving to the intuitive and the intelligent: 'blood and brains and spirit, thee...join for true felicity' was a line from his verse that serves as a text for his writing. Oscar Wilde, a fervent admirer, called him 'a prose Browning', such was the vitality of his approach. His tales race along with some verve, galloping along like the rattling coaches in which many of his effulgent characters breathlessly travel. His style is obliquely unorthodox, perhaps a reason for his lack of 20th century popular appeal. In his 1948 biography, Meredith, Siegfried Sassoon speaks of his 'irrepressible energy and obtrusiveness' and this vim, this force, applies to Meredith's inclusion of cricketing scenes in several of his novels.

Such pictures are to be found in *The Ordeal of Richard Feverel* (1859) *The Adventures of Harry Richmond* (1871) and *Diana of the Crossways* (1885). Of his mainstream novels only *Beauchamp's Career* (1876), with its primarily political accent, and *The Egoist* (1879), Meredith's masterly saga of the conceited Sir Willoughby Patterne's romantic problems, appear to omit direct cricketing reference. For example, in *The Adventures of Harry Richmond* (1871) we find the hero, child of an ill-advised elopement, in search of fortune, something after the fashion of a more decorous Tom Jones, and ultimately and safely marrying the English heroine, Janet Ilchester. Harry, freed from school, 'played a single-wicket game, he giving me six runs, and crestfallen he was to find himself beaten; but, as I let him know, one who had bowled at Heriot for hours and stood against Saddlebank's bowling, was a tough customer, never mind his age.' Cricket tells us about Harry's character in an understandable and refreshing manner.

Later, on one of his many trips, Harry finds 'The driver was very eloquent on cricket matches. Now, cricket, he said, was a fine manly sport; it might kill a man, but it never meant mischief; foreigners themselves had a bit of an idea that it was the best game in the world, though it was a nice joke to see a foreigner playing at it!...Well, and I ask why don't more gentlemen take to cricket? 'Stead of horses all round the year! Now there's my notion of happiness...it comprises - count: lots o' running; and that's good; just enough o' taking it easy; that's good...and you say good morning to the doctor and the parson; for you're in health body and soul, and ne'er a parson'll make a better Christian of ye, that I'll swear.' No wonder, awash with this cricketing eulogy, Harry and his companion 'talked of the ancient raptures of a first of May cricketing-day on a sunny green meadow, with an ocean of a day before us, and well-braced spirits for the match.' The essence of how, half way through the Victorian period, cricket was widely regarded is pithily conveyed in the forthright speech of the plebeian driver and the nostalgic thoughts of his higher-born passengers.

George Meredith's most compelling cricket scene is to be found in another early novel, *Evan Harrington* (1861). It is a candid study of snobbery, a theme close to George Meredith's heart. Evan Harrington is the son of a tailor of lordly ambition and many debts. His three sisters have made what the late 20th century would have termed upwardly mobile marriages and they are anxious to hide their trading origins as they conspire for Evan to wed the eligible Rose Jocelyn of Beckley Court. His sister, Louisa, the preening Countess de Saldar, is especially forward in pressing this design and is a remarkably canny manipulator. Truth will out; there are stratagems galore and, finally, Evan, revealing 'the soul of a gentleman', wins his love, the fresh, independently-minded Rose, and sets off on a diplomatic career.

The autobiographical element of the story adds to the pleasure, particularly perhaps for the cricket-lover. George Meredith was an optimistic, exuberant, brilliant young man of humanist thought - hence his insistence that life itself must be totally valued and appreciated - and bravely athletic disposition. Furthermore, he was himself the son of a tailor and naval outfitter and he uses the not commonplace forename of his grandfather - Melchisedek - for Evan's father's name, and he did have three sisters, no doubt troubled socially by the stigma of their family being in trade.

Thus, in this knowledge, one may see George Meredith as Evan Harrington as, at 'the Green Dragon' tavern, he meets three young gentlemen: 'They were clad in cricketing costume, and exhibited the health and manners of youthful Englishmen of station. Frolicsome young bulls bursting on an assemblage of sheep, they might be compared to...the three young cricketers were hostile from the beginning'. They include Rose's brother, the cavalier Harry, and Evan's rival for her hand, the disdainful young Laxley. Trouble is soon afoot.

There follows the cricket match between the neighbouring villages of Fallowfield and Beckley. George Meredith, like Jane Austen with her exquisitely handled dances, seeks foci where characters may be assembled, in his case often of differing class origins. He chooses the picnic, the grand dinner and the riding excursion as well as the hostelry and the cricket match. In these televisual times the *Eastenders'* 'Queen Vic' and *Coronation Street's* 'Rover's Return' serve the same purpose. The cricket match throws together both major and minor characters, thereby propelling various parts of the plot forward, with letters passed and secrets exchanged. What is notable is that George Meredith manages somehow to give us a vigorous game of cricket without any of the boldly drawn characters losing any of their effect. The cricket is not pushed to the rear, left as a mere back-drop. It is a cleverly organised piece of authorship.

For example, the wily Countess, pursuing her military generalship, as Meredith apostrophises it, flatters the narcissistic Harry: 'You are a great cricketer. What else?...Can you not be told you are perfect without seeking to improve, vain boy? You can play cricket, and you can walk (well), and will very soon learn how to give your arm to a lady. I have hopes for you.' No wonder Harry thought 'what a rattling fine woman this is', even if she found 'creeket', when beguiling another, the MP, Sir George Lowton, 'very unintelligible - indistinct, is it not?' That worthy parliamentarian sees in cricket 'our peculiarity, this absence of extreme centralization. It must be encouraged. Local jealousies, local rivalries, local triumphs - these are the strength of the kingdom.'. The curate, Mr Parsley, 'observed that sound Churchmen unanimously supported the game', while disgruntled Evan, subject to romantic misunderstanding, asks himself why 'he had come on this cricket-field to be made thus miserable?'

Meanwhile the cricket continues with a swing. Nick Frim, the Beckley wicket-keeper - and 'the boys of Beckley rejoice in possessing him' - is 'long-limbed, wiry, keen of eye'. Usually 'he is too sensible of the joys of a grand spanking hit', but he tempers this *bravura* with a 'rare display of skill', eager to impress the apple of his eye, the upper housemaid at Beckley Court, Polly Wheedle. Sadly, 'The foolish fellow did not know that they care not a straw for cricketing fame.'

Here is another excerpt: 'Then again, the last two men of an eleven are twins: they hold one life between them; so that he who dies extinguishes the other. Your faculties are stirred to their depths. You become engaged in the noblest of rivalries: in defending your own, you fight for your comrade's existence...Behold, then, the two bold men of Beckley fighting to preserve one life. Under the shadow of the downs they stand, beneath a glorious day, and before a gallant company...The sons of first-rate families are in the two elevens, mingled with the yeomen and whoever best can do the business. Fallowfield and Beckley, without regard to rank, have drawn upon their muscle and science...

'What a beautiful hit!' exclaimed one of the ladies, languidly watching the ascent of the ball.

'Beautiful, d'you call it?, muttered the squire. The ball, indeed, was dropping straight into the hands of the long-hit-off. Instantly a thunder rolled. But it was Beckley that took the joyful treble - Fallowfield the deeply-cursing bass. The long-hit-off, he who was never known to miss a catch - butter-fingered beast! - he has let the ball slip through his fingers.

Are there Gods in the air? Fred Linnington, the unfortunate of Fallowfield, with a whole year of unhappy recollection haunting him in prospect ere he can retrieve his character...'

It is an intricately woven pattern of the interplay of plot and the clash of character along with a gladsome depiction of cricket and its philosophies. It is difficult to think of another piece of fictional writing which so winningly aligns cricket and story in action; the one is never the subsidiary of the other.

Robert Louis Stevenson very self-deprecatingly believed that he was the model for Sir Willoughby, Meredith's 'Egoist'. George Meredith charmingly demurred: he insisted Sir Willoughby Patterne was all of us. Cricketers and cricket-watchers, of all shapes and sizes, might find 'all of us' among the players and spectators of that Beckley and Fallowfield encounter.

Chapter 7

CURIOUSER AND CURIOUSER - CARROLLIAN CRICKET

'He bowled one ball, and then was taken off, the captain remarking that the ball, had it gone far enough, would have been a wide.' Such spectacular deviation from the ancient virtues of line and length would not normally lead to further cricketing analysis, but the inaccurate bowler was Lewis Carroll. This, is one acknowledged venture into formal cricket, most probably at Rugby School, was recorded by Falconer Madan, who collected reminiscences of Lewis Carroll, the centenary of whose death in 1898, just thirteen days before his 66th birthday, was celebrated a few years ago.

Lewis Carroll was born as Charles Lutwidge Dodgson - he translated and reversed his forenames to find a pseudonym - at Daresbury Parsonage in Cheshire. It was 1832. The early signs of a cricketing connection are not promising. Both at Daresbury and at Croft Rectory, near Darlington, whence the family moved in 1843 with their clergyman father, he showed few signs of athletic attainment. Whilst quiet and uncomplaining, it is probable that the diffident and stuttering young Charles suffered in the rowdy atmosphere of Rugby, with its severe disciplines and rough-and-tumble domesticities. He was at Rugby after the death of Thomas Arnold when that worthy's reforms were under pressure and bullying and excessive fagging had returned in undue measure. It is true he wrote of a couple of framed cricketing pictures in his bedroom at Croft, but, truth to tell, he was no sportsman, and, according to his niece, Violet Dodgson, avoided games at school..

However, he was intently absorbed by child-oriented games and puzzles. The dual adventures of Alice are themselves, whether down the rabbit-hole or through the looking-glass, negotiated through an amalgam of games, like races, croquet, chess and cards. He was especially keen on playing croquet with his child-friends on varied collegiate and clerical lawns. Once established at Christ Church, Oxford, first as a student, then as a mathematics don in holy orders, he proceeded to develop that burgeoning interest - and the strange paradox of his life evolved. On the one hand, was the tall, withdrawn tutor, darkly and conventionally garbed, whose academic studies in logic and maths are particularly well thought of by his scholarly successors. On the other hand, he was a man whose genius lay in that he could 'capture the interest of children and engage their young emotions...He evidently possessed a special gift for understanding children that continually endeared him to them.' It was a mutual attraction, for, as his most modern biographer goes on to write, 'He loved to make them laugh, he invented games to play with them, he encouraged them, he plied them with gifts, photographed them - he simply worshipped them.' Perhaps the two sides of his nature - the technical and erudite with the child-centred imagination - most nearly meet in his photography, in his day a wearisome and messy affair. He is generally regarded as the finest photographer of children produced by the 19th century.

It is perhaps fairer to say of Lewis Carroll, as of so many of us, that he enjoyed games whilst not being very proficient in their performance, and also that he much preferred the more serene delights of croquet and cricket than the rough-house of the football codes or the bestiality of bloodsports which, unusually for his era, he heartily condemned. His diaries include some positive reactions to cricket. In May 1857 he logs 'a strange accident in catching a ball at cricket' which befell his younger brother, Wilfred. He was 'struck between the third and fourth fingers, tearing a wound in his hand.' Much later, in September 1882, we find the 52-year-old Lewis Carroll at Eastbourne, where he 'succeeded in bringing together, for a game of cricket, Stuart, Bertram, Basil Brunton, and Claude and Philip Lonsdale.' He does not say whether he undertook any bowling duties himself.

He was also an interested spectator of cricket, as he was of rowing. On Saturday 17 September 1856, 'we went down afterwards and saw the end of the Christ Church and All England match. We were beaten in one innings with about 50 runs to spare.' This, of course, was a prime example of a fixture played by one of the famed Exhibition teams of mid-19th century, whereby itinerant troupes of talented professionals plied their trade against local and normally inexperienced amateurs and, in so doing, spread the construct and techniques of cricket to the furthest corners of the kingdom. Haygarth supplies the details. The England eleven, with George Parr and Julius Caesar among the runs, made 278, while XVIII of Christ Church could only muster 130 and 77, Edgar Wilsher being the chief wicket-taker.

Lewis Carroll travelled on occasion to Lord's. He attended the Varsity Match on 21 June 1855, after paying 'a long visit' to the Royal Academy. He 'stayed to the end of the 1st innings of Cambridge (139) and to see Oxford in.' It is said to have been 'a marvellously close contest, and, according to a contemporary source, 'the hitting - and the cricket generally - is described as very brilliant.' W.J.Kempson, who later fought in the Chinese campaign of 1860, steadied the Cambridge innings which Lewis Carroll watched, with A.Payne taking 7 for 42, before his dashing 35, not out, enabled Oxford to reach 146. The Cambridge captain, G.R.Johnson, later a New Zealand politician, took 4 for 39. After a poorish start, Cambridge rallied to 152 in their second attempt, after which B.M.Randolph, a student at Lewis Carroll's college, scored 61, leading Oxford to an exciting "three-wickets" victory.

A year later Lewis Carroll went to the Magdalen College ground at Cowley Marsh, Oxford, on 19 May *1856*, 'to see the Oxford and Marylebone match.' He saw the first day of another close engagement. The MCC scored 139 and 124, with the professionals, John Lillywhite and John Grundy, bolstering the batting. In the second innings Hon.W.S.Fiennes bowled superbly to take 8 for 56. The University made 125, with B.M.Randolph, with 37, again figuring, along with C.D.Marsham, 39, the top scorers, and 112, with H.Veitch making 38. Grundy, Lillywhite and another professional, James Dean, were the chief wicket-takers. MCC won by 26 runs.

Having established him as having a passing interest in cricket, it is high time that Lewis Carroll's two literary allusions to cricket are revealed. Both are in verse, although one of them - *The Ligniad* - is not so well-known as the other. Carroll had a college friend, George Girdlestone Woodhouse, a man who had smilingly befriended the shy Lewis Carroll at his first undergraduate dinner - 'your husband was the very first who spoke to me', he wrote to his friend's widow many years later. Woodhouse was the son of a Shropshire vicar and was himself ordained, serving as Perpetual Curate at Upper Gomal, Staffordshire and then Vicar of Yealhampton in Devon. Like many 'Muscular Christians' of the age, he combined the surplice with the flannels and was a useful cricketer. He would, one thinks, have variously gladdened the hearts of Anthony Trollope and Thomas Hughes.

In May 1853 Carroll composed a mock-epic poem of some hundred lines in his honour. It was entitled *The Ligniad*, with an obvious nod towards Virgil's *Aeniad* and with a typical play on 'lignum' meaning 'wood.' The poem begins in Miltonesque fashion and has echoes of Alexander Pope's *The Dunciad*. It praises the several gifts of Woodhouse before launching into the cricketing finale, recorded below. Rarely published, it ends with a typically

Carrollian pun about Woodhouse's shortness of stature and demonstrates overall that Lewis Carroll did have some knowledge of the game.

> But now my Muse, approaching higher themes,
> Shrinks from the task in trembling, for the field,
> Green and smooth-shaven, spreads before her sight.
> The wickets pitched, the players ranged around,
> And he, the hero, in his glory there;
> A sight to dream of, not to write about!
> Then fare thee well, greatest of little men,
> In Greek, in Latin, in the cricket-field;
> Great as bowler, greater as a bat,
> But as a 'short slip' greater yet than that.

It was rather later, in 1879, that Lewis Carroll published his better known cricketing verse, this time on a more solemn note. Earlier in 1867, as well as in 1879, Carroll vigorously opposed the proposal of the Oxford University Convocation to allow the university cricket club to have their ground in the Parks. Lewis Carroll was an arch-conservative, in the genuine sense that he was anxious to preserve hallowed rights and traditions, although in his castigation of greed and other sins consequent on private or, indeed, institutional enterprise he could be quite trenchant. His opposition to the Parks proposition illustrates this stance neatly. Not only was he shaken by the revolutionary notion that organised cricket should suddenly be introduced to the leafy and relatively unspoilt Parks, he was also anxiously concerned for the leisure pursuits of the poorer inhabitants of Oxford who might be denied their wholesome promenade through that bosky terrain.

In the fashion of the day, of which he was an acknowledged master, he circulated around the college senior common rooms his polemical verse, a parody of Oliver Goldsmith's *The Deserted Village*. It was called *The Deserted Parks*. A couple of representative stanzas from the poem are:

> Amidst thy bowers the tyrant's hand is seen.
> The rude pavilions sadden all thy green;
> One selfish pastime grasps the whole domain,
> And half a faction swallows up the plain;
> Adown thy glades, all sacrificed to cricket,
> The hollow-sounding bat now guards the wicket.
> Sunk are thy mounds in shapeless level all,

Less ought impede the swiftly rolling ball;
And, trembling, shrinking from the fatal blow,
Far, far away thy hapless children go.
Not so the loss. The man of wealth and pride
Takes up a space that many poor supplied;
Space for the game, and all its instruments,
Space for pavilions and for scorers' tents;
The ball, that taps his shins, in padding cased,
Has wore the verdure to an arid waste;
His Park, where these exclusive sports are seen,
Indignant spurns the rustic from the green;
While through the plain, consigned to silence all,
In barren splendour flits the russet ball.

There is now no more traditional venue for (sadly, very occasional) first-class cricket than the Parks at Oxford, a ground where one is able to sit, in carefully chosen positions, as if in timeless calm, with no artefact of a post-1914 date to sully the view. It must surprise us a little to be reminded of a moment when this time-worn observance was itself the invasive novelty. We may wonder how Lewis Carroll, all these years on, would assess, first, the transformation of what he saw as a crude and selfish intrusion into reverential custom, and, next, the erosion of that long practice of good cricket in the Parks by ever more modern conditioning.

Of course, Lewis Carroll's greatest contribution to human destiny was his capture of the attractive truth that children are more than 'little men' or (significant title) 'little women', to be trained for and held in abeyance until adulthood. He instinctively understood that childhood has its own autonomy and rationale. The classics - *Alice's Adventures in Wonderland* in 1865; *Through the Looking-glass* in 1872 - that arose from his creative delight in this sensibility are revered by students of children's literature as the beginning of a new millennium in that field, almost the origins of the discovery of childhood in this modern sense, as if the years BC were 'Before Carroll' and those AD 'After Dodgson'. Beforehand, children had had to make shift with books primarily intended for an adult audience - the satirised political intrigue of *Gulliver's Travels* and the political symbolism of *Robinson Crusoe* are two fascinating examples - or with very serious moralising tracts and rhymes. Lewis Carroll upset the literary apple-cart so conclusively that his child-oriented parodies of such dull, improving verses were soon well-remembered where, thankfully, the originals were forgotten.

His recognition, unconscious or otherwise, of the 'child-likeness' of children was of major significance. By speaking directly to children in a cultural grammar and vocabulary intelligible to them, he attacked, at a stroke, the age-old view that children should be transposed as swiftly as possible into adults. Childhood came to have its own special identity. Lewis Carroll's *rapport* with children was, then, of a piece with that more enlightened approach which, since the publication of Jean-Jacques Rousseau's *Emile* in 1762, had very slowly taken hold. Thomas Arnold, legendary head of Carroll's old school, would have had none of it: for him, boys were intrinsically irredeemable; the task was to struggle with their animal nature that a Christian gentleman might emerge as soon as possible.

About the time 'Alice' was becoming famous, there were social changes in train that assisted this switch in children's fortunes, particularly with the lessening necessity, given improved technologies, for child labour, first in middle-class then in working-class households. In effect, this created a socio-economic space in which 'childishness' could blossom. The market-place became involved, with, for instance, children's clothes having some independence of design, rather than them being costumed as mini-adults, of which the tiny sailor-suit is a notable example. Children's games began to have a commercial aspect, with Ludo and Happy Families, the portraits done by Lewis Carroll's illustrator, John Tenniel, in the vanguard. The idea of the children's party arose in this epoch. Hitherto, they had been included in family gatherings or excluded entirely. For instance, they inherited games like Blindman's Buff and Postman's Knock, hitherto a province for the coy flirtatiousness of their elders.

In the long haul, the atmosphere engendered by this revolution was good for the extension of pastimes, among them the playing of cricket, for the value of 'play' in the lives of children and young people was accepted, if only to a limited degree, and, sadly, it is a concept that, having been apparently adopted with some enthusiasm in the 1950s and 1960s, has been subjected to the unthinking Puritanism and hollow severity of politicians and purported educational administrators over the last two decades. We have forgotten the injunction of the wise American philosopher and educator, John Dewey, that education is not 'preparation for' but 'participation in.' Nonetheless, the Carrollian legacy is by no means all squandered and we have reason to be appreciative that, in major part because of his unseen influence, the lives of children are, by and large, happier.

As for Alice herself, the focus for all this cultural change, there is a solid connection between her and cricket, at least in her real personality. Alice's model was Alice Liddell, the pert and winsome daughter of Henry George Liddell, the Dean of Christ Church during Carroll's career in Oxford, and of his equally formidable wife, Lorina. Alice was his favourite of the three Liddell sisters with whom Lewis Carroll made affectionate friends and for whom he invented his entrancing tales. 4 July 1862: that was the 'golden afternoon' when, on a boating picnic, there was the first narration of *Alice's Adventure's Underground.*

Throughout his life Lewis Carroll seems to have struggled more or less scrupulously with a sexual prompting in regard of pre-pubescent girls, quelling any extravagant physical leanings, channelling the impulses perhaps into the springs of creative action. His upbringing and religion enforced a strictness and rectitude about this, with, his sympathetic biographers urge, a price paid in the 'nocturnal hobgoblins' that invaded his bedroom, filling him with guilt, however much he persuaded himself that his interests were aesthetic, even spiritual. Thus in terms of social relations, his existence was a constant string of fond friendships, doomed to eventual rejection as the maidens neared womanhood.

There is some evidence that, in 1863, then aged 31, Lewis Carroll proposed a betrothal with Alice, then aged 11, in years when, it should be noted, the legal capacity for marriage was 12 for females and when age-gaps between men and women were often wide. It may have happened decorously, even teasingly, with a hopeful view of a later marriage. Whatever the case, there was a rupture and the intimate attachment of Carroll and the Liddell girls was at an end. Once more, he was rebuffed, this time by the chief fount of his obsession with what he called 'child nature.'

Then in the early 1870s Alice had a vain romance that might have provided the plot for a musical comedy of *The Student Prince* typology. Prince Leopold, fourth and youngest son of Queen Victoria, became a student at Christ Church and the two fell in love. Alice's mother, an unrepentant huntress for high-born and well-endowed suitors for her daughters, was very much the stimulator of this incipient liaison. Leopold's mother was not amused. The Queen quickly married off her not very healthy and haemophiliac, if wayward, son to Princess Helen Frederica of Waldeck-Pyrmont, the German princess later taking the title of Duchess of Albany.

For Alice, it was a question of two remarkable suitors down and one, with a cricketing connection, to go. Enter Reginald Gervis Hargreaves, of Eton and also of Christ Church, where he was a pupil of Carroll's. Alice and he were married in Westminster Abbey in 1880. The two previous men in her life were treated very differently. She wore on her wedding dress a brooch presented by the absent Prince Leopold: 'he simply could not bear to see her being married', it has been suggested, 'to another man.' The censorious Mrs Liddell removed mention of Lewis Carroll's gift - a fine water-colour - from the wedding present list.

R.G.Hargreaves was regarded as 'a surprising choice', for, although sociable and kind, he was somewhat pedestrian in intellectual matters, certainly compared with his alert and clever wife. He was born in Accrington in 1852, and his family, moving rapidly from farming to prosperous success as calico printers, was like a template for the age. They were upwardly mobile, buying, with hard-earned brass, the stately home of Cuffnells in Hampshire. It was set in an estate of 160 acres and was sanctified by the fact that George III had slept there. Hargreaves, then, was among the first generations of self-made industrial families who wrapped themselves in the insignia of the landed gentry - to the disgust of Richard Cobden, radical guru of Manchesterism, who regarded as apostasy such grovelling of the 'shopocrats' to what he scornfully termed 'the clodpole aristocracy'.

The newly-weds lived at Cuffnells, where 'Regi' soon became the personification of local squiredom. Shooting, fishing, golfing, balls and parties, the Conservative Association, flower shows, the magistrates' bench - they all fell within his Jorrocks-like sway. Cricket was an important part of this. He was heavily involved with the Lyndhurst and New Forest clubs, and also with Hampshire. He played twelve matches for the county between 1875 and 1885, scoring 544 runs, highest score 46, for an average of just under 14 and taking 15 wickets for 426 runs. His *Wisden* obituary quotes a description of him as being 'a good hitter, fields well at cover point, and bowls slow underhand.' Neil Jenkinson, the admirable Hampshire archivist, provides the additional information of Hargreaves' Presidency of the county, 1891-93; of his becoming a vice-president in 1893; and of his periodic attendance at committee meetings until 1920.

It is evident that, in many ways, Reginald Hargreaves was the complete antithesis of Lewis Carroll, to whom it is thought that Alice's marriage caused heavy suffering. Anne Clark, Alice's biographer, has written of how the new Mrs Hargreaves inherited her parents' snobbish social-climbing. Father and children were 'never allowed to forget their social class. There was no hobnobbing with the people in the village. 'Regi' was daring enough to introduce a professional cricketer into the New Forest cricket team, but this man was not permitted to socialise with the rest of the team because of his inferior status. Artisans were not allowed to use the gentlemen's changing-rooms, much less join them for refreshments and conversation after the game.'

In these regards, the 'acutely class-conscious' Alice was the child of her time. She was also a quick-tempered disciplinarian, strict, even a trifle cruel, to servants, revealing a petulance which Lewis Carroll, never one to shirk that kind of truth, hints at in his 'Alice' portrayals. It was not the happiest of marriages. The Hargreaves' estates and fortunes crumbled somewhat, reaching the point where Alice was forced to sell off her Carroll first editions and valuable notebooks; two of her three boys, Alan and Leopold (the Prince was his godfather) were killed in the Great War; the third son, Caryl (Carroll?) was something of a wastrel and there were 'raised voices and banged doors.' There was always a sadness about Alice, although having deliberately shunned the socially inferior Dodgson family throughout her married life, she briskly rallied in 1932 when the commemorations of Lewis Carroll's birth were in full swing on both sides of the Atlantic.

Reginald died and was buried in the family grave at Lyndhurst in 1926, aged 73. The *Times* said that 'none who had the privilege of knowing 'Regi' Hargreaves could fail to recognise in him a quite uncommon fineness of spirit...Until the last year or two he was a faithful spectator at Lord's for the principal cricket matches and a well-known figure in the pavilion.' Thus both the creator of the fictional Alice and the husband of the factual Alice may be numbered among the legions who have watched the cricket at Lord's.

Such are the curious links between Lewis Carroll and cricket. At the end, his invocation to *Through the Looking Glass* may offer an apposite phrase for the romance of cricket: 'for happy summer days gone by, and vanish'd summer glory.'

Footnote: some of these reflections were included in an article, 1898; *Lewis Carroll at Lord's and elsewhere, in The MCC Cricket Yearbook*, 1997-98. I have been generously helped in the drafting of this chapter by two of the world's most distinguished Carrollian scholars: his biographer, Professor Morton N.Cohen of New York, and Edward Wakeling, the modern editor of the Lewis Carroll diaries.

Chapter 8

WILLOW, QUILL AND ENGLISHRY

Cricket is fondly regarded as the epitome of Englishness, just as there is an implied compliment in the adjective 'English' when preceding the noun 'Literature.'

''Tis the King of Anglo-Saxon games - the type of our strength confessed;
Where the charms of perils bravely dared inspires each manly breast.'

So runs *The Cricketer's Song*, first sung in 1859. In 1833, John Mitford argued in *The Gentleman's Magazine* that 'cricket is the pride and privilege of the Englishman alone. Into his noble and favourite amusement no other people ever pretend to penetrate.' In 1851 the dedicated cricket archivist, Rev. James Pycroft, had written that 'the game of cricket, philosophically considered, is a standing 'panegyric' on the English character: none but an orderly and sensible race of people would so amuse themselves.' In 1927 Sir Theodore Cook, editor of *The Field*, spoke of how cricket values were 'drawn from the most deep-seated instincts of the English race - the instincts of sportsmanship and fair play. In 1945 Neville Cardus claimed that 'none except the people of England or of English-speaking countries has excelled at cricket', going on to state that this was because cricket 'somehow holds the mirror up to English nature.'

We have noted how George Meredith embraced some of this thinking into his novels and for exactly the purpose of demonstrating 'Englishry'. It is true, too, that cricket is still largely the province of the old imperial realms which, by the death of Queen Victoria, covered a quarter of the earth's land surface and, with 700 millions, a quarter of the world's population. From its peak in the 1890s to its rapid dismemberment after the second world war, it was a remarkably short-lived Empire, but it providentially coincided with cricket's glorious days: cricket followed the trade which followed the flag. The peril lay in the supposition that cricket was somehow an integral part of English stock, hinting at a crude Lamarckism, whereby, in that alternative version of Darwinian evolution via acquired characteristics, an aptitude to keep the left elbow well up was inherited. That theory was famously derided by the observation that a man with a wooden leg does not have children similarly endowed.

One must look to nurture rather than nature for the Victorian affection for cricket and its religious and moral connotations as part of the Imperial mission. Like many other such traits, it arose from the socio-economic construct of the time. It had little to do with ethnic inheritance. It was not 'in the blood', any more than the Welsh zeal for choral music is the consequence of some mysterious gene or hereditary St Cecelia's tonsil. Wales, as a result of certain social and other components, has produce a sub-culture in which music is encouraged and praised and, in cyclic development, people cling to and reinforce their regional *persona*, rather as 19th century Nottinghamshire produced an abnormally high proportion of professional cricketers. The real question, then, is what created the kind of national culture in Britain that, in turn, made manifest a special brand of sport, in particular, cricket, and, in parallel, a special brand of literature, in particular, the family novel?

There may be no gene-bank for the straight bat but there may be such a phenomenon as national character, determined by the social environment. A nation is, in Benedict Arnold's evocative phrase, 'an imagined community.' Nations seek to find and preserve their identity through an array of flags, anthems, heroes and, of course, nationally-appropriate activities like, in England, cricket and literature. Citizens, in their turn, energetically display the traits they have come to believe embody their nationality. What is intriguing is that, because the driving-force is not eugenic but cultural and social, that identity is subject to the changes wrought in those areas.

According to Jeffrey Richards, arguably the United Kingdom's leading cultural historian, the Victorian version of Englishness differed markedly from that of earlier times. For instance, 17th century Englishmen were typically seen as wild regicides and insurrectionists. In his study, *Films and British National Identity* (1997) Richards explains how two complementary elements created a sea-change in British character by the coming of Queen Victoria. One was Evangelicalism, with its earnestness of purpose and its leaning toward puritanical abstention. The other was Chivalry, a gloss on the later 18th century concept of 'decency', with its emphasis on a quiet courtesy. All this was associated with the rise to prominence of a largely industrial or capital-oriented middle class. The result was a transformation - even a purification - of society and of how society regarded itself.

The perceptive social historian, Harold Perkin, puts it with categorical power in his *The Origins of Modern English Society* (1969): 'Between 1780 and 1850 the English ceased to be one of the most aggressive, brutal, rowdy, outspoken, riotous, cruel and bloodthirsty in the world and became one of the most inhibited, polite, orderly, tender-minded, prudish and hypocritical.' One pertinent official example may be seen in the legal system. According to V.A.C.Gatrell, in his award-winning study, *The Hanging Tree, execution and the English people,*1770-1868 (1994), the numbers of executions rapidly declined, from over 500 in the years 1816-1820 to 51 in the years 1836-1840, the result of a combine of increased pardons, decreased prosecutions and the first fruits of an abolition of capital offences. Public executions were banned from 1868, but this, too, was chiefly envisaged as a matter of civil order and, in some ways, the hanging behind closed prison doors was, if anything, more horrific for the condemned person. Indeed, it is strongly urged that the outright abolition of capital punishment was long delayed as a consequence of hiding away the apparatus of state execution. What mattered was the public and private face of docile and well-behaved conduct.

The relative suddenness of the switch to a more orderly society helps explain the abrupt modification of cricket from the sinful, rollicking, gambling sport of the Hanoverian and Regency times to the saintly, quasi-religious, morally acceptable pastime of the Victorian age. The two notions of Evangelicalism and Chivalry had political faces, the former underwriting the ideology of the Liberal and later the Labour Party, always, as the old saying went, more Methodist than Marxist, while Tory paternalism was linked firmly to the latter. Together they acted, it has been argued, as counterweights against the depredations of rampant capitalism, for both were keen, from differing standpoints and with differing emphases, on public and voluntary intervention for the benefit of society at large.

In literary terms, the key figure was the perfect English gentleman, a combine of stoicism and courteous valour. He was a cross between Phileas Fogg of *Around the World in Eighty Days* (1873) and *The Scarlet Pimpernel* (1905). It is interesting to note that the one was created by a Frenchman, Jules Verne, who hated the Victorian English, and the other by a Hungarian, the Baroness Orczy, who loved them. Both P.Fogg and Sir P.Blakeney might have captained England at cricket; both - Douglas Jardine; the Hon.F.S.Jackson? - perhaps did.

To run ahead a little, Jeffrey Richards would take the persuasive view that, about 1960, Britain underwent another rapid transformation, with equally telling effect on its national character. The post-war accent on affluence and materialism led to what, in his 1980 book of that title, Christopher Lasch called 'the culture of narcissism.' Self-gratification, with an eschewal of civic and personal responsibilities, became more of the norm, and, although much has been gained by way of improved and much welcomed physical quality of life, the price is paid in social unrest. Crime, just to take one illustration, halved in proportionate terms between 1857 and 1901 and then rose 40 times over the last century. There were 791 reported woundings in 1920 and 95,000 in 1980. The major political parties have lifted anchor from their Victorian roots, with the privatism, usually associated with the Thatcherite dogma, of the Conservative Party contested by the technocratic but un-radical 'modernising' of New Labour. Cricket finds itself struggling to retain its traditional character in the brave new world, whilst literature, too, has challenges to face.

To the degree that this analysis has credence, it postulates a period of some hundred and twenty years when our national identity was a mix of stiff upper lip and a kind word. We have already remarked some of the effects of this in the writings of Anthony Trollope and Charles Dickens and, in passing, those, on behalf of Chivalry, by Sir Walter Scott: we will have cause to revisit these concepts when we examine the pastoral image of cricket in literature and also the place of cricket in schoolboy stories. What might also be re-emphasised is that this cultural commonalty pervaded both middle - class and aspiring working-class ranks. For roughly this same period, if mainly at its core, say, 1870 to 1914, there was a remarkable conjunction in this respect.

It amounted to an united culture and the notion of a cross-class enterprise, such as a cricket team, is all of a piece with its times. A distinctive characteristic of Victorian culture was its integrated nature. It contrived to be both hierarchical and synthesised. There is no doubt it was a class-ridden society. But the cultural norms were constant. Even if the seats or other placements were severely separated, it was the same sermon; the same landlord; the same sports team; the same railway journey from the same station; the same theatrical performance; and the same pierrots or military band playing on the same pier breathing in the same ozone.

The cultural icons of the Victorian and Edwardian age provided material accordingly. The prime exponents of the family novel, discovered and sustained a massive following across the classes. It is important to stress the reading habits of the manual workers of the age. It was calculated that, in Middlesborough in 1907, a quarter of this class read good books as well as newspapers and that a half read newspapers. In his *England; 1868-1914* (1979) Donald Read describes the growth of cheap editions for the self-improving working man and woman. Within two years of its launch in 1905, W.T.Stead's Masterpiece Library sold 9 million copies of its con-densed Penny Novels and over 5 million of its Penny Poets. In 1906 J.M.Dent initiated its successful Everyman Library series, which had already published 750 classics from the humanities and the sciences by 1914, to pro-vide 'a democratic library at the democratic price of one shilling.'

There was a cross-generational as well as a cross-class component. Prudent self-censorship meant that all the writing was accessible to maid or child, at a time when prurience reigned. For instance, Nancy in *Oliver Twist'* might be recognised by the knowing adult as a prostitute, but it was unsaid and, for the rest, ignorance was bliss. Nor was literature the only field where this happened. Gilbert and Sullivan, with D'Oyly Carte the shrewd impresario, created the first-ever light music industry with their series of Savoyard urban ballad-operas. By the time Arthur Sullivan died in 1900, over 6000 London and almost 30,000 provincial performances of their joint works had been enjoyed; by the time William Gilbert died in 1911, 2 million copies of his libretto had been sold - at the height of their popularity, comic operas like *HMS Pinafore* retailed 10,000 copies of the score a day. *The Mikado* is the most produced musical play ever known; 3% of the population saw its first run of 627 performances.

The incisiveness was phenomenal. The dexterous construct of each comic opera meant that there was always a couple of 'parlour' or 'shop' ballads, a stirring march, a cheerful quartet, a madrigal, a churchy slice of pseudo-reli-gious music and so on. From the budding amateur tenor round his Pooter-type cottage piano, via the bandstand - by the late 19th century there were 50,000 brass bands, including, significantly, a thousand organised by the Salvation Army - and the barrel-organ, to the whistling errand-boy, it was a complete cult. 70,000 arrangements of gems from *The Gondoliers* were sold in the few weeks after its opening. The music was cleverly written down within the scope of amateurs: on 30 April 1879 there occurred the first-ever amateur production of a G&S opera - *HMS Pinafore* at Kingston-on-Thames. By the end of the century 3000 amateur performances were being licensed every year. Interestingly, at about the same time that W.G.Grace and company were carrying cricket to the outside world, Gilbert and

Sullivan were beginning a similar conquest musically - theirs was the first transatlantic major musical export and the last such Britain to America traffic until the Beatles.

Moreover, Gilbert and Sullivan, with their 'intelligent pantomime', made the theatre respectable for Victorian family audiences, to the point where many contemporaries remarked on the church-like nature of the proceedings. Evangelicalism and Chivalry were wonderfully combined, for instance, in the splendours and frivolities of *The Yeomen of the Guard.* There remainded rough and refined peripheries, but to nothing like the degree before or since. In many ways this cultural integrity was to stand the passage of time, despite severe disruption during and after the first world war. The cinema inherited the newly respectable theatre audiences. With censorship imposed, a couple of generations of cross-class family audiences were wooed, with crime not paying, even for Jimmy Cagney, in the last reel, with virtue rewarded, and with love requited, albeit none too carnally.

The radio was an even more influential manipulator of this consensual culture. The public service ideals of the BBC, as determined by Lord Reith, sustained the middle-brow front of what would now be termed 'Middle England'. During the late 1930s, the 1940s and the early 1950s, when radio reigned supreme, the social and cultural values were quite narrow. The music, the humour, the talks, the plays, the magazine programmes - they all fell within a restricted code of ethical valuation. Few, incidentally, complained; indeed, everybody listened and, for the most part, enjoyed. It is no accident that radio and cricket still go together as fluidly as Hobbs and Sutcliffe or that John Arlott, 'the voice of cricket', came to the fore in the heyday of radio. Cricket, cerebral, traditional, unhurried, temperate, exactly fitted the temper of those days and radio caught the mood acutely. What makes all this doubly compelling is that the very stuff of this cultural provision expressed the actuality of first-class cricket, with its strict class combination yet separation. We all know of the separate dressing rooms, pavilion gates, 'card' nomenclature, travel and hotel arrangements for Players and Gentlemen, although they were all engaged in the same enterprise.

The foreign visitor might have been amazed to see rich man and poor man disporting themselves together. The sight of workmen paying a tanner to watch Ranji bat was a peculiar one to the alien eye. To the ordinary Victorian it did not seem at all odd. Their entire life-styles and cultural artefacts were predicated on that unity of the social segments within the same circle: the mainstream analogues of the 'pro-am' character of cricket at this stage of its evolution were the factory-owner/foreman, the master/butler and the colonel/sergeant-major duos. Each of those pairings expresses the same acceptance of a particular lot within a prescribed entity. Often it is the subordinate who is the more ardent keeper of the covenant - the butler concerned for the family escutcheon; the sergeant-major anxious about regimental honour. Note that they are not the lowly mill-hands, the estate-workers or the private soldiers; they are the elite of their own complicatedly nuanced class.

It was the ex-professional who coached the public schoolboys in the nets. It was Wilfred Rhodes who, reputedly, strode into lessons at Harrow to release pupils for his expert tuition. Imagine the gall of that. It is akin to the RSM, in charge of the regimental discipline, loudly scolding the junior officers for below-par drill. Intriguingly, the middle and upper-classes tended to use the expertise of the lower middle and working-classes for their children's tuition in specialist areas: the governess and the nanny figure; the retired NCO running the OCTU drill; a bevy of maids, gamekeepers, grooms, later chauffeurs and other technicians.

It was, in fact, the 1914-1918 war that helped to destroy the waning potency of that consensual culture of Victorian and Edwardian England and by the 1960s, if not before, it had well-nigh vanished. Ironically, as society became supposedly more democratic and egalitarian, the cultural aspects grew more pluralistic. The strength of pluralism lies in the width of available choice. Nowadays, the poles of newspapers - *Sun/Times* - of radio and television programming, of films and art-forms are unbelievably wide compared with previous generations. There are very few novels that are read by those of every social background and age-echelon; there is both wham-bang limited overs' cricket and five-day Tests.

There is something for everybody, with little censorship or control, and this has something to recommend it. Its possible weakness lies in there being few cultural 'Jacks of all trades', few social binders and concords that everyone shares. Perhaps the soap operas, with their massive followings, are the nearest to the old style. As the gap widens, the middle ground weakens - and that is exactly where cricket lay. Its structure was - and remains - as wedded to Victorian cultural values as a family novel or a Savoy opera. Its teams were composed of rigidly defined combines of middle and working class personnel; its watchers reflected, in microcosm, a similar classification of the nation. Happily for themelves, professional cricketers rightly negotiated their way out of the stern duality of that exacting mould and, through the leadership of men like Wally Hammond and Herbert Sutcliffe, they became, like other members of the upper proletariat, 'embourgeoised': the story of Henry Cotton mirrors this change in regard of the lot of golf professionals.

What is absolutely clear is that, by the time the designation of Players and Gentlemen was abandoned prior to the 1963 season - and the date is very close to the approximate year of 1960 utilised as a landmark by Jeffrey Richards - in favour of the general appellation of 'Cricketers', all those involved were, in practice, 'Gentlemen'. They may have lacked some of the associated urbane graces, but in financial terms and by other indices - life-style, including car, house, holidays and so on - they were all distinctly middle class, bearing in mind that the middle class proportion of the populace had sprung from under 30% to over 50% in the post-1960 years.

On a fast-changing cultural terrain, first-class cricket finds it difficult to preserve a modicum of support, let alone the broad consensus of backing it once enjoyed. It is significant that W.S.Gilbert, that uncannily effective arbiter of late Victorian taste, constantly and deliberately used culinary metaphors to describe his overwhelming success. He saw himself as the chef, seeking 'the gastronomic mean', as he called it. He was keen 'to supply a meal of one dish at which all the community are to sit down'. *Supreme de caville* might prove 'insipid' for 'the butcher's boy in the gallery'; 'baked sheep's head' might well 'disgust...the epicure in the stalls'. The answer was 'rump steak and oyster sauce for all'. As late as 1900 he again asserted that 'tripe and onions' and 'sweetbread and truffles' might alternately dismay or satisfy stalls and pit. 'A plain leg of mutton and boiled potatoes', Gilbert claimed, 'is the most stable fare of all'.

For a creditable period of maybe eighty years, first-class cricket also provided 'a stable fare for all'. Now our cultural requirements are much more *a la carte* and much less *table d'hôte*. First-class cricket faces something of the same crisis as the classical novel and for the same reasons.

William Makepeace Thackeray watched over that rich pageant of 19th century Englishness with a kindly, worldly eye, one never long free from the tear of melancholy. For his had been a sad upbringing. Born in Calcutta in 1811, his father, an employee of the East India Company, died soon after and, unhappy at school, irresponsible at college and with his patrimony lost in

Indian bank failures, he leaned towards his mother, a lady of decided Evangelical tendencies. In 1836 he married a penniless Irish girl, Isabella Shawe, and, yes, once again there was a literary marriage doomed to sorrow. They had three daughters, one of whom died in babyhood, and one of whom, Minny, married Sir Leslie Stephen, the scholarly critic, himself the child of Evangelical kin, and whose daughter by a second marriage was Virginia Woolf. In 1840 poor Isabella had to be privately confined because of her mental instability and Thackeray lived as a virtual widower, his later close friendship with Mrs Jane Brookfield terminated by her irate husband. Nor was the novelist destined to be long-lived: he died in 1863, aged 52.

Having studied art and exerted himself in journalism, W.M. Thackeray made his name as an authoritative chronicler of the passing scene, in particular as the recorder of the English middle and upper classes when they were at their most powerful and intransigent. Mocking but rarely malicious and never embittered, his irreverent, sceptical and, on occasion, pained accounts form, in his words, 'a sort of confidential talk.' He was compassionate enough, for he was constantly aware of the ambivalence of human motives: few of his villains have no redeeming trait; few of his heroes avoid some human fault. 'We are for the most part...', he wrote, 'foolish and selfish people...all eager after vanities.'

Vanity Fair (1847/48), with its incomparable portrait of the defiantly roguish Becky Sharp, was, of course, his greatest work, but there were also his historical novels, like *Henry Esmond* (1852), his self-explanatory *Book of Snobs* (1848, originally presented in *Punch*, 1846/47) and the sequence of '*Pendennis*' books (1848-62) which really describe mid-19th century high life in lucid fashion. The middle story of the three is *The Newcomes*, published 1853/55, and it acts as a fictitious illustration of the Harold Perkins/Jeffrey Richards' thesis about the composition of Victorian national character. The leading character, Colonel Thomas Newcome, a veteran of India, exhibits the strict doctrine of the 'Evangelical' and the *politesse* of the 'Chivalrous' in his dealings with his family and acquaintances, not least with his son, the sturdy and agreeable Clive, like Thackeray an incipient artist, and a chief protagonist of the plot.

Some wry play is made of the Clapham Set, 'the resort of the most favoured amongst the religious world', for it was in the well-to-do, still partly rural suburb of Clapham where, inspired by the work of the anti-slavery campaigner, William Wilberforce, such moral conviction most notably thrived.

Elsewhere he extols, slightly tongue-in-cheek, the virtues of the 'well-bred English lad' who 'holds his tongue, and listens to his elders: his mind blushes as well as his cheeks: he does not know how to make bows and pay compliments like the young Frenchman: nor to contradict his seniors as I am informed American striplings do. Boys, who learn nothing else at our public schools, learn at least good manners, or what we consider to be such.' Or, as Thomas very sincerely instructs his son, 'if we can't inherit a good name, at least we can do our best to leave one, my boy.'

Thomas Newcome, after many intricacies of story line, comes to a sad and impoverished ending, as a black-gowned pensioner of Grey Friars, his *alma mater*. In one of the most famous of that large category, the fictional Victorian death-bed-scene, he feebly murmured "Adsum!", and fell back. It was the word we used at school, when names were called; and lo, he, whose heart was as that of a little child, had answered his name, and stood in the presence of The Master.' Thackeray had attended the Charterhouse from 1822 to 1828 and, in location and style, Grey Friars is a direct borrowing. We witness both Thomas and Clive as pupils there, during a time when, in reality, the school was, like others of its kind, on the march, recruiting boldly from up-and-coming families like the Newcomes. Before 1780 there had barely been 80 scholars but it sprang to as many as 480 during Thackeray's schooldays, before further falls and rises.

The public (that is, 'endowed', as opposed to 'private') schools were not havens of serene erudition, and violence, official and unofficial, was rife. W.M.Thackeray elsewhere ruefully nicknamed his seat of learning 'the Slaughterhouse', but he allows Thomas and Clive a modicum of pleasure there and this gives us just a glimpse, no more than that, of cricket. We discover Thomas at school, about the time Charterhouse was beginning to play cricket against other schools, 'bartering a black eye, per bearer, against a bloody nose drawn at sight, with a school-fellow, and shaking hands next day; playing at cricket, hockey, prisoners' base, and football, according to the season; and gorging himself and his friends with tarts...' When he runs away, after some dispute, to the home of his old nurse and is pursued by his father, 'Tommy, scared out of a sweet sleep and a delightful dream of cricket, knew his fate; and getting up out of bed received his punishment without a word.' These *soupcons* of cricket help to suggest the normality, the openness, of the Colonel-to-be.

As a parent, he escorts Clive to visit some family members and finds his nieces' governess, Mademoiselle Lebrun, who is 'forced to keep the eyes of lynx' on her charges, horrified that they are 'playing at criquette' with local youngsters. The amiable colonel say, 'Well, my dears, I should like to have a game at cricket with you, too.' Here is more tiny coding: the foreign despair at the English fondness for sport and the games-loving English gentleman responding affably and civilly.

Finally, as the Colonel lies dying, his 'little gown-boy' from Grey Friars visits him 'and sat by the bed with an awe-stricken face; and then gathered courage, and tried to amuse him by telling him how it was a half-holiday, and they were having a cricket-match with the St. Peter's boys in the green, and Grey Friars was in and winning. The Colonel quite understood about it; he would like to see the game; he had played many a game on that green when he was a boy.' To the end, the Colonel preserves his trusting goodness and candour, with cricket, in his dotage as in his infancy, typifying his gentlemanly virtue.

It has been said of Thackeray that 'he wrote to be read aloud at the long Victorian family evenings', and, although he may be a trifle prolix for the more laconic modern taste, the conversational pace and colour of his prose reminds us of the place of the serial family novel in Victorian domestic life. It should cause no surprise that *The Newcomes* is nicely sub-titled 'the Memoirs of a Most Respectable Family.'

Years later, early in the 20th century, John Galsworthy narrated his *Forsyte Saga*. The title's pun is sardonic: as Galsworthy wrote of late Victorian England, it 'had no Future, for England then expected its Present to endure, and rode its bicycle in a sort of dream.' Born in Surrey in 1867, he was educated at Harrow and Oxford and briefly practised at the bar. Thereafter he became a prolific playwright, concentrating on social injustices - for instance, *The Silver Box* (1906); *Strife* (1909) - as well as erecting his still popular monument to the travails of three generations of a family steeped in Victorian middle class mores. The long sequence began with *The Man of Property* in 1906, with an interval to *In Chancery* in 1920 and To Let a year later. Three more novels, plus two 'interludes', formed the second part of this chronicle and it was published in 1929, Galsworthy died in 1933.

The saga begins in 1886, at the acme of Victorian prosperity and puissance. The chief protagonist, Soames Forsyte, personifies the narrow-minded possessiveness of the Victorian moneyed classes, centrally in his urge to own, as he would a work of art, his beautiful, if, to him, frigid Irene. Her lovers, the somewhat Bohemian architect, Bosinney, and Soames' more relaxed and courteous cousin, Jolyon, reflect the other side of the medallion of the 19th century English gentleman. Soames is 'Evangelical' to a grievous, anal-erotic fault; Bosinney and Jolyon are 'Chivalrous', without some of the necessary disciplines of mind and commitment.

The Old Harrovian, John Galsworthy, chooses the Eton and Harrow match at Lord's for one of his memorable settings for this personal conflict. It is a fixture which in itself tells the story of England's new-found purity. In 1796 the Eton authorities banned a match arranged with Westminster School and, on their return from a miserable defeat at Hounslow Heath, the Eton eleven were soundly flogged by their headmaster for their defiance and for subsequent misbehaviour, a distinctive case of adding injury to insult. In 1861, already a keynote date on the social calendar, 700 carriages and 7000 spectators paraded at Lord's for the Eton and Harrow match. Cricket's conversion to virtue, in historical time, had been sudden and precipitate.

In *The Man of Property*, Soames Forsyte, the veritable upholder of that title, lunches at and perambulates about Lord's during the Eton and Harrow game. He is isolated among throng of thousands and there, amid 'six thousand top hats, four thousand parasols', he spots the hauntingly lovely but distant Irene, naturally the focus of flattering attentions. It is a clever selection of staging. The values of the public school and of sportsmanlike cricket at Lord's, together with the fashionable pomp of a London occasion, paint a back-cloth of late Victorian Englishness. The proprietorial Soames, the loner in the crowd, so near and yet so far, is thwarted in this glittering public arena and psychologically unable to contact the object of his distorted desire. It is not an idle choice of venue. As with George Meredith in *Evan Harrington*, if more fleetingly, character, plot and setting are perfectly unified.

Sprawling, luxuriant, multifarious, the famed novels written or set principally in the pre-1914 era ranged in subject matter and commentary over our domains throughout an epoch when, confident and buoyant, Britain ruled the waves. The severally critically acclaimed novels of the later 20th century are not, of course, worse than their predecessors, but they tend to be more allusive, more sophisticated, more refined, more explicit and more acidic in flavour.

They cater for a mainly adult and educated middle-class audience. They do not penetrate deeply into the population. They are aimed at a fairly small minority, rather as now is first-class cricket.

Footnote: some of the analysis in the early pages of this essay was taken from the article 'Can Cricket Adapt?' *Cricket Lore* vol. 3 issue 6.

Chapter 9

VILLAGE GREEN, COUNTRY HOUSE AND THE PASTORAL IMAGE

When the late 19th and early 20th century cricket antiquarians examined the origins of cricket, they located them much further back in time than some modern scrutiny might allow. By homing in on selective, sometimes obscure, references, such as 'creag' in the Royal Household Wardrobe accounts of Edward I in 1300 (thought by an expert modern analyst, Dr Derek West, perhaps to be a synonym for 'griasch', a kind of nine-pins) or a papal illumination of the 14th century showing a man and boy with clubs and ball, they convinced themselves, and, thus, generations of cricket-lovers, that cricket had enjoyed a long inheritance.

When one carefully considers the social milieu in which these activities purportedly took place, and the general character of 'disportment' among the children and lower classes among whom cricket is said to have originated, it becomes apparent that, although some of these pastimes were labelled 'cricket' or something similar, no regular definition of what that really meant has been discovered. In his famed Dictionary, published in 1755, Samuel Johnson defines cricket as a game 'in which the contenders drive a ball with sticks in opposition to each other'. The true doyen of British cricket historians, H.S.Altham, dismissed this as a 'less happy' error, but it may have been that Samuel Johnson knew of a version of 'cricket' which had this hockey-like flavour.

It is not until about the era of Dr Johnson, or perhaps just before in the early 1700s, 400 years after the date proposed by some commentators, that the three necessary elements - the use of the title, cricket; a description of the game under that label recognisable as cricket today; and an acceptance of its validity over a sizeable tract of land, say, the home counties - were in place. That authoritative cricket historian, Peter Wynne-Thomas, has astutely argued, in possibly the most rational analysis of these issues, that cricket is three-dimensional, a complicated amalgam of a trio of sporting typologies: throwing (as in bowls); hitting (golf, tennis, hockey) and running (athletics), so much so that the likelihood of a latish start is compelling. Moreover, our modern mind-set invokes the idea of the fixture, whereas, for all kinds of social and economic reasons, much cricket was played <u>among</u> its small group of protagonists rather than <u>between</u> teams.

Even when sports clubs were more formerly established, the prevalent concept was that they were 'sides' clubs, with members meeting regularly and picking up teams. When Newton Heath (Lancashire and Yorkshire Railways) started a football club for its workers in 1878, little realising that one day it would be the mighty Manchester United, it, too, was a 'sides' club, with, doubtless, cries of 'you can't have David Beckham two nights running' rending the Mancunian evening peace. Envious fans of Manchester United's crestfallen rivals might be forgiven for wishing that this powerful club might revert to its former model. In short, in football as in cricket, there was not so much urgency for codified rules when much of the play was so localised and autonomous. The 'nationalisation' of sporting laws was often quite a late development, with, for instance, the association football laws agreed no earlier than 1863 when the Cambridge University brand was widely accepted.

Insofar as this and like testimony is persuasive, it raises an equally pertinent question: why did cricket's pioneer historians put so much energy into insisting that cricket has a lengthy story? The amount of documentary investigation undertaken by the likes of James Pycroft, P.F.Thomas, H.T.Waghorn, G.B.Buckley, F.S.Ashley-Cooper and others is truly astonishing, and all credit must be paid to those intrepid explorers of the primary sources for the sheer comprehensiveness of their discoveries. History, however, has two components: information and interpreters. New facts do sometimes appear to challenge old explanations, but, as palpably, interpretations of the same data alter in that the interpreters' thinking is fashioned by their own cultural values. It is, in part, a natural pendulum effect, whereby successive groups of historians re-examine the same facts and offer a different weighting to them. Our childhood heroes, Richard Lionheart and Alfred the Great, have not had such a good press as late, whereas those rascals of our schooldays, King John and Richard III, have enjoyed a modicum of rehabilitation. Such reappraisal is often undertaken in terms of contemporary mores. For example, in the wake of the collapse of Empire and troubled consciences about imperial values, several derring-do Union Jackites - Robert Clive and Cecil Rhodes are examples - have allegedly been shown to have feet of clay.

There is no final judgement, and, in turn, that should act as a warning, in that the redress of previous findings in an essay such as this are, of course, subject to the same relativist perils. This is cricket history as seen from the stance of the late 20th and early 21st centuries. That said, it is clear that an older generation of cricket archivists chose to discern in ostensibly controversial data very early signs of cricket. Why did they opt for the 'wine' (the older the vintage...) as opposed to the 'chicken' (the fresher the bird...) viewpoint?

It is common ground that, after about 1830 and as part of the cleansing evangelical movement, cricket became heavily 'Christianised' and was adopted by the church and the public schools as the builder of English character and as a medium for Christian ethics. It was a leading aspect of the Victorian desire for 'rational recreation' a counter to licensed premises and other dens of vice. Yet it did not require that cricket have a long-term ancestry. The immediate preface to this had seen the stimulation of cricket as an outcrop of the gambling mania of the 18th century, and this had been excoriated by right-thinking clergy and school-masters. The wagers were immense, and, for instance, 'form' was a borrowing from horse-racing, that is, data to assist with betting.

So it would have made sense had the evangelical and 'Muscular Christian' advocates sought new foundations of a righteous nature for cricket. The opposite illustration of basketball is instructive. In exactly that same convention of developing a physical activity with a distinctly moral dimension, the Rev. James A. Naismith fashioned an entirely new game at the International Young Men's Christian Association Training School in the United States in 1891. Of course, there might have been a simple and straightforward urge to justify cricket by reference to its ancestral past: there was and is a body of cultural opinion which derides ephemera and innovation and insists on longevity as the respectable yardstick of 'classical' merit. That is the keystone of the small 'c' conservatism of the human mind. Christian institutions have especially been adept at 'stealing the Whigs' clothes', adopting pagan festivals with aplomb - did not 25 December welcome 'the Birth of the Unconquered Sun' at the end of the Roman Saturnalia and did it not mark the virgin birth of the Persian sun god, Mithras? - and adding a comforting sense of familiarity by so doing. Thus it was not long before Hambledon, in reality the Las Vegas of 18th century gambling, with the team's managers sometimes backing the opposition with big stakes, became the 'cradle of cricket', the Bethlehem of 19th century piety.

Beyond that, there is possibly another more specific reason why, with sub-stantial urgency, cricket's early historians sought to give cricket so prolonged a lineage. Britain's industrialisation, earlier and, initially, more pronounced than in any other country, led to considerable cultural unease. Even in the 1980s it was suggested that one reason for the nation's economic malaise was an intellectual and political establishment that remained *chary* of the ugli-ness and artificiality of the manufacturing processes. In the second half of the 19th century there was a discernible reaction against what some saw as industrial blight. Speaking of 'the characteristic mythical Britain of travel posters', that cogent historian, E.J.Hobsbawm, has shown how 'the heavy incrustation of British public life with pseudo-medieval and other rituals, like the cult of royalty, dates back to the late Victorian period, as does the pretence that the Englishman is a thatched-cottager or country squire at heart'.

Other illustrations of this tendency include the then current affection for the historical novel, inspired by the earlier success of Sir Walter Scott's *Ivanhoe*, with its classic tournament at Ashby-de-la-Zouche, and exemplified by Charles Kingsley's *Hereward the Wake* (1866) or Charles Reade's *The Cloister and the Hearth* (1861). The younger Dickens embraced some of this back-ward-looking spirit, and the Pickwickian coach and horses still festively adorns our Christmas cards. In architecture and the arts, and under the potent influence of men like Augustus Pugin, there was the restoration of a 'vibrant medievalism' as an antidote to industrial and urban perils.

Politically, 'the medieval dream', as it has been termed, had been stimulated earlier in the century by the highly-coloured Tory pageantry of the Young England movement, with which Benjamin Disraeli was closely associated, and even the radicals had the 'Merrie England' concept to excite them, the attractive notion of a common Arcadian past unspoilt by rampant commer-cialism. It was the time of the great revival of folklore, the very term a Victorian coinage, with Cecil Sharp, by Edwardian times, a key figure in the collation of rustic songs and legends. (They tended to be bowdlerised; when, in infants school, we innocently warbled, say, *Strawberry Fair*, we were unaware that this succulent fruit was formerly an analogue for female sexu-ality. Goodness knows what that ballad's refrain of 'Rifle-triffle; fol-de-did-dle-di-do' actually meant)

Little wonder, then, that, in such an atmosphere, cricket was deemed to be a pastoral pastime, with a heavy emphasis on the village green and the remembrance of shepherd boys romping on the downs. The fact that the growth of cricket depended very largely on urbanism and the steam train for its mature success was disregarded: the old-style 'county' became the focus for first-class cricket, when, in practice, its locale was the thriving commercial cities and flourishing market towns and seaside resorts. The countrified 'gentleman' of 'the Forsyte Saga' convention became the middle-class embodiment of cricket; thus, fielding a team such as 'the Gentlemen of Surrey', or whatever county, could be part of the normal routeway to full 'county' status.

Wise cricket historians, like C.L.R.James or John Arlott, have taught us to view cricket as the social expression of its times. Similarly, cricket historians reflect their times. Hence the industrious and persistent fathers of cricket history firmly expected to find the fountainhead of the most important of games in medieval times, and probably interpreted their findings accordingly. Historical research in general in that period tended to seek for explanations of the same ilk. The great constitutional historians, William Stubbs and F.W.Maitland, were, for example, busily tracking down English legal and institutional origins directly to Anglo-Saxon and Anglo-Norman sources.

The later Victorians were as anxious to find their cricketing as well as their constitutional roots in pre-modern soil and a substantial amount of fiction, either based on or including reference to, cricket, utilised this tendency to convincing effect. Several authors, undeniably, take refuge within the noble portals of Lord's, but, somehow, that majestic bastion escapes affinity with the grime and stress of urban life, existing, at least in literary consciousness, in calm and dignified Regency grandeur. It is almost as if a stately home had accidentally found itself translated to metropolitan environs.

For the rest, the Oval, built on a former cabbage-patch before the great expansion of London, has suffered, with some equanimity, cycles of urban extension, finding itself first all but rural in situation, then built-up well-to-do, then suburban, then working-class and now inner-city. It has rarely attracted, in spite of the notoriety of its gas-holders, the pens of many well-known authors. The same goes for those major centres of authentic cricket development and prestige in the central and north midlands, at Trent Bridge, Old Trafford, Headingley and Edgsbaston. Although they constantly tell the truth that first-class cricket is irrefutably an urban game, and the larger the conurbation the more likely the cricket, for self-evident reasons, to be the more strongly supported, fiction writers have shied away rather from such venues.

Instead their concentration has been on the pastoral image of cricket. It is not a false one: cricket, of course, has been and is played in the countryside. It is more that it gives a slightly misleading notion of the incidence of the game. During the reign of Queen Victoria the British population switched its weighting: in 1837 the majority of her subjects were rural; in 1901 the majority were urban in location. However forceful the aggrieved cries of the countryside lobbyists, the fact remains that well over 90% of the population of the United Kingdom lives in urban areas, that is, districts with 5000 or more residents, occupying but 11% of the land. The proportion of the labour force working in telephone centres is now almost as many - less than 2% - of those working in agricultural and allied trades. Yet the rustic vision of cricket continued to dominate.

Literature has been especially shrewd in its observation of this backward-looking, bucolic effect. In *The Newcomes*, the Thackeray novel examined in chapter 8, the pretended ancestry of the appropriately-titled Newcomes is mocked as follows:

'It was but in the reign of George III that Mr Newcome first made his appearance in Cheapside...on a wagon...and some bales of cloth...though if it could be proved that the Normans wore pigtails under William the Conqueror, and Mr Washington fought against the English under King Richard in Palestine, I am sure some of the present Newcomes would pay the Heralds' Office handsomely...these Newcomes have got a pedigree...which proves the Newcome in Cromwell's army, the Newcome who was among the last six hanged by Mary for Protestantism, were ancestors of this house; of which a member distinguished himself at Bosworth Field; and the founder slain by King Harold's side at Hastings had been surgeon-barber to King Edward the Confessor...'

Admirers of the Savoyard comic operas may recall how W.S.Gilbert derided the late Victorian *penchant* for claiming remote but honoured forebears. Major-General Stanley in the *Pirates of Penzance*, first performed in 1880, believes that he has purchased a proud lineage along with a grand property: 'With the estate, I bought the chapel and its contents. I don't know whose ancestors they were, but I know whose ancestors they *are*.' Five years later, in *The Mikado*, Pooh-bah, the pluralist Lord High Everything Else, goes even further, describing himself as: 'a particularly haughty and exclusive person, of pre-Adamite ancestral descent. You will understand this when I tell you that I can trace my ancestry back to a protoplasmal atomic globule.'

It will be readily understood that this retrospective yearning for an olde-worlde stake for one's existence is closely related to and fed the 19th century view of Chivalry, already alluded to in respect of Sir Walter Scott and other authors and also as a clause in the cricketer's creed. Predictably enough, the anthologies of cricket literature teem with cricket in sylvan settings. From as early as 1832 Mary Russell Mitford, in *Our Village, Sketches from Rural Life, Character and Scenery*, was arguing that there was nothing 'more animating or delightful than a cricket match', so long as it was 'a real solid old-fashioned match between neighbouring parishes, where each attacks the other for honour and a supper, glory and half a crown a man.' She does 'not mean a set match at Lord's Ground, for money, hard money...an affair of bettings, and hedgings and cheatings.' She extols the country virtues, with an early reference - 'your blacksmiths are capital hitters' - to a beloved stereotype, while there is even a definite case of sledging, when 'the pretty boy, David Wills' makes his debut among adults, 'who talked to him, and stared at him', such that he 'was seized by a fit of shame-faced shyness, that he could scarcely hold his bat, and was bowled without a stroke, from actual nervousness.' That happening seems to have been repeated at the highest level a number of times since 1832.

A breezy, frolicsome soul, Mary Russell Mitford (1787-1855) supported her spendthrift father, a Hampshire doctor, from her writings, chiefly concentrating on her knowledge of the village of Three Mile Cross, near Reading. She helped rediscover the countryside for the urban middle orders and her notion that village green was preferable to the city venue has always had energetic support. Derek Birley, in his comprehensive *A Social History of English Cricket* (1999) quotes a letter she wrote in 1823 about a major game: 'There they stood ...silent, solemn, slow - playing for money, making a business of the thing, grave as judges, taciturn as chess players - a sort of dancers without music, instead of the glee, the fun, the shouts, the laughter, the glorious confusion of the country game.' Derek Birley percipiently points out that, in 1907, the E.V.Lucas edition of John Nyren's memoir of Hambledon, first published in 1833, fuelled the engines of the on-going nostalgia for the verdant life. A year later, E.V.Lucas, himself a cricket writer and poet - for example, his *Driving to the Match*, with 'the brown-armed peasants in the hay', from his *Willow and Leather* - of pastoral urges, attacked the mechanistic 'hard utilitarianism and commercialisation' of first-class cricket in phrases that have a distinctly modern ring. As Derek Birley makes clear, the reality was sometimes different to the ideal - he cites a Berkshire clergyman in that same year, 1907, who said it was 'a fond delusion' to believe that village cricket was widespread.

Nonetheless, the dream was a persistent one. Almost a hundred years after Mary Russell Mitford had eulogised village cricket, Siegfried Sassoon, in his *Memoirs of a Fox-hunting Man* (1928) sustained the idyllic vision in the famous Flower Show Match. It took place in one of the opening summers of the 20th century, with the narrator, 'young master George', home on holiday from Ballboro' School, playing, 'an awkward overgrown boy, fielding anxiously at mid-on', for Butley in the annual tussle with Rotherdene. The Butley band plays *The Soldiers of the Queen*, the fair and flower show are in full swing on the verges of the game, and the social mix of parsons, spinsters and yokels is tidily done. For instance, dignified William Dodd, 'a sort of unofficial Mayor of the village' combines the roles of saddler, electoral teller, churchwarden, cricket captain and leading light of the Horticultural Society. The winning run comes, via a quickly-taken single from the young schoolboy, in the last over with one wicket to fall, and all is well with the world.

The book was part of a semi-autobiographical trilogy, to which Siegfried Lorraine Sassoon (1886-1967) added three more volumes of childhood autobiography. Ballboro' is Marlborough, where he was schooled, before moving on to Cambridge. He wrote some early cricket verse and, later, among his 1926 *Satirical Poems*, there is *The Blues at Lord's* ('...One fact seems sure;/That, while the Church approves, Lord's will endure.'). A useful school and college cricketer, he retained an active involvement in cricket into his riper years, especially on the ground of his residence, Heytesbury House, with the peak of his career perhaps being a few games with Kent Club and Ground.

The story has been many times told of how Siegfried Sassoon, after meritorious service with the Royal Welch Fusiliers in the 1914-18 war, turned to pacifism. The poet, Robert Graves, persuaded the War Office to treat this as a medical rather than a disciplinary matter and, saved from the bullet of the firing squad, the troubled warrior was instead subjected, in company with Wilfred Owen, to neurological inquisition in an Edinburgh hospital. Sassoon turned from the pale Anglicanism of the unappealing Rotherdene rector, Parson Yalden, and the indignant Toryism of Aunt Evelyn of Butley, to Roman Catholicism and to Labour politics, including the job of literary editor of *The Daily Herald*. His world irrevocably shattered by the First World War, there is thus a brittle ring to the sentiment, and yet, inevitably, the charming Flower Show Match is widely quoted as an invocation of beguiling rusticity.

There are legion of instances of village cricket, including one in Edmund Bucknell's *Linden Lea* (1925), where an Old Wykehamist assists Norton to victory over Wendlebury, and another in R.C.Hutchinson's *The Unforgotten Prisoner* (1933), complete with squires and parsons of cheerful mien. They invariably demonstrate the deference of the lower and the paternalism of the upper orders, assembling together for cricket in a fashion that the liberal historian, G.M.Trevelyan, would have adored, given his ingenuous but much-quoted opinion about how cricket might have saved the French chateaux from Revolutionary arson. Some of these fictional matches are close in style to the Country House or 'Hall' and village fixtures, also much deployed to reflect this rural idyll, despite Mary Russell Mitford's trenchant view of them: '...a pretty fete in a gentleman's park,' she scoffed, 'where one club of cricketing dandies encounter another...where they show off in graceful costume to a gay marquee of admiring belles...the whole being conducted according to ball-room etiquette, so as to be exceedingly elegant and exceedingly dull.'

Effete or not, novelists have constantly found in them a pleasant and effective background. Such an occasion in a stately home brings together characters and throws them together in varied conflict, whilst, at the same time, readers enjoy the vicarious delights of country life and activities, such as cricket. In an excellent little book, *Country House Grounds of Leicestershire and Rutland* (1997), E.E.Snow identified no less than 76 such 'rural palaces' where cricket was played, at many of them of a high standard, within his chosen area. By way of perspective, it might be mentioned that, in 1851, 4000 landowners possessed a half of our native soil, their large estates encompassing the farms of over 200,000 normally compliant tenants, and with their yearly revenues soaring into six figure fortunes. From about the 1840s until the trauma of the Great War, there was a busy round of Country House cricket, often with a festival week and often with a visit from a regimental team or from one of the itinerant amateur elevens, like I Zingari (formed in 1845), Quidnuncs (1851), Free Foresters (1856) or Incogniti (1862).

While, at much the same time, the professional Exhibition teams toured the nation, this elaborate mesh of young gentry inter-crossed the great houses, a week-end here, a week there, establishing the place of the 'Gentleman' in cricket circles and providing a nursery for county cricket. Indeed, so potent was the effect of this cult on the development of county cricket that Richard Hill, the indefatigable editor of *Cricket Lore*, the journal which has done so much to open up opportunities for the rational deliberation of cricket, past and present, has maintained that the present county club, with its subscriber membership and other attributes, still retains some of the aura of this kind of private garden party.

Small wonder that authors have found a beneficent source for their tales on the manicured lawns of these halcyon days, all the while appealing to their readers' appetite for nostalgia. J.C.Masterman's *Fate Cannot Harm Me* (1931) is a case in point. Having played the Hunt, the Old Uptonians and the Foresters, George Appleby's Fincham play his 'Saturday match' against Sir Anstruther Oliver's Besterton, with Merton, most discreet of butlers, as one of the umpires. The match, which is not all that closely linked with the main story, revolves round the comeuppance received by Colonel Murcher-Pringle, who contrived to be 'angular and self-opinionated, dogmatic and fussy at the same time.' Sir John Masterman, at one time Provost of Worcester College, Oxford, played for Oxfordshire and the classier touring sides, like I Zingari, Free Foresters and Harlequins; he also played four first-class games.

Another example, of which there are many, may be taken from E.R.Eddison's a *Fish Dish in Memison* (1941). This is the second of a trilogy of novels about an imaginary sphere, which, after a fashion of its era in the manner of James Dunne's once highly regarded *An Experiment with Time* (1927) or the J.B.Priestley 'Time' plays, such as *Dangerous Corner* (1932), *I Have Been Here Before* (1937) and *Time and the Conways* (1937), explored the mysteries of the temporal dimension. There is, however, a chronological window of opportunity for an Edwardian Country House cricket match, with Lord Ammering's eleven opposed to Colonel Playter and his Hyrnbastwick colleagues. All is coolly elegant, as a group of some five score worthies, some titled, some of high military and naval rank, observe and comment upon the cricket. 'Just too perfect for words', murmurs Lady Southmere.

'And so', this enchanting passage concludes, 'amid great merriment, chaff and mutual congratulation, the game came an end.'...as did the period, in the tragic chaos of the first world war, which, among other mindless horrors, slaughtered these amateur 'cracks' by the thousand. The grim agricultural depression of the last quarter of the 19th century and the application of industrial tenets to agrarian practice had already undermined the old way, a system which had given employment to approaching a fifth of the labour force as late as 1871 - although it must be added that the average labourer's wage in mid-19th century was a weekly 9s 7d (48p) and the annual income of a maid-of-all-work as little as £9, that is 18p a week, apart from bed and board. The collapse of the great estate has come to be a cultural analogue for the disintegration of late Victorian and Edwardian society, with Country House cricket one of the vanishing ingredients. The 1984 film, *The Shooting Party*, set in 1913, starring James Mason and taken from the Julian Bond story, offers a matching symbolism, as the behaviour of Sir Randolph Nettleby and his guests prefigure the coming of Armageddon.

The crumbling breakdown of the old-style agrarian stability was, of course, the underlying theme of the novels and poetry of Thomas Hardy (1840-1928). A rare reference to cricket in the Hardy canon touches on this grimmer view of English pastoralism. *The Mayor of Casterbridge* (1886) details the tragic fall of the guilt-stricken Michael Henchard, which, for example, in the way the incoming Scot, Donald Farfrae, with his modernising tendencies, takes over Henchard's old-fashioned business, acts as a portent of the replacement of the organic rhythms of the countryside by more soulless business practice.

When Susan Henchard, his shamefully wronged wife, returns to Casterbridge, that is, Dorchester, Michael Henchard invites her to meet him secretly at the Ring, a Roman amphitheatre just outside the town. It is not a spot of good omen. It had been the site of the town gallows; in 1705 a woman had been strangled and burnt there by official order; 'crimes might be perpetrated there unseen at mid-day.' Hardy continues, 'Some boys had latterly tried to impart gaiety to the ruin by using the central arena as a cricket-ground. But the game usually languished for the aforesaid reason - the dismal privacy which the earthen circle enforced, shutting out every appreciative passer's vision, every commendatory remark from outsiders - everything except the sky; and to play at games in such circumstances was like acting to an empty house. Possibly, too, the boys were timid, for some old people said that at certain moments in the summer time, in broad delight, persons sitting with a book or dozing in the arena had, on lifting their eyes, beheld the slopes lined with a gazing legion of Hadrian's soldiery...' The melancholy Hardy, observer of humanity's vainly feeble struggle against indifferent fate, knows that Henchard, for all his defiance, will die a miserable death. Poor Susan herself dies soon after their somewhat halting reconciliation. The two characters are smothered and shrouded by a pitiless providence, just as even cricket has been killed off by the gloom of their concealed rendezvous.

By and large, however, authors have sought a happier image in the delights of cricket and rural life. A final and picturesque illustration of the affection for rusticity in cricket fiction is the choice of names for imagined county teams. It is true that Ernest Raymond's young hopeful, T.J.Budlier, actually plays for Middlesex at Lord's in *To the Wood No More* (1954) and Sir Home Gordon also uses Middlesex in his 1921 story, *That Test Match*. This tends to create an odd effect, with real and made-up names mixing unsatisfactorily. One might prefer the Full-Montyshire of dreamt-up Ersatz-counties, such as Hillfordshire versus Meadshire in one of Mrs Murray Hickson's love-stories, or Glebeshire in Graham White's *Cricket on Saturday* (1947) or Downshire, the county team in Dudley Carew's *The Son of Grief* (1936). Then again, the felicitous Ian Peebles chimes in with Midshire and Boffshire in his *Talking of Cricket* (1953), whilst Ginger Stott, courtesy of J.D.Beresford, is *The Hampdenshire Wonder* (1911). So many of them have a pastoral lilt, with not even the occasional Northshire dispelling the prevailing air of leafy quietude.

The pastoral literature of cricket fits an arc into a circle of fictional and factual, of real and envisioned, circumstances. It tells us what village and stately home cricket was like, and what we are pleased to think it was like, the whole entering our consciousness, the reality and the dream difficult to separate. By the by, Loamshire, overall, appears to be the most used county name in fictional accounts. One would love to be a Loamshire member, for every game is not only enthralling but the outcome is in doubt until the last dramatic over.

Chapter 10

WIMSEY AT THE WICKET; OR, RAFFLES OUT ON BAIL

'With five minutes to go, Wimsey watched the first ball of the over come skimming down to him. It was a beauty. It was jam. He smote it as Saul smote the Philistines. It soared away in a splendid parabola....The match was won.'

Lord Peter Wimsey is one of the exceptions to the rule that, for a number of cultural reasons, the shrewdest of fictional sleuths have not been renowned for their cricketing expertise. Sergeant Cuff, Sherlock Holmes, Sexton Blake, Miss Marple, Hercules Poirot, Adam Dalgliesh, the inspectors Appleby, Wexford, Wycliffe, Frost and Morse - none of these has been noted for the fiery delivery or the firm on-drive, even if Morse's progenitor, Colin Dexter, has declared, along with a thousand or two others, that his unfulfilled ambition was to open the batting for England. From Sergeant Cuff's horticulture, as made manifest in Wilkie Collins' *The Moonstone* (published in 1868, usually acknowledged as the first 'detective' story) to the brooding poetry of P.D.James' Dalgliesh (introduced a century later in *Cover Her Face* in 1962) they have all chosen rather less physical pursuits than cricket for their few leisure hours.

That is not to say that cricket and crime fiction do not mix as well, one is tempted to remark, as cricket and crime fact. The persistent P.L.Scowcroft, demonstrating just as much investigative stamina and zeal as any of his inquisitive heroes, has tracked down numerous examples and logged them in a series of pieces in *The Journal of the Cricket Society*, beginning in 1977 and through to 1990. Sapper's *Ronald Standish* (1933) has that investigator save a fast bowler, on duty against the Free Foresters, from unfounded suspicion; Nicholas Blake's *A Question of Proof* (1936) is about a teacher who, plausible scenario, slaughters his headmaster during a thrilling prep school match; Barbara Worsley Gough's *Alibi Innings* (1954) involves a murder victim who 'forfeits our sympathy' with her total lack of interest in cricket; even C.P.Snow (1905-1980) better known for his *roman fleuve*, the 'Strangers and Brothers' series about the maze-like corridors of power, includes a detective, seeking inspiration at an empty Lord's cricket ground, in his first novel, *Death under Sail* (1932); MCC colours are the clue to the mystery *Case with*

Ropes and Rings (1949, republished 1975) by Leo Bruce; Ernest Bramah who, apart from his creation of the diffuse storyteller, Kai Lung, also invented the blind detective, Max Carrados (1927, reprinted 1978) who enjoyed, before Wilfred Rhodes did the same in reality, listening to matches at Lord's...these and many more.

It is also true that in one TV Morse adaptation, *Deceived in Flight* (1989), the uncomplaining Sergeant Lewis, phelegmatically played by Kevin Whateley, displays some tidy bowling and fielding skills, scarcely appreciated by his crossword-solving, classically educated senior, and he is knocked out for his pains with a cricket bat in an Oxford college ground pavilion. Happily, he recovers to help his master track down the murderous drug smugglers who are utilising the joys of cricket touring as a cover for their illicit trade.

Curiously enough, Sergeant Gavin Troy, the rather naive associate of Chief Inspector Tom Barnaby, has also swapped hand-cuffs for batting-gloves. In an episode of ITV's *Midsomer Murders*, based on the characters created by Caroline Graham, he is interrupted in the middle of a productive bowling spell by a scream from the score-box, where a somewhat unsavoury youth, Charles, having been unjustly dropped from the team, has been stabbed whilst marking down a single. The match is between venemous rivals, Fletcher's Cross, captained by Ian Frasier (Terence Rigby) and Midsomer Worthy, whose skipper, the authoritarian Robert Cavendish (Keith Barron) is at the centre of the mystery. His young and beautiful wife, the scheming Tara, is disposed of with eight blows from her devious step-son's True-Blade cricket bat, and only the acute deductions of Barnaby, played by John Nettles, formerly Bergerac, the detective, saves Cavendish from a not altogether undeserved throat-cutting. The episode is nicely titled *Dead Man's Eleven*; Imelda Staunton, who combines Born-again Christianity, sexual ardour and theft in her role as the son's secretary, remarks that, had Jesus played a sport, it would have been cricket, and purists would sniff with disapproval at the knowledge that this charming village green fixture is a league match.

Otherwise, of the classic detectives of fiction, Lord Peter Wimsey is one of very few to have been also a distinguished cricketer. Lord Peter, of Eton and Balliol was born, courtesy of Dorothy Leigh Sayers (1893-1957), in 1890, second son of the 15th Duke of Denver; he played for Oxford prior to the First World War, making 112 in the 1911 Varsity Match. There was something of the Scarlet Pimpernel about his detective-work, with the sharpness of mind and the depth of knowledge disguised behind the mask of aristocratic lethargy. His creator was born in Oxford, where she also studied, after a childhood in the Fens where her father was vicar of Bluntisham-cum-Earith, the sort of place-name that might crop up in the detective yarns of the era. As well as a few non-Wimsey crime tales, there are a dozen or so books on the actual Wimsey shelf, in the later ones of which appear cricket-loving Harriet Vane, a precursor of the bright female companion (as opposed to the dull male of the species, like Watson) such as Simon Templar's Patricia Holt or Paul Temple's 'Steve'. Probably the best-known stories are *The Unpleasantness at the Bellona Club* (1928), *The Nine Tailors* (1934), and *Busman's Honeymoon* (1937). Thereafter she abandoned detective fiction for serious translation, especially of Dante, and to write religious drama - her somewhat stereotyped radio sequence about the life of Christ - *The Man Born to be King* - was broadcast in 1941-42 to considerable acclaim.

It was in *Murder Must Advertise* (1932) that Lord Peter most effectively displayed his cricketing prowess. Using his second and third fore-names, Death Bredon, he worked *incognito* in Pyms Advertising Agency (Dorothy L.Sayers had real-life experience of that profession and the text includes her ominous pre-view of the ad-mass). 'Bredon's' task was to determine the reasons for the sudden and violent death of a previous employee, and, not without further portents for today's society, the story revolves around the flushing out of a large-scale and murderous drugs-ring.

Toward the end of the novel - it is interesting how often cricket matches are used as the base for the *denouement* of a plot - the Pyms' office enjoys its annual fixture with Brotherhoods, one of its client companies. Purists will happily note that it is a two-innings game. Although 'Bredon' coyly plays the role of a fortyish man of decent Country House cricket standards, an elbow cracked by his opponents' quick bowler leads him to forget himself and the Oxford blue emerges rampant, his delectable 83 being the mainstay of an unlikely victory. At the same time, his exciting sporting ventures cause his identity to be revealed, and the Pyms' captain, Tallboy by name and suspect by character, is on the alert. However, all is cleared up in a matter of pages, although - for, as Dorothy L.Sayers came closer to foregoing detection for religiosity, she grew ever more solemn - there are sadnesses, notably Jim Tallboy's redemptive act in allowing himself to be killed rather than face the disgrace of a sordid drugs-related murder trial. Incidentally, the key to the initial death was Tallboy's keen fielding and accurate throwing; from a convenient skylight, he had catapulted a small object at the blackmailer, Victor Dean, causing that miscreant to fall down an iron staircase and break his neck.

Although, for modern ears, the Sayers dialogue is sub-Wodehousian for the upper crust characters and Cowardesque, after the prim fashion of *Cavalcade*, for those from the lower orders, here is an author of erudite background, so that some of the literary reference is pleasing, even if the advertising subtext occasionally goes into overdrive. As for the cricket, it is an excellent description of a game that fills its slot in the unfolding story with lucid aplomb. According to Clifford Jiggins ('a Hundred for Lord Peter', *The Cricketer*, November 1990) there are brief cricket references in several of the other stories, including a walk, 'under a fire of glances'. across the quadrangle of an Oxford women's college in *Gaudy Night* (1935), which Lord Peter compared with 'the long trek from the pavilion at Lord's' at a vital juncture.

As P.L.Scowcroft's diligent researches showed, there have been many cricketing scenes in what might be disrespectfully termed the second class of thriller-writing. The English detective, private or official, has, in fiction, adopted a more fastidious *persona*, than - although one does not speak from intimate professional experience - those who in reality uphold the law. They are bookish and civilised and this chimes in perfectly with the literary view of cricket, most urbane of diversions. Fictional murders also have a habit of happening in a discreet location, where the number of suspects may thereby be restricted to manageable proportions - that is why the country house or the boarding school, with its statutory cricket match, is such a gift to the mystery writer. Not for Lord Peter Wimsey the house-to-house interviewing of an entire estate or the DNA testing of a huge population. As if programmed by some clever Marxist conspiracy, an unusually large proportion of the victims are members of the upper middle classes, conveniently corralled in penny numbers at one of those secluded elite locations.

Some titles are explicit. Cyril Allington's *Mr Evans: a Cricketo-detective Story* (1922) and *Blackmail in Blankshire* (1949) are two such, while there is also, leaving little to the imagination, *The Amazing Test Match Crime* (1939) by Adrian Alington, *The Test Match Murder* (1936) by Denzil Batchelor, and *Testkill* (1976) which Clifford Makins co-authored with that lordly batsman, Ted Dexter. In mid-20th century John Creasey, somewhat after the fashion of the Saint or, on television, the Avengers, created the Toff. True to his given character, he found himself mixing cricket and crime in *The Mark of the Crescent* (1935) and *A Six for the Toff* (1955). The amazingly well-read Gerald Brodribb, in the updated version of his original 1950 roster of cricket fiction, includes others with tell-tale titles: Hal Pink's *The Test Match Mystery* (1940), James W.Kenyon's *Peter Trant; Cricketer-Detective* (1944), E.& M.A.Radford's *Murder isn't Cricket* (1946), Nancy Spain's *Death before Wicket* (1946), Alfred Tack's *The Test Match Murder* (1948), Osmington Mills' *No Match for the Law* (1957) Stanley Shaw's *Sherlock Holmes at the 1902 Fifth Test* (1985). Homicides at Test matches abound. It amounts to a light industry.

Curiously and, for those wearied by the self-confident success of a string of suave sleuths, satisfactorily, the forces of literary law and order on the cricket field are conspicuously out-pointed by the master-criminal of the cricketing arena. Raffles, amateur cracksman and amateur cricketer, is the name with which to conjure. There is a gallery of literary characters that is recognised by all, whether or not they have read the texts: Alice, Sherlock Holmes, Oliver Twist are specimens. The closest one to entry from cricketing fiction is Raffles. He was both the Amateur Cracksman and the Amateur cricketing 'Crack'.

A.J.Raffles was a bowler, whereas, both in reality and fiction, the upper crust of cricketers have tended to be fluent batsmen, unfolding silky cover drives across the glistening greensward. The point is that Raffles was about the business of taking professionals on at their own game, and this applied to policemen and burglars as well as cricket 'pro's'. The tales constantly portray him as outdoing all of them, not too scornfully and not with disdain. He was out to prove himself a more effective house-thief and bowler than the plebeian workers in those trades, and, not content with outwitting the plodding police himself, he also excelled them in unmasking fellow-burglars from the lower orders.

The key lies in his legendary sobriquet, 'the amateur cracksman'. The term was used in its proper social connotation, synonymous in cricketing circles with 'Gentleman'; indeed, 'the gentleman cracksman' would have been a more accurate descriptor. Just as there were some 'shamateurs' who were surreptitiously paid for playing cricket, Raffles was not an amateur thief in the sense of his being voluntary work. He has sometimes been compared with Robin Hood, but he never mastered the second element in the Sherwoodian economic equation: he robbed the rich...but he kept it for himself. He stole to keep himself in the manner to which he felt he should be accustomed, luxuriously in the Albany, Piccadilly. Furthermore, he inducted Bunny, an ex-fag from his school-days, into being his slavish adherent and accomplice. Over the stories hang - the first, *The Amateur Cracksman*, was published in 1899 - *a fin de siecle* miasma, a slightly self-pitying, restless, decadent whiff.

'As a cricketer', said Bunny, 'I daresay he was unique. Himself a dangerous bat, a brilliant field and perhaps the finest slow bowler of his decade...' His interest was solely in playing. 'Cricket', declared Raffles, 'like everything else, is good enough sport until you discover a better...but I'd chuck up cricket tomorrow, Bunny, if it wasn't for the glorious protection it affords a person of my proclivities'. In the first cricket described in the tales, Raffles places sovereigns on the stumps, 'with the professionals bowling like demons for hard cash'. Raffles loses eight or nine coins, but the practice is valuable and, he who laughs last, he scores 57 next day against them.

Such shrewdness informed his bowling. Bunny describes 'his perfect command of pitch and break, his beautifully easy action, which never varied with the varying pace, his great ball on the leg stump - his dropping head ball - in a word, the infinite ingenuity of that versatile attack. It was no mere exhibition of athletic prowess, it was an intellectual treat.' Bunny spotted the 'affinity' between bowling and burglary; both were a 'combination of resource and cunning, of patience and precision, of headwork and handiwork, which makes every over an artistic whole.'

At Lord's for the Gentlemen against the Players, he took 3 for 41 out of the first four wickets to fall, which, as Raffles remarked, 'isn't so bad for a slow bowler on a plumb wicket against these fellows'. This was the occasion when Raffles was stung by Lord Amersteth's invitation to play Country House cricket at Milchester Abbey: he was 'venomous' because he had been asked 'as though I was a 'pro' myself.' Off he went in his I Zingari blazer to play against the Free Foresters and the Gentlemen of Dorset, but, ineluctably, Lord Amersteth's valuables came to play a major part in the subsequent plot.

The sort of cricketing analogies found in other literature are cleverly utilised in the Raffles' stories. Raffles is quick to compare the attitudes of 'Players', at both cricket and larceny, referring to them both in the old-fashioned styling of 'professors'. Talking of professional burglars with eyes on the pearls, he says that 'they see the pegs, and they mean to hit 'em, but that's all they do see and mean'. For, of course, Raffles obtained a measure of excitement from the polished style of both his off-breaks and his break-ins, leading George Orwell to write in his 1944 essay *Raffles and Miss Blandish in Horizon* (Miss Blandish, for whom there were 'no orchids' was a literary *femme fatale* of the era) 'in the eyes of the true cricket-lover it is possible for an innings of ten runs to be 'better' (ie more elegant) than an innings of a hundred runs'.

Nonetheless, the double life was morally, as well as materially, perilous. Social disgrace was, needless to say, worse than death for the Amateur Cracksman. Suicide was not an option: 'I'd rather be dropped by the hangman's noose than throw my wicket away', so it was off to the Boer War, the faithful Bunny still at his master's side. After three lost encounters - 'all three pegs', groaned Raffles... 'neck and crop, neck and crop.' - he sought out the guilty spy - 'I'm mad keen on bowling him out with my own unaided hand - though I may ask you to take the wicket'. This last to Bunny, never the brightest of cricketers nor burglars, of whom Raffles rather patronisingly requests 'the kind of fluke I always trusted you to make when runs were wanted.' The spy summarily dealt with, it is Raffles' turn to find 'redemption in a hero's death on the Veldt.' Delivering cricketing metaphors to the end, he says of the Boer sniper who kills him: 'By Jove, though, I believe he's having an over at me'.

Stumps were not irretrievably drawn for Raffles. He was, so to speak, recalled from the pavilion to continue his innings. There were four original volumes of Raffles stories. Later other writers were to take up the character and there was also stage presentations, beginning with a New York production in 1903, starring the matinee idol, Kyrle Bellew. There were some half a dozen silent Raffles films, including one featuring House Peters and directed by King Baggot in 1925. John Barrymore also played the role, but it was the Ronald Colman version of 1939, and the shot-by-shot re-make by David Niven in 1940 which really carved out a cinematic *niche* for the sophisticated burglar.

Written by John van Druten for Sam Goldwyn, and co-starring Olivia de Havilland, Raffles was the ideal vehicle for the refined, carefree David Niven, and it sparked off a mini-convention of courtly thieves, among whom Cary Grant and George Sanders may be especially remembered. There were to be flavours of Raffles in popular literature, too. He became something of an icon.

His creator was Ernest William Hornung. The son of John Peter Hornung, he was born in Middlesborough in June, 1860, but, after schooling at Uppingham, ill-health compelled him to go for two years to Australia, the setting for two of his novels, *Bride from the Bush* and *Stingaree*. He wrote over twenty other novels, a volume of war poems and a book of war reminiscences, while his school story, *Fathers and Men*, which includes some cricketing action, is well-regarded. The critic, Hugh Caister, suggests that Hornung was a little like Raffles, in that he might have been more successful 'had he bothered. But he did not bother. Raffles came to him once, and he wrote a minor classic.' E.W.Hornung lived during the later part of his life at Partridge Green, Sussex, and he died at St Jean-de-Luz, Basses-Pyrenees, France, in 1921, aged 54.

An MCC member, he had many cricketing connections. In 1893 he married Constance Doyle, the sister of Arthur Conan Doyle, to whom the first Raffles book was dedicated. Conan Doyle always had a special affection for the eloquence and charm of his brother-in-law, despite his apprehension over 'Willie' Hornung's glorification of a criminal - and perhaps because there is the mocking air of a Holmesian parody about Raffles. The parallels are evident enough. Where Conan Doyle created the gentleman detective, dismissive of the earnest efforts of the constabulary as well as a match for the most cunning villain, and with a loyal henchman, Doctor Watson, to marvel at and record his doings, so did his brother-in-law create the gentleman crook of similar leanings, even unto the sudden mood-swings.

As for Hornung the cricketer, Conan Doyle wrote, 'Hornung was the best-read man in cricket lore that I have ever met, and I am sure he would have excelled in the game itself if he had not been burdened by short sight and villainous asthma. To see him stand up behind the sticks with his big pebble glasses to a fast bowler was an object lesson in pluck if not in wicket-keeping.' To elect, in the face of myopia and breathlessness, to be a wicket-keeper is anti-Falstaffian, a setting of valour above discretion. Perhaps Raffles was his fantasy as well as his creation.

Conversely to his brother-in-law, Conan Doyle introduced very little cricket into his wide range of writings. Among a scattering of mentions, there was the famous yarn, *The Tale of Spedegue's Dropper* (1928) wherein Tom, the school-teacher hero, emerges from obscurity to baffle the Australians with his mountainous full tosses; apparently the author had once been so deceived by an accidental 'donkey drop.' It is well-rehearsed that Sherlock is named after F.J.Shacklock, who took 497 wickets in his 117 matches, principally for Nottinghamshire, including four in four balls against Somerset at Trent Bridge in 1893; and that Sherlock's brother, Mycroft, was named after Thomas and William Mycroft, the Derbyshire professionals, the former of whom was on the Lord's ground staff for years. For all that, as Jeremy Malies relates, in a finished biographical essay on Arthur Conan Doyle, 'a posse of literary sleuths has shown that Sherlock Holmes never so much as mentions' cricket.

The omniscient detective first demonstrated his uncanny skills in 1887 in *A Study in Scarlet.* Soon the stories were all the rage and the *Strand Magazine,* where most, from 1891, were to be read, saw its circulation rocket upwards. Collected volumes - *The Adventures of Sherlock Holmes* in 1892 and *Memoirs of Sherlock Holmes* in 1894 - soon followed. He also diversified into historical and science fiction, with *The White Company* (1891) and *The Lost World* (1912) respectively serving as examples. Born in Edinburgh in 1859, he soon turned aside from the Roman Catholicism of his family upbringing and schooling at Stonyhurst and proceeded to read medicine at Edinburgh University, where he fell under the spell of criminal psychologist, Joseph Bell, the model for Holmes. He practised medicine, but became a full-time writer from 1891. He was married twice, first to Louise Hawkins, who died of tuberculosis, and then to the delectable Jean Leckie, in whom Jeremy Malies sees something of Irene Adler, the only woman brilliant enough to warm Sherlock's notoriously chilly emotions. His son, Kingsley, died in 1918, after being invalided out of the army, following valiant duty on the Western Front. Conan Doyle himself died in 1930 at Crowborough in Sussex.

Bluff, generous-hearted, energetic of mind and without pretension, Arthur Conan Doyle was very much the late Victorian and Edwardian gentleman. A man of many interests, his friends were to include W.G.Grace and the young Douglas Jardine, such unlikely cricketing fans as Rudyard Kipling ('the flannelled fool at the wicket...') and Jerome K.Jerome, as well as Harry Houdini. He was as fit as a fiddle and devoted much of his time to a range of sports, including, like Doctor Watson in this and other respects, rugby. It does seem surprising that, given his fascination with the exact scrutiny of evidence, he permitted his boundless obsession with Spiritualism, in part encouraged by Tinkerbell's creator, J.M.Barrie, to blind him to some photographic hoaxes.

These included the infamous Cottingley fairy photographs of 1917, fabricated by two young girls, Elsie Wright and Frances Griffiths of Bradford.

There was nothing fairy-like about his hefty interventions on the cricket pitch as forthright bastman and cunning bowler. Of all famous writers, he has some claim to being celebrated as the most competent cricketer-author. Sir Arthur Ignatius Conan Doyle, to greet him with his complete title, played an enormous amount of good club and similar cricket, including busy spells with various authors' and allied teams, such as the Allahakbarries. Moreover, he also played ten first-class games, all for MCC, between 1900 and 1907. His highest score was 43, for MCC against W.G.Grace's London County side at the Crystal Palace in 1902, but it was in 1900, in the same fixture and on the same ground, when his authentic moment of glory arrived.

He had W.G.Grace caught off his bowling by the wicket-keeper, William Storer. It was Conan Doyle's one and only first-class wicket, but he picked the perfect victim. Nor was his feeling of triumph diminished by the fact that W.G.Grace had already scored 110 before he was out. Conan Doyle wrote an amusing ode to commemorate that event, a verse which ends with the well-known lines:

> Did I give Storer the credit,
> The thanks he so splendidly earned?
> It was mere empty talk if I said it,
> For Grace was already returned.

Conan Doyle and 'Willie' Hornung played cricket together, these two authors, related by marriage, who had contrived to originate the fictional master-sleuth and master-criminal of their generation. But if Raffles was a superior cricketer to the ascetic, violin-playing, cocaine-sniffing Holmes, his inventor was the inferior sportsman. E.W.Hornung's *Wisden* obituary is as curt as it is censorious, with not a whisper of Raffles: 'was a keen cricketer, but was not in the eleven whilst at Uppingham.' Oh dear, what a humiliating, negative dismissal! But E.W.Hornung did have the imagination to envision Raffles and there are hundreds who made the eleven at Uppingham who would have liked to have made so proud a mark.

And E.W.Hornung is reliably credited with the excruciating re-phrasing of the salient line of the ballad, *Home, Sweet Home,* on the subject of his brother-in-law's eminent investigator: 'though he might be more humble, there's no police like Holmes.'

Footnote: some of the material on Lord Peter Wimsey was used in a piece in *The Journal of the Cricket Society* (vol. 20 no.1 Autumn 2000) and on Raffles in an article in *MCC Cricket Yearbook 1998-99* (1999).

Chapter 11

PETER PAN, NOT OUT; AND JEEVES FOLLOWS ON

James Barrie might have made a reasonable selection as Lewis Carroll's bowling partner. After each delivery, he said, he would sit down at mid off to observe whether the ball reached the other end, 'which it sometimes did.' His lethargic method did have the advantage that, if dissatisfied with a delivery, he could run after it and bring it back. This confessed expert on slow cricket spoke of games in Spain of such snail-like pace that players willed the continuance of them to their second son. Such was the whimsy of this gentle figure, whose love of cricket possibly surpassed that of any other professional writer.

When J.M.Barrie first came to London, he eked out a precarious existence with congenial articles under the all-embracing pseudonym of 'Anon', chiefly for the *St. James's Gazette.* He had been pointed towards a lighter approach by John Morley, politician, editor and friendly biographer of William Gladstone. His editor, his initial Mentor, was Mr Greenwood; the reader is not vouchsafed knowledge of his forenames. J.M.Barrie had a silk hat, regarded as a necessary piece of headgear for the literary 'assault on London', and, years later, he found copies of those old articles in the ancient leather hat-box that had protected his tokenistic silk hat. In 1930 he privately published fifty issues of this collection of ephemeral pieces and in 1937 they were made available to the public, with an introduction by Stanley Baldwin, under the title *The Greenwood Hat,* in honour of 'our beloved editor.' The articles were published between 1885 and 1887. They consisted of the original copy, to which a commentary of recent date was appended. The whole is an unthreatening compound of youthful musing and mature reflection.

The eighth such article was called 'Ladies at Cricket', the description of a cheerful game between a girls' school and a team of neighbouring women, all bedecked with flowers and in excellent humour. James Barrie's forty years-on addition is, in fact, the tale of the Allahakbarries, so that, unusually in cricket circles, one is able to enjoy the story of the foundation of a real cricket team written by its founder, a genuine author. Having enjoyed cricket in his native Scotland, James Barrie soon found his way to Lord's 'and did not dare speak to anyone' during his first summer. He was soon befriended by the artist, Thomas Gilmour, and the writer, Marriott Watson: 'Sometimes the three of them went for long tramps in Surrey, oftenmost to lovely Shere, in which village, 'over the butcher's shop', Meredith told me he had written one of his novels.' It would be pleasing to believe it was one of his novels, as scrutinised in chapter 6, with happy cricket references, and George Meredith was to be Barrie's most encouraging adviser.

Barrie continues: 'On these occasions they talked so much about cricket that it began to be felt among them that they were hidden adepts at the game and an ambition came over them to unveil.' They challenged Shere to a game, although some of the team had to be coached in the railway compartment on the way to the match, including counsel on which side of the bat to employ. Two African travellers were on the team-list, Paul du Chaillu 'of gorilla fame' - he discovered them, along, apparently, with pygmies - and Joseph Thomson, the African explorer, who turned out in pyjamas. A mock-despondent Barrie asked them what he called the 'African' was for 'Heaven help us' and the reply 'Allahakbar' was adopted in the plural for the team's not altogether politically correct appellation. Soon it was changed 'with complimentary intention' to Allahakbarries. That first game was lost heavily, Barrie's side ousted for a meagre eleven runs.

The next time Shere was played they had to recruit a protesting artist and 'a soldier sitting with two ladies outside a pub.' This unknown warrior carried the Allahakbarries to victory and was last seen 'sitting outside another pub with another two ladies.' The club flourished, playing 'a few matches yearly for several summers, that first one being the most ignominious.' Arthur Conan Doyle was regarded by J.M.Barrie as the main exception to the 'depressing rule' that 'the more distinguished as authors his men were the worse they played.' For all that, he introduced key players on occasion, among them J.C.Snaith, already met as early as chapter two, S.S.Pawling, who played three first-class matches for Middlesex in 1894 and was a noted club cricketer, and the writer, H.V.Hesketh-Prichard. It is claimed that one of his characters, 'Don Q', was the basis of the Zorro cinematic industry, sparked off in 1920 by Douglas Fairbanks, revitalised by Tyrone Power in 1940, and still thriving today. He, that is Hesketh-Prichard, not Zorro, played in 86 first-class matches and took 339 first-class wickets, mainly for Hampshire, in the Edwardian era.

There were others. A.E.W.Mason was a perilously quick bowler of a length uncertain enough 'to hit square leg in the stomach.' Everyone will remember his 1902 adventure yarn, *The Four Feathers*, set during the 1890s Sudan campaign and filmed first in 1929 and then more memorably in 1939, with John Clements and Ralph Richardson. The presence of C.Aubrey Smith and the screen-play of R.C.Sherriff, playwright of the cricket drama, *Badger's End*, provided some cricketing flavour. A.E.W.Mason also created the detective, Inspector Hanaud, who first tracked down crime in *At the Villa Rose* in 1910.

Augustine Birrell, who 'once hit so hard that he smashed the bat of Anon, which had been kindly lent him' and, far from grieving, 'called out gloriously, 'Fetch me some more bats.'', was the essayist - *Obiter Dicta*, for example, in 1884, 1887 and 1924 - and biographer - for instance, *Charlotte Bronte*, in 1887. He was perhaps better known as Liberal MP for West Fife from 1889, as President of the Board of Education from 1905 to 1907 when he became a not very impressive Chief Secretary for Ireland, an unenviable post he resigned in the wake of the 1916 Easter Rising. There was also the novelist and poet, Maurice Hewlett, who made his early name with the medieval romance, *The Forest Lovers*, in 1898; E.V.Lucas, the essayist, Punch contributor and author of the 1907 cricket book, *The Hambledon Men*; Owen Seaman, assistant editor of *Punch*; together with Alfred Parsons; Bernard Partridge; Henry Ford; Charles Furze; Charles Whibley, names not perhaps too well recollected a hundred years on.

However, there was that favourite son of Walsall, Jerome K.Jerome (and, by way of casual information, the K stands for Klapka) whose absorbing tale, *Three Men in a Boat* (1889), of an accident-prone cruise on the Thames, remains very popular and whose 1907 play, in more serious mood, *The Passing of the Third Floor Back*, is still occasionally performed. According to J.M.Barrie, he 'once hit two fours', while Will Meredith, son of the Victorian novelist, 'would have excelled in the long field but for his habit of shouting 'Boundary' when a fast ball approached him.' George Meredith, in his own character of 'Old Mel' in *Evan Harrington*, was a Vice-President of the Allahakbarries to whom 'telegraphic communications about the state of the game' had to be forwarded.

The 'dear enemy' of James Barrie's eleven was Madame de Navarro, the actress Mary Anderson, whose husband, Antonio F.Navarro was sometime captain of the Broadway club in Worcestershire, 'the scene of contests and suppers of Homeric splendour.' The bewitching actress, who always called the game 'crickets', had 'a powerful way' of detaching a star opponent for a beguiling stroll, after which he 'would tell Anon that he had promised to play for her in the second innings.' An entrancing interpreter of Shakespearean leading ladies, Mary Anderson, who was of American German parentage, published her stage memoirs, *A Few Memories*, in 1896. As Barrie, in the person of Anon concludes, 'In their love for her the Allahakbarries tried to let her side win, but were so accomplished it could not be done...The Allahakbarries were invincible.'

James Barrie's private Allahakbarries booklets, twelve copies of nine pages in 1893 and fifty copies of 33 pages in 1899, eventually attained high value on the bibliograhical mart, but the latter, with an introduction by Don Bradman, was given a cheap reprint in 1950. In these mementoes of his cricketing past, James Barrie characterises his colleagues and himself in mildly demeaning fashion; for instance, of one worthy; 'the worst batsman in the world. equally at home with the ball.'

Cricket buffs are indebted to James D.Coldham for his long interest in the fascinating linkages between cricket and the arts, as, indeed, for his dedication to cricket scholarship in general. He was born in 1924, worked for the Crown Agents Office and served with the Welch Regiment, aside from building a massive library and an astonishing knowledge of cricket. A fastidious researcher, he was for fourteen years editor of *The Journal of the Cricket Society*, still as prestigious today, polished by the humane values of its editor, Clive Porter, as James Coldham made it during his incumbency. His obituary in *The Cricketer* in 1987 properly appears on a page alongside one of his own notices, for he had provided many of that magazine's obituaries for a number of years. As well as writing some and contributing to other cricket books, James Coldham also published many articles, principally in *The Cricketer*, including several on the topic of writers and cricket. A sincere word of appreciation is also due to that tower of the cricketing academy, Peter Wynne-Thomas, who, from his intricately detailed indexing of *The Cricketer*, has been able unerringly to indicate where lie the gleaming nuggets.

James Coldham described how James Matthew Barrie, born in Kirriemuir in 1860, fell in love with cricket at Dumfries Academy and how, after a spell in Nottingham, he came to London, where, from 1887 to 1913, he organised his famous team. They played villages, teams of artists, of pressmen, of actors and even of fire station personnel, normally finding themselves at the pleasantest of venues, such as Esher, Frensham, Farnham, Shackleford, Downe and Sandwich. They were, as James Coldham points out, the true precursors of the Idlers, the Heartaches and other sides of a literary bent, not least the Invalids, on whom attention will be turned in the next chapter.

J.M.Barrie was a tiny, frail, wan figure, his pads seeming to envelop his entire frame, and his batting maxim was 'should you hit the ball, run at once; don't stop to cheer.' He admitted that, in one important match, he 'scored one run' but in the second innings, 'was not quite so successful.' Much of this, of course, was typically self-deprecating. It is reported that he could sturdily keep an end up, whilst Conan Doyle told of how 'he bowled an insistent left-hand good length ball coming from leg.' He fielded close to the wicket, but, according to James Coldham, 'he was sometimes incommoded by his pipe.'

James Barrie was knighted in 1913 and, expressionless and inoffensive in tone, he was much in demand as an after dinner speaker at major cricket functions. His romantic view of cricket was very genuine. He spoke in 1934 of cricket being the gift of the gods, a ball tossed down to us as 'a winged word about playing the game...the immortals left it at that because cricket is the only game they play themselves.' For him the rural cricket match was 'surely the loveliest scene in England and the most disarming sound.' He visualised in his mind's eye that from 'the ranks of the unseen dead for ever passing along our country lanes, the Englishman falls out for a moment to look over the gate of the cricket-field and smile.'

James Barrie was a sentimental man. Where other authors might have escaped to the joys of cricket from the rigours of the typewriter and the terror of the dead-line, his fancifulness about cricket was at one with his literary approach - and both were of a piece with his philosophy of life. When he writes about cricket fictitiously, this becomes apparent. In his book, *The Little White Bird*, published in 1902, there is a game of cricket played against 'a ragged yew' between the adult narrator and a diminutive boy, not coincidentally named David. During this little tussle among the branches, a catch is dropped but the child-batsman is distraught: ' 'I am a cad,' he said in distress, 'for when the ball was in the air I prayed.' He had prayed that I should miss the catch, and as I think I have already told you, it is considered unfair in the Gardens to pray for victory.'

That degree of sensibility, perhaps mawkish to the more austere mentality, was evident throughout Barrie's life, whether at work or at leisure. He did not insert much cricket into his writings, as did others, for plot or characterisation; it was more that the same sentiment imbued his affection for the game, his view of humanity and the way that was manifested in his work. The expert on Scottish literature, Alexander Mackie Scott, has explained how J.M.Barrie never recovered from the trauma, aged six, of the death of a brother and the resultant grief of his stricken and much-loved mother. Himself the ninth child of the ten born to an Angus weaving family, he automatically aligned himself with the Kailyard school of Scottish writers who flourished toward the end of the 19th century. Kailyard, or cabbage-patch, was coined by Ian Maclaren, writer of such collections as *Beside the Bonnie Briar Bush* (1894), while S.R.Crockett, author of *The Stickit Minister* (1893) was another of this small and briefly popular group. Homespun, sentimental tales of Scottish village and small town existence were their *forte*, and J.M.Barrie made his early name with the homely *Auld Licht Idylls* (1888), *A Window in Thrums* (1889 - 'Thrums' was his name for Kirriemuir) and *The Little Minister* (1891), later dramatised in 1897 as his first theatrical success.

This taste for the sentimental overflowed into the supernatural, especially when, once settled in London, he turned to the stage for his principal livelihood. He married the actress, Mary Ansell in 1894; it was a painful experience in the extreme, and they were divorced in the 1900s. There were no children. It is difficult to assess whether the marriage collapsed because of the continuing effect of his childhood crisis or whether its failure merely exacerbated his incapacity to stare reality in the face. As A.M.Scott and other commentators have explained, J.M.Barrie made his name and fortune by reflecting through the prism of his plays and stories an unwillingness to face change, in particular human growth and death. That, naturally, has an appeal to all. The remarkable attraction of *Peter Pan*, first staged in 1904 at the Duke of York's Theatre, bears testimony to this ingenuous desire to avoid the hazards of growing up and 'the awfully big adventure' of dying. Apart from 1940, it enjoyed an endless and unprecedented series of London seasons, itself almost an advertisement for eternal youth, and, although, with its appetite for star-lit 'principal boy' Peter Pans and 'heavy' Captain Hooks, it became part-cult and part-panto, no one could deny its enduring power. With the help of a Walt Disney cartoon version in 1953, with Bobby Driscoll doing the vocal honours for Peter Pan, it is a name which has entered the gallery of literary immortals.

In 1897 James Barrie had met the wife of Arthur Llewellyn Davies, Sylvia Llewellyn Davies, to whom he expressively referred as 'little mother', and through her five small sons he re-lived the experiences of early childhood, telling them the Peter Pan stories (some of them were included in *The Little White Bird*), just as Lewis Carroll had earlier related his Alice fantasies to the Liddell girls. Sylvia Llewellyn Davies died in early widowhood and two of her sons, for whom Barrie became guardian, died tragically young. The real world continued to taunt him with its grim incursions. Where others might temporarily yearn for the allure of childhood or occasionally wish older age might not advance quite so rapidly, J.M.Barrie was overwhelmed by these concepts, his disenchantment with adult life well-nigh total.

Not least among the practical features of his attitude was that he was able to compete theatrically with the pre-1914 emphasis on dramas of social con-science and criticism, associated with George Bernard Shaw and the sober Ibsen. Peter Pan, 'the boy who would not grow up' outwits the scheming pirate, Captain Hook and, in effect, the rather grumpy Mr Darling, the two parts generally being played, in casting of some significance, by the same actor. The pagan immortal, Pan, is celebrated; the Never Land becomes a child's Shangri-La; and, incidentally, the name Wendy is popularised. The national sorrow over the blood-letting of the 1914-18 war probably con-tributed to its consolidation as an annual memorial to escapism.

Because of the public identification of Barrie with Peter Pan, it is sometimes forgotten both how successful were his other plays and how they, too, med-itated on the theme of dire adulthood, usually with fanciful plot-lines. To take three examples, *The Admirable Crichton* (1902; it was filmed in 1957, with Kenneth More as the eponymous butler) finds Lord Loam and his fam-ily shipwrecked on a desert island, under which conditions his manservant becomes king, a humorous parable on the artificialities of adult social cus-toms. Then *Mary Rose* (1920), less chirpily, concerns the misery brought to herself and others by a little girl who, in antithesis to Peter Pan, cannot grow up. Most pertinently, in 1917, *Dear Brutus*, relates the unrelentingly harsh morality fable of a group of failed adults who, allowed a magical second chance to redeem themselves, blow the opportunity again through defects of temperament and personality.

Although welcome as speaker and cricket captain, J.M.Barrie was agonis-ingly shy in any private encounter. Christopher Brookes, in *His Own Man, the Life of Neville Cardus* (1985) records the bizarre episode when the doyen of English cricket writing visited the playwright, an event Neville Cardus wrote about in his own *Autobiography*, published in 1947. The combine of Cardus, the incessant talker with a grand fondness for Peter Pan, and Barrie, the painfully reticent cricket buff who wished, above all, to listen to cricket gossip, was an intriguing one, but, when Neville Cardus stayed at James Barrie's Adelphi Terrace House flat, he barely caught a glimpse of him. Shyness and bronchitis, itself, one feels, but an excuse, paralysed the author and Neville Cardus was abandoned to the tender mercies of Thurston, a butler of embarrassing haughtiness, and Barrie's sister, the fey Maggie, a lady of spiritualist leanings, carrying messages from across the ether from Cardus' mother, whereas, in fact, despite Neville Cardus' public statements to the contrary, she was still alive. It was all very disconcerting, with Barrie 'the most fleeting of presences,' although the friendship endured well enough thereafter. Further consideration will be given to the Peter Pan phenomenon in the later examination of schoolboy stories and cricket. However, it is revealing to document how complex and yet how entire was the personality and work of J.M.Barrie, the arch-sentimentalist, finding comfort from what for him was a frighteningly adult world in the fanciful delights of stages he could people with imperishable children and village fields he could inhabit with friends bound together in boyish pastime. Peter Pan may have been deathless: Sir James Barrie died in 1937.

Apart from the Allahakbarries, J.M.Barrie joined with his literary comrades in other guises. *The Cricketer* published the results of several matches, especially for a score or so years before the Great War, involving authors, actors and, in particular, artists - the Artists' XI thrived, even unto arranging its own 'country house' cricket week in 1905, including a fixture with the Allahakbarries at Farnham Park. Major, later Colonel, Philip Trevor, in his 1901 book, *The Lighter Side of Cricket*, reminiscences about these matches. He found Conan Doyle to be 'solid, four-square...untiring' and not unlike W.G.Grace; E.V.Lucas to be 'a pretty bat'; J.C.Snaith 'an excellent one'; but that A.E.W.Mason and J.M.Barrie, despite 'a most business-like cap and blazer done in colours of his own invention', did not 'appear to take the game very seriously. Philip Trevor joined the Allahakbarries and, on occasion, James Barrie, rather than Conan Doyle, captained the authors. At a post-match supper, J.M.Barrie proposed the toast to 'the Leader of the Opposition', *aka* the Artists' skipper, and described him as 'one of the best captains in the room.' Arthur Conan Doyle and James Barrie were once partners in the theatre: in 1893 they provided the book for Richard D'Oyly Carte's rather weak Savoy production of *Jane Annie; or the good conduct prize.*

'Still rather the schoolboy', in Philip Trevor's slightly dismissive phrase, the young P.G.Wodehouse - the man whom Alan Gibson would describe as 'the most distinguished writer ever to take cricket as a main theme' - turned out for both the Authors and the Allahakbarries, including six matches at Lord's for the Authors. In the last of these, in 1911, he made 60 and took 7 for 75. The knowledgeable Murray Hedgcock has drawn together P.G. Wodehouse's cricket prose in his 1997 compendium, *Wodehouse at the Wicket* and his school stories will fall under the lens in the chapter on that topic. Moreover, in an article, 'a Plummy Century', in the Spring 2000 edition of the *Bodyline Books* catalogue, the same resourceful author outlines something of Wodehouse's actual cricketing experience in 1900, his final school season.

Born in Guildford in 1881 and with the forenames Pelham Grenville foisted upon him, he was educated at Dulwich College, but then - Oxford denied him because of a collapse in family funds - became a reluctant employee of the Hongkong and Shanghai Bank in Lombard Street, although the bank, like so many offices then, ran a cricket team. He was a quick bowler and, troubled with poor eyesight, a very late order batsman. He sometimes opened the bowling at Dulwich with Neville Knox, later of Surrey and twice for England. Benny Green, generously hailing his hero as 'the most fecund comic writer in the history of comic literature' has related how P.G. Wodehouse enjoyed his proudest hour, and one he could recall in loving detail seventy years later, in 1899. As *Wisden* sonorously recalls, he took seven wickets in the Tonbridge School first innings. This haul of 7 for 50 included the wicket of Kenneth Hutchings, the future Kent and England bat, who was killed in action in 1916. P.G. Wodehouse may have been less graphic in recounting that Tonbridge assembled 247 runs, Hutchings making 74, while Dulwich collapsed for 77, with the author making a duck. Murray Hedgcock's regretful conclusion is that P.G. Wodehouse was 'never more than a moderate player', not so competent as his older brother, Armine, another flowery choice of forename.

Benny Green, in his delectable *P.G. Wodehouse; a literary biography* (1981) has retailed the manner in which the author, soon rejecting banking for comic journalism, moved from school to adult stories, carrying his cricket bag with him, until, on moving across the Atlantic, 'we see the Dulwich College fast bowler heading unobtrusively for the pavilion for the last time.' In novels and in short stories like *How's that, Umpire?* cricket had featured strongly, but now he had to 'banish cricket from the fictional Eden of his imaginary world.' *Piccadilly Jim*, published in 1917, was 'the last time the game was presented as a symbol of the Higher Life.' The Transatlantic bridge is negotiated in the scene where Bayliss, the august butler, attempts to explain cricket to the baseball addict, the exiled Bingham Crocker, who 'is reduced to abject wonder' by the information that Hayward has scored 67 runs by all himself. The baseball/cricket chasm, as a token of the USA/UK divide is a familiar one, but here it is, of course, wittily handled. Golf, widely accepted on both sides of the ocean, was to be the sporting substitute for Wodehouse.

Initially in collaboration with Jerome Kern and Guy Bolton, P.G.Wodehouse contributed hugely to the American stage musical, his felicitous lyrics strengthening the somewhat febrile and weak construct of Anglo-American musical comedy. *Oh, Boy!* (1917) and *Oh, Lady! Lady!* (1918) are examples. He later worked with the Gershwin Brothers, George and Ira, Irving Berlin and Cole Porter, contributing, for instance, to the Porter hit show, *Anything Goes,* in 1934. Probably his finest single achievement in this bustling field was the provision of the lyric of 'Bill' in Jerome Kern's *Showboat* in 1927. It is of interest that, aside from his other incarnation as comic novelist supreme, P.G.Wodehouse helped introduce to the American musical stage the concept of subsuming lyric into book, characterisation and plot. The frothy musical comedy, on either side of the Atlantic, had become a flimsy excuse for singing and dancing, and Wodehouse assisted in the renaissance of the well-crafted and integrated musical entertainment. In so doing , he was preparing the ground for the post-1940 emergence of the American musical play, of which *Oklahoma!* (1943), *Guys and Dolls* (1950) and *West Side Story* (1957) might be offered as compelling illustrations.

In this regard, as well as in the drafting of intelligent, bright lyrics, P.G.Wodehouse was indebted to his guru, W.S.Gilbert. One may note the fresh-paint smartness of Wodehouse's lyrics in his cricket poem, *Missed!* A typical verse runs:

> By the handful my hair (which is auburn)
> I tore with a wrench from my thatch,
> And my heart was seared deep with a raw burn
> At the thought that I'd foozled that catch.

These cadences hint at the Gilbertian facility with rhyming and the librettist and producer of that long series of Savoyard comic operas had just one moment for cricket himself. This was in his plaudit, previously mentioned, to the liberated English girl, hymned by Mr Goldbury, a company promoter, in the rarely performed G.&S. opera, *Utopia Limited*, a late offering, overshadowed by the Italianate glories of its predecessor, *The Gondoliers*. Among other sportive exploits,

> At cricket, her kith will lose or win -
> She and her maids, on grass and clover,
> Eleven maids out- eleven maids in -
> And perhaps an occasional 'maiden over!'

The young Wodehouse, 'a shrinking flowerlet' in his own phrase, met the crusty Gilbert, by now something of a squire-like figure, with a touch of Doctor Dolittle, given his zoological *entourage*, at the playwright's home, Grim's Dyke on the Harrow Weald. The youth was suitably overawed, like most of Gilbert's visitors, but one impression may have stuck fast. Although Wodehouse may have abandoned fictional cricket, he never forgot the real thing. He maintained a lively interest, supported the legendary Hollywood club, wore the Warwickshire tie and liked to be reminded of Dulwich cricket. It is well known that he named his impeccable butler after Percy Jeeves, born in Yorkshire in 1888, who took 199 first-class wickets in 49 matches for Warwickshire and was regarded as exhibiting high promise before being cut down in action in France in 1916. P.G. Wodehouse had seen him play in 1913, a summer in which the bowler Jeeves took 106 wickets for an average of just under 21. Almost in commemoration, Jeeves the paragon first appears to 'save' but never to 'reconstitute' the imbecile Wooster in *The Man with Two Left Feet*, published a year later in 1917. *My Man Jeeves*, in the same year, continued the exquisite pattern that was to run, so happily, to scores of stories, long and short.

Commentators have guessed at Jeeve's fictional derivations, with the stoic Phipps, valet to the Wooster-like Lord Goring in Oscar Wilde's elegant comedy of manners, *An Ideal Husband*, first staged in 1895, high in the lists. However, on the side of reality, there are claims for W.S. Gilbert's butler, the blandly impregnable Warmilow, an ex-actor who gave 26 years of service to Gilbert and who may well have contributed to Wodehouse's intimidation when he lunched with the master.

Maybe he saw, for all his palatable writing gifts, something of Bertie Wooster in himself. He occasionally betrayed an incautious naiveté, never more so than in Berlin in 1941, when, after being interned while staying in his Le Touquet villa by the invading German troops, he broadcast light-hearted talks about his experiences. These were transmitted in still-neutral America and Wodehouse was to become a USA citizen in 1955. He was reviled in war-scourged Britain as a traitor, with the sober-sided author of, among other novels, *Fame is the Spur*, Howard Spring, and William Connor (the implacable Cassandra of *The Daily Mirror*) fuelling the fire. Government files reveal that the authorities judged him vain and stupid rather than treacherous and it seems that American intelligence agencies were later to use his scripts as a model of how to react if pressed to collaborate in that way. Nonetheless, reconciliation was a long time a-coming and it was 1975, just weeks before his death, that this long-lived author of nearly a hundred books was knighted.

The Arcadian world of Jeeves and Wooster, as of Beach and Lord Blandings, is a timeless one. Loosely set in the inter-wars years, it is a planet apart, Tolkien-like in its exclusive autonomy, with its own language, replete with literary allusion, an upper-class argot and a procession of audacious similes. It is a Never Land, akin in its ageless quality to Peter Pan's abode. Benny Green has indicated in some detail how P.G.Wodehouse was heavily influenced, as was H.G.Wells, by J.M.Barrie and his seductive, romanticised view of professional writing. As calm and amused cricket captain and as felicitous writer, he very much admired Barrie.

Apart from the obvious comparison of Crichton and Jeeves, one should also bear in mind the trenchant judgement of J.B.Priestley (himself the writer of an admiring essay on his fellow-Yorkshireman, 'Sutcliffe and I' in the collection *Open House*). In *English Humour* (1976) Priestley claimed that P.G.Wodehouse 'was really a schoolboy...no ordinary schoolboy, but a brilliant *super-de-luxe* schoolboy...His sexless young women...and his formidable bullying aunts, all belong to a schoolboy's world.' He is, says Priestley, enjoyed by those who 'still have a schoolboy somewhere in us' and the author himself behaved like 'an elderly schoolboy.' The concept of 'permanent adolescence' will be addressed more fully in chapter 17, but the notion of Bertie Wooster and his inventor as schoolboy-men is an entrancing one and, although Barrie's mind-set was even younger, it draws them ever closer together. One can easily imagine J.M.Barrie making, in similar circumstances, musing, trifling broadcasts from Berlin.

Thus do the slow bowler and the fast bowler share some common ground, in personal as in professional matters, as well as in their devotion, itself boy-like, for cricket.

Chapter 12

CRICKET BETWEEN THE WAUGHS

Somerset Maugham was born in Paris in 1874 and after yet another unhappy experience for an author at school, this time at King's School, Canterbury, he studied philosophy and medicine, before turning to full-scale writing and extensive travel, with his companion, Gerald Haxton. He died in 1965. He dubbed himself one of the leading 'second-raters', although the popularity of his novels, such as of *Human Bondage* (1915) or *The Moon and Sixpence* (1919), and of his razor-sharp short stories, remains high. In 1930 he published his spirited anti-romantic, *Cakes and Ale*, and the narrator describes as follows the protagonist of the action, Alroy 'Roy' Kear, the son of a colonial officer, educated at Winchester and New College, Oxford, who has found his first employment as a private tutor:

'I knew him first soon after he had resigned from his tutorship to devote himself exclusively to literature, and he was then a fine, upstanding young man, six feet high in his stockinged feet and of an athletic build, with broad shoulders and a confident carriage. He was not handsome, but in a manly way agreeable to look at, with wide blue frank eyes and curly hair of a light-ish brown: his nose was rather short and broad; his chin square. He was something of an athlete. No one who has read in his early books the descriptions of a run with the hounds, so vivid and so accurate, can doubt that he wrote from personal experience; and until quite lately he was willing now and then to desert his desk for a day's hunting. He published his first novel when men of letters, to show their virility, drank beer and played cricket, and for some years there was seldom a literary eleven in which his name did not figure. This particular school, I hardly know why, has lost its bravery, their books are neglected, and cricketers though they have remained, they find difficulty placing their articles. Roy ceased playing cricket a good many years ago and he has developed a fine taste for claret.'

Roy is thus first seen in the Edwardian years, but one forms the impression that Somerset Maugham was also looking through half-closed sceptical eyes at the inter-wars' period. His impish critique, mischievous and knowing, angles in on a pairing of half-truths, in that from the 1880s, but especially in 'the long week-end' between the two world wars, *litterateurs* appeared to play cricket unceasingly and, by and large, their names were not the most eminent in the roll-call of major English Literature.

The Great War traumatised traditional English life and, with it, cricket. It may be convincingly argued that, such was the malign influence of the carnage after a century of, more or less, freedom from continental warfare, cricket was petrified at that point, luckily, an excellent juncture at the zenith of its golden age. In format and methodology, and, apart from the money-spinning roulette wheel of numberless limited overs' fixtures, it has changed little, certainly compared with most other sports. The County Championship, with just two grudging admissions and, more significantly, no evictions, since 1918, is a stationary, concrete monument to that thesis, particularly compared with its restless, evolving existence among the bold Victorians. A reincarnated W.G.Grace, having observed with respect the overall improvement in fielding and the latest variation on the LBW law, with glee the shortened boundaries and the fielding and bowling restrictions in some competitions, and with quizzical astonishment the vast betterment of pitches and equipment, to say nothing of the protective armour, would assuredly proceed to make 2000 runs a calendar year the world around.

A picturesque example lies in the hullabaloo over the reintroduction of coloured clothing after its replacement for a relatively short period by white dress. That later 19th century adherence to the purity of white attire was in kilter with the religiosity of the day, with the white-garbed acolytes reverentially following the druidically surpliced umpires from the sacristy of the pavilion to the altar of the wickets for the celebration of 'the holy game.' The score-book is a basic symbol of Victorianism: it is both the double book-keeping ledger in which Newman Noggs or Bob Cratchit might have scratched monetary accounts and the book of judgement, as encapsulated in Grantland Rice's sombre verse about the 'One Great Scorer.'

A macabre illustration of the switch to religion has been supplied by the well-known military historian, John Keegan. Before the Battle of Waterloo in 1815, and although it was a Sunday, there was scarcely a whisper of religion in the damp June air. The Duke of Wellington had procured a handful of Anglican chaplains, but these were for chasing Methodism, deemed to be subversive of the martial hierarchy, from around the camp-fires. His officers and the 'long-nosed bugger', as the Iron Duke was less imposingly if more affectionately nicknamed by his soldiers, treated religion with cool disdain and the other ranks regarded it, by and large, with rude irreverence. A hundred years later before the Battle of the Somme in July 1916, a majority of the soldiery went willingly to church parade, judging this to be a necessary and ritual preparation for battle, and many of these men met a painful death, pitiably clutching their bibles in shell-hole or dug-out.

Yet the bitter price of the Great War secularised the population quickly. The God-head that was agonised over by Victorian thinkers, like Charles Darwin, T.H.Huxley, George Eliot and Thomas Hardy, as so lucidly recorded in A.N.Wilson's 1999 study, *God's Funeral*, was so effectively killed by the 1914-18 War that the modern historian, Ross McKibbin, has firmly concluded that, by mid-20th century, 'England was by formal criteria - meaning, usually, church attendance - one of the most secular societies in the world.' Cricket, however, despite its massive reliance on ecclesiastical support in its formative years as a discrete sport, did not lose as much ground as one might have expected. Its penetration into the social environment was profound and this was as true on a world basis. One of the ironies of the collapse of the British Empire is that, when the soldiers, the officials and the missionaries had fled the field, it was cricket that ubiquitously remained. Across large tracts of the post-imperial *regnum,* cricket proved more of a stayer than the English version of Christianity.

Cricket, especially in England, adopted an aesthetic instead of an priestly character. It was played from memory, from a memory of a lost, if idealistic, world of Edwardian calm and spaciousness. Importantly, cricket's establishment fought the war to return to the past it cherished, not so that in the future homes fit for heroes might be erected. Paralysed by the bloodbath, they aborted the confident Victorian belief in continuing revolution and opted for a grave traditionalism. It was not distressing; when Wally Hammond was batting it was comely and when Don Bradman was batting it was compelling. It was more trance than coma. Cricket was rather like the lovely but 'dead-pale' Lady Of Shalott, of Tennyson's mournful poem, floating down the stream 'till her blood was frozen over.'

Thus the soul of cricket was less religious and more artistic - and this may have helped to account for the influx of author-cricketers, enjoying, often at a modest level of ability, cricket as a socially and culturally intriguing exercise, not as a moral and character-building experiment. As Somerset Maugham's jocose comment suggests, there were plenty of writers, including himself, who found that whole exercise somewhat puerile and shallow, a contempt in a long tradition represented by Horace Walpole, John Ruskin and - 'the well-fed Englishman...cannot even play at cricket or football; he has to work at them' - George Bernard Shaw. Rudyard Kipling, although not opposed root and branch to cricket, had believed that it was excessively worshipped, to the detriment to the sort of education necessary, in his fearful mind, to withstand the nation's enemies. He also felt that one had 'to hit an Englishman more than once on the jaw before he will take a thing seriously': hence his tart comment that the Englishman should be turning to more important responsibilities than 'casting a ball at three straight sticks and defending the same with a fourth.'

It would be a gross over-simplification to mark out the ground in the style of Cavaliers and Roundheads, of sensible traditionalists *versus* progressive aesthetes, of middlebrows against eggheads, but it might be fair, as an approximate guide, to suggest that the writers in question edged toward or hovered about this or that pool of emphasis. In retrospect, it might be judged that the cricket-playing writers were not so much, as Somerset Maugham waggishly hinted, not published as not so well-remembered. Classical literature is to some degree a matter of enduring vintage: a generation or two must pass before, in most cases, one might dare arbitrate on whatever that lasting quality is. D.H.Lawrence and Evelyn Waugh and Virginia Woolf have enjoyed a longer innings, therefore, than some of their contemporaries who mixed the business of writing with the pleasure of cricket.

Certainly the names that appear on the score-cards of varied authors' and allied elevens mainly belong to what is sometimes known as the 'Georgian' school. The label derives from the poetry published in the early years of the reign of George V. This verse was, although not exclusively, naturalistic and uncontroversial, providing, for much of the rest of the century, the engaging and harmless rhyming fodder of a million classrooms, with odes, for instance, by Robert Brooke, Walter de la Mare, W.H.Davies and John Masefield. The likes of Ezra Pound, T.S.Eliot and the Sitwells, Edith, Osbert and Sacheverell were loudly critical and their more modernist approach was, for instance, incorporated in the annual poetic collection, *Wheels*, at much the same time. One might note, in passing, that Osbert Sitwell, although entered for MCC on the day of his birth, raised the wrath of his grandfather, Lord Londesborough, founder of the Scarborough Festival, when he fell into infant slumber during an exciting passage of county cricket. Of his grandfather's cricketing gala on the Yorkshire coast, he was to write that, in 'the tents that blazed with the ties of the cricketing clubs and the port-wined faces of the *aficionados*' he was forced to watch 'this, to me, always unattractive and lengthy game.'

Over the years a looser conflict of these 'Georgian' and the 'Modernist' attitudes developed. A pertinent case-study may be examined in the careers and relationship of the Waugh brothers, who were not as *sympatico* as their cricketing antipodean namesakes. They were the sons of Arthur Waugh who, at the tender age of 35, had been appointed managing director of the ailing publishers Chapman and Hall, with its Dickensian and Meredithian connections, and still employing a 'misanthropic clerk' who remembered Anthony Trollope, clad in hunting pink, banging his crop on the reception desk, impatient for service. Arthur Waugh coped with kindness and with capability and it is not irrelevant to this analysis to recollect that 'with characteristic earnestness, he organised an office cricket team to restore team spirit.'

Evelyn Arthur St John was born in 1902; his elder brother, Alexander Raban, in 1898, with the latter's indoor cricket threatening to destroy the quietude of the household and the repose of the new-born babe. The pro- and anti-cricket seeds were immediately sown. Arthur leaned toward the manly, boisterous Alec, instructing him in cricketing technique, whereas Evelyn, a reluctant cricketer, 'could not share in the surrogate religion of Lord's and *Wisden*. Frightened by his brother's forcefulness, he preferred the company of his mother...he loathed cricket, which rivalled Christianity as a staff of life for his father and brother.'

For his part, Alec, not unlike his hero Charles Dickens, detested shows of world-weary diffidence, and threw himself enthusiastically into the lessons and games of Sherborne School, with his father insisting that his scores be telegraphed to him, subsiding into near-ecstasy when Alec's persevering innings won the House Cup. To Arthur's admirably restrained dismay, Alec's fervour led him into deep waters. In 1915 he was asked to leave, and spent a term in a kind of scholastic limbo, having been discovered in homosexual activity. Off he went to the wars and to the precocious writing of *The Loom of Youth* (1917), based on his Sherborne experience and to which readers may return in chapter 17 where cricket in school stories is the theme.

Effectively barred from Sherborne, Evelyn Waugh was hustled off to Lancing and Hertford College, Oxford, both of which he felt were a little beneath him, and where he seemed to drift between rebellious behaviour and bouts of hard work. However, small and clumsy, he never came to terms with the cult of sportsmanship. Both brothers had failed first marriages. Alec married Barbara Jacobs, the daughter of the writer W.W.Jacobs. Some will remember his salty short stories of dock-yard and coastal shipping, collected into volumes like *Light Freights* (1901), although perhaps his gruesome tale, *The Monkey's Paw*, is his best known prose. That alliance folded quickly, possibly unconsummated. Evelyn married the quite highly born Evelyn Gardner in 1928, the year he was converted to Roman Catholicism, but they divorced in 1930, following her flight, to Evelyn's chagrin, with another man. Both later married more contentedly, Evelyn to Laura Herbert, the mother of Auberon Waugh, in 1937. Evelyn Waugh served in the Royal Marines during the 1939-45 war, proving to be, by some accounts, unpopular with his men. He died in 1966, whereas Alec lived on until 1981, mostly living abroad.

Alec Waugh wrote many novels, reasonably successful in their time, but largely now forgotten: *Island in the Sun* (1956), with lots of sexual and racial tension on a West Indian isle, may be the sole survivor, some of that the result of the 1957 film with a star-strewn cast of James Mason, Joan Fontaine, Dorothy Dandridge, Harry Belafonte and Joan Collins. For his part, Evelyn Waugh became Britain's leading satirical novelist, prospecting a seam of gleaming black diamonds. *Decline and Fall* (1928), *Vile Bodies* (1930), *Scoop* (1938), *Put out more Flags* (1942), the more pensive *Brideshead Revisited* (1945), *The Loved One* (1948), the military trilogy, *Sword of Honour* (published as a set in 1961) are proud gems picked from a distinguished assortment.

Snobbish, on occasion malicious and petulant, Evelyn Waugh could be a difficult person, but few would deny his dark comic genius, and it is fair to add that Alec Waugh was never envious of his younger brother's greater critical acclaim. There was no bitter animosity between them, but they were as men apart. Martin Stannard, who has adeptly and painstakingly traced these threads in *Evelyn Waugh; the early years, 1903-1939* (1986) concludes: 'it is hard to imagine how two brothers, both of whom became famous novelists and both of whom shared an affectionate home, could grow up strangers. But that is precisely what happened.' Martin Stannard also insists that this alienated relation was coloured by their work: 'his father's and brother's absorption in what seemed to (Evelyn) Waugh a second-rate literary world frustrated and bored him.'

Nonetheless, Alec Waugh combined cricketing pleasures with writing duties, exactly as Somerset Maugham suggested. He has written of how, as a part-time worker in his father's publishing house, he found he had five days a week free for good club cricket in the 1920s. He did not have a 'home' side but spread his talents over a wide range of touring and other sides, including the Stoics; the Thespids; the Old Broughtonians (raised by Clifford Bax who composed, among much else, the poem, *Cricket Days*, 'when summer had burst the poppy and skies were brazen') Richmond, the Chiltern Ramblers, captained by the lawyer, E.E.Carus-Wilson. His most famed team was the Invalids, celebrated in legend and lore, and with A.P.Herbert, Hugh Walpole, Dudley Carew and the broadcaster Howard Marshall among the hundred or so *literati* enrolled on the team-sheets, and with luminaries such as G.K.Chesterton and Hilaire Belloc, both, after their fashion, Anglophile to an immense degree, among the occasional spectators.

Alec Waugh has described how its founder, the poet, J.C.Squire, was inspired by a visit to a military hospital in World War I. The Invalids' colours were hospital blue and orange in broad stripes; their badge was crossed crutches. This authors' team was, of course, made famous by A.G.Macdonell's tribute to its mixed skills in his *England, their England*, published in 1933. It is quoted as everybody's favourite piece of amusing cricket writing; it has been endlessly anthologised; the blacksmith, 'breasting the slope superbly like a mettlesome combination of Vulcan and Venus Anadyomene' and delivering the first ball as 'a high full toss to leg, of appalling velocity', has entered the gallery of literary prototypes. A.G.Macdonell himself was coached at Winchester and, of quick-steeled temper, something of a lusty hitter; his 1938 book, *The Autobiography of a Cad*, is another mirthful tribute to his humour.

'The account' affirms Alec Waugh, 'was not a caricature.' Fordenden, home of the fictional opponents, was, in parts, the villages of Bridge, Ditchling and Fordcombe, and the organisation was as surreal and as casual as the bemused Scot, Donald, the Macdonell character, relates. Alec Waugh has helped to identify the combatants. The stout wicket-keeper was Cecil Palmer, the publisher; the somnolent outfielder was J.B.Morton, *Beachcomber of the Daily Express* (Will Hay's *Boys will be Boys* film in 1935 was based on Narkover school featured in his newspaper column); the fiery major was one-time parliamentarian Reginald Berkeley, writer of *The Lady with the Lamp* (the vehicle for the 1951 movie, *The Lady with a Lamp*, starring Anna Neagle as Florence Nightingale) and one of the first-ever 'wireless' plays, *The White Chateau*...and 'the famous novelist', Robert Southcott, was Alec Waugh.

'The next player was a singular young man. He was small and quiet, and he wore perfectly creased white flannels, white silk socks, a pale pink shirt and a white cap. On the way down in the *char-a-banc* he had taken little part in the conversation and even less in the beer drinking. There was a retiring modesty about him that made him conspicuous in that cricket eleven, and there was a gentleness, an almost finicky gentleness about his movements which hardy seemed virile and athletic.' Soon, 'holding his bat as delicately as if it was a flute or a fan', he was the hero of 'a mob of screaming urchins' as, 'delirious with ecstasy', they were recovering the ball from hayfield, tavern bar and trout stream. If Alec Waugh is right and that this no caricature, cricket fans may confirm the judgement that, for all the other's superior literary gifts, one would probably opt to spend an afternoon with Alec rather than Evelyn.

Robert Southcott's skipper, Mr Hodge, was J.C.Squire, untidy, short-sighted and unorthodox as a cricketer. But he was large-hearted, describing himself 'as a centipede with a foot in a hundred worlds.' One is again indebted to the accomplished James Coldham. Writing in *The Cricketer Spring Annual* (1957) he concisely summarised Sir John Collings Squire, the man, the cricket sponsor and the writer. J.C.Squire was born in Plymouth in 1884, and, after his education at Blundell's School, Tiverton and St John's College, Cambridge, he became a poet and critic, most notably as the founder-editor of *The London Mercury* in 1919. This journal became the chief focus for Georgian poetry and, by extension, the Georgian tendency, with its sympathetic feel for English tradition, history and countryside. Jack Squire also wrote a little about cricket, including the introduction to Neville Cardus' 'Cricket' contribution to the *English Heritage* series, of which he, Squire, was one of the editors, as befitted his stance on that concept. Among other titles were, predictably, *English Folk-song and Dance*, *The English Inn* and *The English Public School*.

E.W.Hornung was involved in the conversations that led to the establishment of the Invalids in 1920 and for many years they sustained a goodly fixture list, once trouncing Lords and Commons at the Oval and, on New Year's Day, 1929, beating the Hampshire Esquimos on Broadhalfpenny Down, Hambledon in an act of peaceful resistance against the encroachment of football on the cricket season. The Invalids were also resurrected after the Second World War. J.C.Squire was knighted in 1933 and John Betjeman, unsurprisingly, given his own sources of inspiration, edited Squire's collected poems, published in 1959, a year after his death. Jack

Squire contrived to stand as a Labour candidate in the 1918 general election and as a Liberal candidate in the 1924 parliamentary contest, but he combined such leftish tendencies with a perhaps not incompatible conservatism about cricket's pastoral heritage. That excellent historian of cricket's inter-wars era, Jack Williams, records how, in 1930, J.C.Squire wrote of cricket's 'rural root', claiming that 'few men...would not rather play on a field surrounded by ancient elms and rabbit-haunted bracken than on a better field with flat black lands or gasworks around.' He felt that, in village cricket, 'the distinctions in life are temporarily forgotten: for the time being we live in an ideal republic where Jack is as good as his master, but may be a little better...' One thinks of Charles Dickens' advice on the running of the Gad's Hill cricket club or of Hugh de Selincourt's adroit filleting of the class composition of the Tillingfold eleven.

After the precedent of Arthur Waugh's man-management strategy, J.C.Squire doubtless combined his undeniable love of cricket with a device for in-breeding team spirit among his colleagues and followers. There does seem to have been any number of Authors' XIs at this time, as well as publishing house teams. W.A.Darlington was a sound opening bat and had captained his Cambridge college side. He was drama critic of *The Daily Telegraph* for some fifty years, but he had made something of a name with his fantasy of *Alf's Button*, the farce of the tommy who, with a button fashioned from Aladdin's lamp, finds himself with a genie to make life in the trenches more bearable. It was filmed, with Leslie Henson in the (silent) title-role in 1920, and with 'talkie' sequels, one in 1930 with Nervo and Knox, the other - *Alf's Button Afloat* - in 1938 when that manic duo was joined by other members of the Crazy Gang, Flanagan and Allen and Naughton and Gold, together with Alastair Sim. Another was Herbert Farjeon, revue sketch writer, dour opening bat and brother of Eleanor, the imaginative children's writer. His amusing account of the Herecombe and Therecombe match, from his 1946 miscellany, *Cricket Bag*, that two-ball engagement, with its involuntary declaration and its interminable bowler's run-up, is another 'must' for the anthologies. He claimed that his own bowling was 'slow off the pitch and quick off the bat.'

The author, Nigel Balchin, was a reasonable wicket-keeper: he played for Dauntsey's School in 1927 and Wiltshire in 1930, while J.R.Sheffield went one better - he kept wicket for Essex in 177 games between 1929 and 1936, and he had 196 first-class catches and 54 stumpings, along side which he wrote the thriller, *Bolivian Spy*. Bernard Hollowood, a noted editor of

Punch, played, like his father and two brothers, for Staffordshire. One could continue: the writers who played cricket a little; the cricketers who wrote a little...it is an endless list. They testify to the alignment of literature and cricket before and after the First World War.

However, just as Anthony Trollope reminded that the clergy were not all cricket nuts, the antagonism engendered between the traditionalists and the modernists, especially after 1918, demonstrates that all was not peaceable on the literary-cum-cricketing front. Sir John Squire was a forceful influence in literary affairs between the wars, leading the clique of 'Georgian' writers, referred to by their foes as the 'Squirearchy.' These were not simply ideological squabbles: influence and control might dictate where the commissions were offered and who received how much for what pieces. A.G.Macdonell pokes mild fun at the Hodge/Squire figure, as 'a poet, and therefore a theorist and an idealist', as a bowler who 'detested in theory' Lancashire, the land of factories, and 'loved in fact' Worcestershire, realm of 'English apples and Mr Stanley Baldwin.' He portrays him, tankard in hand, rarely tearing himself away from the consoling comforts of 'the Three Horseshoes.'

Evelyn Waugh, a virulent enemy of John Squire and all for which he stood, was more waspish. Eager to spread the rumour that the poet was imbibing not wisely but too well, he wrote to his friend, Tom Driberg, later the Labour politician, then William Hickey, the gossip columnist for Lord Beaverbrook's *Daily Express*, to tell him that 'J.C.Squire has taken seriously to drink at last.'

Chapter 13

CRICKET: THE PLOT THICKENS

Once we move from the realm of books and stories devoted solely to cricket, the incidence of cricketing references in fiction is, it must be confessed, largely incidental. As we have noted, it helps, sometimes with no more than a brief allusion, to delineate a character or provide a hint of background. On occasion, however, we may find novels where quite an extensive episode is employed to develop or augment the plot. Two such were L.P.Hartley's *The Go-between* and E.M.Forster's *Maurice*.

A word or two, by way of introduction, about the authors. Edward Morgan Forster was born in London in 1879 and educated at Tonbridge School, which gave him a jaundiced view of public school values, and at King's College, Cambridge, an institution with which he enjoyed a life-time's attachment. His childhood was dominated by adoring female relations and he spent much time with his mother, until her death in 1945. He died in 1979 at Coventry, having a year before been awarded the Order of Merit. Although not a boisterously public personality, E.M.Forster enunciated and believed in a strong sense of individuality. He was the first President of the National Council of Civil Liberties; he served as a non-combatant with the International Red Cross in the Great War and he was active in opposition to the censorship or suppression of books such as Radclyffe Hall's lesbian-oriented book, *The Well of Loneliness* or D.H.Lawrence's *Lady Chatterley's Lover*. He is famously recollected for his brave saying that, faced with the choice, he hoped he would have the courage to betray his country rather than his friend.

In his great and beautifully crafted novels, such as *Where Angels Fear to Tread* (1905) *A Room with a View* (1908) *Howards End* (1910) or, much later, in his contribution to the libretto of the Benjamin Britten 1949 opera, *Billy Budd*, based on Herman Melville's story, this fervour for personal freedom and emotional impulse, liberated from the narrow bonds of conformity, is important. It is interesting how, in the current generation, his justly acclaimed novels have been the source of sumptuous and perceptive filmic and televisual portrayal, not least in respect of *A Passage to India* (1924) said by some commentators to be the best novel about Asia by a European. Wisely and directly, he pursued the *motif* of the social barriers that separate individual from individual, very much the theme of *Maurice*.

Leslie Poles Hartley was the younger man, although Forster outlived him. Born in 1895 at Whittesley, Cambridgeshire, he was educated at Harrow and Balliol College, Oxford, and he fought with the Norfolk Regiment in the 1914-18 war. Coming from a moderately privileged background, he led a fairly leisurely life of literary practice, spending almost all his time after his military service in Venice, whilst, when in England, living at Bath. As well as writing a number of delicately etched novels, he wrote literary criticism, for, among other journals, *The Spectator*. It was with his trilogy *The Shrimp and the Anemone* (1944), *The Sixth Heaven* (1946) and *Eustace and Hilda* (1947) that he sprang to prominence, although his best-known novel is certainly *The Go-between*, which won the Heinemann Foundation award. L.P.Hartley died in 1972.

He was the child of his age. Many of his stories examine the Freudian idea of the effects of early childhood on adult development and his polished style was carefully but not slavishly based on the approach of Henry James. John Betjeman said. 'of all the novels L.P.Hartley has written I think *The Go-between* is the best...(it is) in the best tradition of fiction.' Certainly Hartley's handling of the hazy sheen of a hot thunderous pre-1914 summer is sublime: it is slumberingly torpid, but with portents of electric shocks in the air.

The books have some common elements. Some two-thirds of the way through each novel there is depicted the yearly match of the great estate against the local villagers and tenant farmers. Although the 'hall' servants may sometimes complete the former team, it is basically Gentlemen *versus* Players in miniature, in the proper sense of social rather than economic status. Both are set in the Golden Age of cricket prior to the first world war, with the action of *The Go-between* occurring during the Boer War at the turn of the century and that of *Maurice* some years later. Both matches include three players who are somehow involved in the romantic thrust of the plot, which turns, in essence, on the love-interest being cross-class. This made manifest a strong, but by no means exclusive, Victorian convention. It was reflected in the good old pantomimic tradition of Cinderella and Prince Charming or Aladdin and Princess Balroubadour, in the Dickensian canon with Estelle and Pip in *Great Expectations* or Florence and Walter Gay in *Dombey and Son* and in the grand Savoyard prescription where Mabel and Frederic in *The Pirates of Penzance* or Josephine and Ralph Rackstraw in *HMS Pinafore* find romance beckoniong across the social boundaries. Moreover, in another adherence to fictional orthodoxy, the third character in the two novels under review is an upper class rival lover.

Then there are two main differences. *The Go-between* was published in 1953, and - 'the past is a foreign country; they do things differently there' - it represents the view of an older man looking back from about that juncture to his boyhood. *Maurice* was published in 1971, but it was finished by E.M.Forster as long ago as 1914, just after the imagined time of the action, although only then perused by private eyes. That explains the second contrast, for *Maurice* is a story of homosexual love, which the author had insisted could only be published after his own death and after the demise of others who might have been hurt by its subject-matter.

Leo Colston is 'the Go-between' for Marian Maudsley, the daughter of the local landed magnate, and a smallscale tenant farmer, Ted Burgess. They are engaged in a clandestine and passionate love affair, sinful for its sexual boldness, its coupling of the upper class girl with the lower class farmer, and for the fact that she is affianced to Lord Trimingham. Leo, on holiday at the Maudsley country house, Brandham Hall, is innocently drawn into acting as messenger between them and, as innocently, the cause of their being discovered. The trauma of that revelation, and the sight of the protagonists in ardent embrace, robs Leo of his own sexuality and he lives out an impotent and celibate existence.

The cricket match provides an ironic mirror of that crucial act, presaging it with elegant symbol. The village team 'distressed' Leo by 'their nondescript appearance; some wore working clothes, some had already taken their coats off, revealing that they wore braces.' He could not believe that 'you could succeed at a game unless you were dressed properly for it. It was like trained soldiers fighting natives. And then it crossed my mind that perhaps the village team were like the Boers, who did not have much in the way of equipment by our standards, but could give a good account of themselves, none the less; and I looked at them with new respect.' The paragraph is a precise summation of the pre-1914 view of class and its import, a significance that is lucidly measured in and by cricketing terms.

A 'pretty' correct, if eventually disappointing, innings by Lord Trimingham and a prudent, solid knock from Mr Maudsley, the land-owner, give the Hall 'the very respectable score' of 142. However, Ted Burgess, a mighty but, conversely, unorthodox hitter, looks like winning the game for the village, when Leo, acting as twelfth man, catches him out at square leg with only three runs required: Burgess, caught sub, bowled Lord Trimingham, 81, reads the scorebook. It is only a matter of time before Ted Burgess is 'caught out' again by Leo, this time in flagrant breach of all the social mores of the age. There are tears after bed-time. Burgess brings to an end his life's innings, short and rumbustious as it has been, by blowing out his brains. The respective life-styles are cleverly reflected in their sporting technique and approach. Lord Trimingham, impeccable in manners as in cricketing deportment, marries Marian and she gives birth, it transpires, to Ted's child.

Maurice, like Leo, is a visitor at a stately home, when he is recruited to play for the Park against the village. 'Maurice hated cricket', wrote Forster, 'It demanded a snickety neatness he could not supply...he might be bowled by or punished by some lout, and he felt it unsuitable.' Leo's Boers are Maurice's louts. Like Hartley's 'Hall' eleven, the 'Park' side includes servants. The well-to-do suburbanite, Maurice, had discovered his homosexual nature at Cambridge under the tutelage of Clive Durham, now owner of the Penge Estate, the scene of the action, and, having found within himself a heterosexual constitution, a passingly happily married man. He is to arrive late for the match, as he is canvassing the local constituency in the safe hope of becoming its MP. Simcox, a footman, asks Maurice to captain the team instead of Clive: 'things always go better', he opines, 'under a gentleman.' Maurice refuses and Alec, the replacement servant-skipper ' 'put himself in first', said a lady, 'a gentleman would never have done that. Little things interest me."

The previous night Maurice had found himself locked in impassioned dalliance with his captain, the undergame-keeper, Alec Scudder. As the game unfolds, and in spite of his dislike of cricket, Maurice enjoys a fruitful stand with Alec: 'and as the game proceeded, it connected with the night and interpreted it.' Perhaps with a lateral glance at all those cricketing friendships in school yarns, with close affection exemplified in winning alliances, Maurice and Alec recall the joys of the night in the partnership of the day.

It might be remarked that, like Burgess, Scudder is not overly working-class, but, as he constantly reminds his lover, of sturdy lower middle-class stock, from, indeed, that echelon of agricultural and industrial tradesmen whence came - H.G. Wells' father, the cricket player, coach and shopkeeper is, as we have already found, an example - many of the Players who joined in cricketing tourneys with the Gentlemen, such as Maurice, Trimingham and Maudsley.

The magical mood of the stand between Maurice and Alec is broken by the arrival of Clive, the former lover who had rejected Maurice to his bitter anger, while there is yet another subordinate metaphor involved. The inquisitive Reverend Borenius, the village vicar, suspects Maurice and Alec of what he sees as foul play and is anxious to put a stop to such scandalous behaviour. Maurice stolidly refutes his aspersions and then, when the clergyman bowls his cunning twisters, 'Alec blocked Mr Borenius's lobs.'

Not altogether convincingly, not even, apparently to E.M.Forster himself, the smooth upper-class Maurice and the rougher lower-middle-class Alec abandon their respective positions and circumstances and form a continuing relationship. The shining batting partnership, despite its being clouded by the appearance of the one-time, neo-Platonic lover, Clive, who also represents, like Lord Trimingham, the right side of the social tracks, emblematically prefaces the fruitful life-alliance of Maurice and Alec. Perhaps, as E.M.Forster elsewhere opined, 'Fate is the umpire, the Hope is the ball.'

Even such a brief examination as this of the two novels reveals a further correspondence between them. Like so many novels, there is an autobiographical element. On the one side, L.P.Hartley was writing, in his late fifties, from the stance of a similarly middle-aged man looking back to a dreadful crisis of boyhood in a time when he, the novelist, was also of that youthful age. On the other side, E.M.Forster was writing from the viewpoint of his own social and sexual difficulties at the point of their occurrence, but the public were not able to hear this testimony until many decades later.

Like the great Victorian novelists, E.M.Forster essayed at a broader intellectual sweep than L.P.Hartley, questioning the way a dull and hidebound society trammelled the nonconforming individual, especially in matters of class, gender, race and sexuality. L.P.Hartley, perhaps turning his back, along with many of his contemporaries, on the horrors they had experienced in the trenches, spoke little in his writings of such vistas. Rather was his the more fastidious preoccupation with the personal torments of the psyche.

Yet both turned to cricket to illuminate the truths they wanted to tell. What a glorious game is cricket in that it is capable of offering such scope for psychological and social illustration. Although these two stories differ in that one has an unhappy and the other a happier ending, they both benefit from the deployment of the cricketing analogue. Whether it is being 'caught out' or having 'a good partnership'. to say nothing of 'blocking' someone's probing queries, or possibly being 'stumped' by them, *The Go-between* and

Maurice spell out once more the parallels between life and cricket.

Even James Joyce sought symbolism in cricket. It is no more than a couple of paragraphs, but the prospector for the gold-dust of cricketing allusions in classical literature soon learns to count his blessings in tiny specks. James Joyce was a contemporary of E.M.Forster: he was born in Dublin in 1882 and, after a life of voluntary exile, accompanied by his partner, Nora Barnacle, he died in Zurich in 1941. Unwavering in his devotion to a modernist approach to writing and, for that reason, the object of censorship and the subject of critical but rarely material success, his two great works, *Ulysses* (serialised 1918-20; published in volume form 1922) and *Finnegan's Wake* (serialised 1928-37; published 1939) stand as emblems of the cultural rebellion against traditional and representative forms. His experimental use of the dream-like 'stream of consciousness' relates him strongly to the abstract painters and sculptors, the modern atonal composers and non-structured poets of the same anti-conventional renaissance.

Originally influenced by the sombre, farsighted Norwegian dramatist, Ibsen, he found, despite the stimulating acquaintance of the playwright, J.M.Synge, and the poet, W.B.Yeats, the attempt to foster an Irish national culture too narrowing and he struck out for a more international perspective. One might see his work as the literary equivalent of Picasso in the studio or of his fellow-Irishman, Samuel Beckett, in the theatre. His earlier book, *Portrait of the Artist as a Young Man*, was drafted in 1904, soon after the leaving of Dublin, but it was not published until ten years later, when it was serialised in *The Egoist*, a progressive journal, with which poets like Ezra Pound and T.S.Eliot had connections, and published as a single volume in 1916.

It is in this largely autobiographical venture that Joyce's cricket is to be uncovered. The novel follows the inner consciousness of Stephen Dedalus from infancy to university, encompassing his teen-age sexual initiation, the gradual impoverishment of his family background and his struggles with sin and the converse temptation of the priesthood. Stephen is educated at Clongowes, very explicitly modelled on a school James Joyce attended briefly, Clongowes Wood College in Kildare, and where the argot - 'smugging' for homosexual behaviour - is as curious as any at an English public school.

Stephen's glasses have been broken in some horseplay. 'That was why the fellows seemed to him smaller and farther away and the goalposts so thin and far and the soft grey sky so high up. But there was no play on the football grounds for cricket was coming and some said that Barnes would be the prof and some said it would be Flowers. And all over the playground they were playing rounders and bowling twisters and lobs. And from here and there came the sounds of cricketbats through the soft grey air. They said: pick, pack, pock; puck: like drops of water in a fountain slowly falling in the brimming bowl.'

The 'fellows' are discussing a 'smugging' incident and the conversation naturally turns to flogging. 'The fellows laughed but he thought they were a little afraid. In the silence of the soft grey air he heard the cricketbats from here and from there: pock. That was a sound to hear but if you were hit then you would feel a pain. The pandybat made a sound too but not like that. The fellows said it was made of whalebone and leather with lead inside and he wondered what the pain was like.'

The luckless Stephen did not have to wonder long. The Prefect of Studies, denouncing him as 'a lazy little schemer' for his tale of broken spectacles, thrashes him cruelly with the 'pandybat'. Recording a true-life incident, Stephen earns the acclaim of the 'fellows' when he plucks up the courage to complain to the Rector, that is, head master of the college, and be heard sympathetically. In his contentment he smells the pleasant rural scents 'in the little wood behind the pavilion...The fellows were practising long shies and bowling lobs and slow twisters. In the long grey silence he could hear the bump of the balls: and from here and from there through the quiet air the sound of the cricketbats: pick, pack, pock, puck: like drops of water in a fountain falling softly in the brimming bowl.' Stephen is returned to benign pasture.

His biographer reports that James Joyce, although in adult life dismissive of any boyish sporting involvement, did play cricket at school and was also a good swimmer. His editor notes that the 'prof' was the captain of the eleven, although the uninitiated might be forgiven for musing over the possibility that it referred to the professional coach. Wilfred Flowers and William Barnes of Nottinghamshire, let alone the great Sydney Barnes, were professional cricketers active in James Joyce's boyhood. It would be pleasing to think that those worthies might have gained access to his flux of consciousness.

That complaisant incidental apart, it is the counterpoint of the soothing sound of leather on willow, before and after, and the vicious noise of leather on hand that is telling. The 'pock' of the ball on bat is possibly as close as a writer has come to relating that distinctive tone in print. The disconcerting cricketing affinity of the dreaded 'pandybat' underpins the contrast; apparently it was also called a 'turkey' because it turned hands red.

There is wider circle of meaning. According to the Joycean scholar, Seamus Deane, the author was 'unforgiving in his analysis of the Irish version of degeneration', accusing his countrymen of 'adherence to deforming systems of belief and modes of behaviour that kept the Irish in bondage', and asserting that 'the conventional systems by which the Irish lived were borrowed, from both London and Rome.' In spite of his appreciation of the intellectual rigour of a Jesuitical upbringing, James Joyce detested the twin captivity of Roman Catholicism and English imperialism. What could be more symbolic of this joint thraldom than the school organised on English public school lines by members of a Roman Catholic order? Seamus Deane rightly castigates the critics who thought that James Joyce's references in *Portrait* to 'the whirl of a scrimmage' relate to Gaelic Football, revived after 1884 for its playing to become a major badge of Irish patriotism. Clongowes plays rugby and cricket like any God-fearing English boarding school. Thus the cricketbat (James Joyce carefully glues the two words together) and the pandybat are physical tokens - 'pock' - of Irish servitude to Whitehall and the Vatican.

Cricket has a lengthy history of literary usage. It is strange to contemplate that the game has both a faint mention in Jane Austen, mistress of the rationally structured, objective novel of social manners, and a firmer footing in James Joyce, master of the freely-flowing, subjective novel of internal emotion; the two as distant in time and styling as a resplendent Mozartian edifice and the unorthodox tonality of an abstruse Schoenberg composition.

Footnote: some of the arguments of this essay concerning L.P.Hartley and E.M.Fortser were included in article, 'Hall and Village' in *Cricket Lore*, vol 3 no 8, Jan.1999.

Chapter 14

AMIS AND MURDOCH:
GROUNDS FOR DEVELOPMENT

It matters not how strait the gate,
How charged with punishment the scroll,
I am the master of my fate:
I am the captain of my soul.

Those famous lines, the last verse of the defiant poem, *Invictas*, were penned by W.E.Henley (1849-1903) who had a leg amputated aged sixteen and who gloried in a reputation for what has been called 'maimed masterfulness'. Such was his forcefulness of character, a dominant quality thrust forward in Invictas, that his friend, Robert Louis Stevenson, modelled Long John Silver on the one-legged poet. Long John Silver, that wily but loveable rogue, joined a small band of literary characters who become and remain household names. We have already met his coevals, Sherlock Holmes and Peter Pan, in these few pages; Billy Bunter awaits our pleasure. The 1934 film of *Treasure Island*, with Wallace Beery making a determined fist of the buccaneering sea-cook, boosted Long John's notoriety, but it was the cheery Walt Disney re-make of 1950 that consolidated his position. Personified by the rolling gait and the equally rolling 'ahhs' of Robert Newton, the definitive Silver, like the Quasimodo of Charles Laughton or the Richard III of Laurence Olivier, was bequeathed to film-goers. 'As tricky as an ageing jockey', was one critic's admiring tribute.

The book of *Treasure Island*, possibly the best-ever adventure story for youngsters, was written in 1883. It was originally devised by R.L.Stevenson (1850-94) for his son, Lloyd, and he was, of course, to enjoy a distinctive career as novelist, essayist and travel-writer. In an essay, *My First Book*, he discusses how long it had been before he had written this his first novel, having never managed to move beyond short stories and other brief pieces. 'All - all my pretty ones - had gone', he wrote, 'for a little, and then stopped inexorably, like a schoolboy's watch. I might be compared with a cricketer of many years' standing who should never have made a run... It is the length that kills.'

It was the late Gerald Brodribb, whose range of fictional reading baffles and astonishes, who indicated that R.L.Stevenson was, in fact, far from being a cricketer and was one of the few writers who deserve Gerald Brodribb's label, 'dissenter.' In another essay, *Child's Play*, Stevenson opined that 'Cricket, which is a mere matter of dexterity, palpably about nothing and to no end, often fails to satisfy infantile craving. It is a game if you like but not a game of play. You cannot tell yourself a story about cricket, and the activity it calls forth can be justified on no educational theory.' One recalls one's school-fellows who hated cricket and found nothing of relish in it or who, because they were less able than the necessary twenty-two, were shunted off round the unappetising cross country course during the summer games periods. In the modern era there were to be plenty of physical education teachers who, with genuine reason, saw little that was physically educative about an activity which involved two intermittently, eleven marginally and nine not at all.

Plenty of writers have, of course, told a story about cricket or included cricket in their tales, often with an educational setting. I am grateful to Charles Oliver, a respected cricket statistician whose elephantine memory embraces other matters beyond runs and wickets, for the reminder about Francis Brett Young's *My Brother Jonathan*. First published in 1928, it is just such an example. Francis Brett Young (1884-1954) was a middle-order novelist, with some thirty books to his credit, several of them located in the south-west midlands and with a medical background that presaged the more popular and often filmed stories of his fellow-doctor, A.J.Cronin (1896-1981), author of *Hatter's Castle, The Stars Look Down* and *The Keys of the Kingdom*.

Cricket runs like a thin thread through *My Brother Jonathan*, with a word here and a paragraph there, especially in the first part of the book. Jonathan is the less favoured son of the aesthetically pretentious, indeed, fraudulent Eugene Dakers, who directs all his adoration toward the younger son, Harold, so dextrous at games and, seemingly, life. Mr Dakers, among a series of local social enterprises, is the energetic organiser of Brimsley Cricket Club, where 'he instructed the youth of Brimsley in the science of keeping a good length and a straight bat.' Harold goes to Harrow, playing for the eleven, and Cambridge, where he gets a blue, with all expenses paid from a trust-fund intended for the honest Jonathan, who is relegated to King Edward's Grammar School and the University of North Bromwich. The gulf between the brothers is exhibited in Harold's silken batting and Jonathan's bulky, ungainly strength as a rugby prop forward. The mood is established in an early childhood game on coconut matting in 'a vast barn-like structure' in the garden of some wealthy acquaintances, where Harold's pretty style confounds the rich family's sons. A row erupts over whether he is out or not, and Jonathan, ever quick to rush to his brother's defence, ends in fisticuffs with one of the other boys.

The main cricketing episode is used to mark out the crisis point of the plot. Harold is playing for Cambridge against Worcestershire at nearby Alvaston. He later plays as an amateur for Worcestershire, as well as enjoying the elegance of country-house cricket. He is batting, as always, distinctively, and his doting father says 'If Hal makes a hundred I shall die happy.' Harold is caught out on the boundary for 66; Mr Dakers is fatally struck by a motor vehicle as he leaves the ground and his body is carried to the casualty department where Jonathan is the doctor in charge. The world collapses. Mr Dakers, a closet corset salesman, has left untold debts, including the costs of the new cricket pavilion at Brimsley. To cap all, Jonathan comes to realise at the cricket match that his love for Edie will ever be unrequited, for she is in love with the mercurial Harold.

Jonathan is forced to abandon his surgical ambitions and take a partnership in general practice with old Dr Hammond in grimy Wednesford, where he is embroiled in a medical feud as lethal as the gunfight at the OK Corral. Cricket takes a back-seat, as the tale winds sorrowfully to its unhappy conclusion. Harold is reported missing, presumed dead, in the Great War; Jonathan marries Edie who is pregnant by Harold, although the alliance remains unconsummated; Edie has a miscarriage; Harold reappears, badly shattered - 'no more cricket for me!', he moans - and Edie rejoins him; Jonathan is infected by a germ when operating on his arch-enemy, Dr Craig; he dies, whispering of his genuine love to Dr Hammond's daughter, the taciturn, Junoesque Rachel, the antithesis of the gossamer-like Edie.

Cricket, then, has its prominent part to play both in the delineation of character and in the forwarding of the plot of *My Brother Jonathan*, probably Francis Brett Young's most well-known novel. Two other very contrasting modern authors also felt that you could tell a story in which cricket had a decisive role, both of them finding that an educational location was acceptable for such a phenomenon.

Kingsley Amis and Iris Jean Murdoch shared a similar life-span that occupied much of the 20th century. Kingsley Amis was born in Clapham in 1922 and Iris Murdoch in Dublin in 1919. Both were educated at Oxford; both did a stint as a university tutor; both went on to write over twenty novels apiece; both published a first novel in 1954; both were appointed CBE, before, in 1990, Kingsley Amis was knighted and, in 1987, Iris Murdoch was made a Dame of the British Empire; Kingsley Amis died in 1995 and Iris Murdoch, after a long illness, in 1999. Her husband, the critic and teacher, John Bayley, has written movingly of those last years of dementia, with such endearing touches as Iris Murdoch's affection for football on television.

Both authors attracted critical acclaim. John Mortimer wrote of Kingsley Amis that 'he was a genuine comic writer' placing him second only to P.G.Wodehouse, while one of Iris Murdoch's obituarists, Peter Conradi, thought she 'was one of the best and most influential writers of the 20th century. Above all, she kept the traditional novel alive.' That might fairly be said of both of them, in that Kingsley Amis showed some of the *panache* of the early Dickens, without the ceaseless dynamism and range of the great Victorian, whilst Iris Murdoch, a recognised scholar, especially of modern philosophy, demonstrated some of the analytical insight of George Eliot, without plumbing quite the same depth of profound calculation. Kingsley Amis nobly said of his contemporary, 'she is a distinguished novelist of a rare kind.'

For all these contemporaneous aspects, their writings were widely different. Kingsley Amis started his career with the explosion of *Lucky Jim*, an antiheroic figure lined up in the 1950s, with John Braine's Joe Lampton in *Room at the Top* and John Osborne's Jimmy Porter, as 'angry young men', making a working-class statement in a middle-class world. All three drifted a little from that left-leaning anchorage and, truth to tell, for all their splendid efforts, none again achieved that same degree of impact. Nevertheless, all Kingsley Amis' novels, such as *That Uncertain Feeling* (1955) or *The Old Devils* (1986) carry a punch and vehemence, more perhaps darkly farcical than overtly satirical. His facetious observation of the *impedimenta* of everyday life is, at times, uproarious, whereas Iris Murdoch, although keen to position her characters with material care, is much more concerned with the inner life and lofty conversation germane to that subject.

For her part, Iris Murdoch produced a regular series of serious novels, probing the psychology of relationships with compassionate if unwavering steadiness, wrestling over motive and response throughout. Heavy with symbolism, the titles of many of her novels are cues to this highly intellectual approach: *The Bell* (1958), *A Severed Head* (1961), *The Unicorn* (1963), *The Sea, the Sea* (1978) and others. Putting the negative side of the equation,

Kingsley Amis' work is possibly a trifle too glib and self-aware for the solemn reader and that of Iris Murdoch a mite too intense and searching for the frivolous one.

In 1957 Iris Murdoch published *The Sandcastle* and just three years later, in 1960, Kingsley Amis produced *Take a Girl Like You*. The Amis story is something of a romp about sexual manners. Jenny Bunn, a probationer infants teacher, journeys from the north to take up her first teaching post at a suburban school. Disarmingly nubile, she attracts the lascivious attentions of many, including her clumsy, doltish landlord, Dick Thompson, and a fellow-lodger, the fake Frenchwoman, Anna le Page. Jenny is attracted to Patrick Standish, a master at the College, the local boarding school, and the plot revolves around his studied attempts to seduce Jenny, hovering, as she is, between reluctance, dictated by her past upbringing, and acquiescence, prompted by her present *milieu.*

The Sandcastle is the close examination of the liaison of a middle-aged house-master, Bill Mor, and an effervescent young artist, Rain Carter, who visits St. Bride's School to paint the portrait of Mr Demoyte, its retired headmaster. They fall in love but agonise over the reverberations of such an affair. Mor's family gang up on him: his daughter, Felicity, tries some DIY Voodoo; his son, Donald, after a hair-raising ascent of the school tower, runs away; while his wife, Nan, seeks to outwit him. They are successful. The couple's plan to live together is aborted before the affair is physically consummated and the reader is left to understand that Bill Mor finds moderate solace in becoming a Labour MP. As in several of Iris Murdoch's novels, the obliquely symbolic meaning of the title is passed over in a momentary phrase or two, when Rain Carter, speaking dolefully of her childhood by the tideless Mediterranean, says 'When I tried to make a sand-castle, the sand would just run away between my fingers. It was too dry to hold together.' Her very name now echoes with a booming resonance.

While so very different in purpose and style, the two novels share a surprising number of resemblances. Apart from closeness of publication and their setting in the England of the 1950s, they both utilise the device of the refreshing, exciting young woman, disrupting the composure of suburban life; they are both located close enough to London for escape to and anonymity within the city - in, typically, the strip clubs of Amis and the art-galleries of Murdoch; the romanticism of the protagonists is stemmed by the Philistine acerbity of, for instance, Dick's wife, Martha, and Bill's wife, Nan.

Moreover, both novels are, in part, about, sexual repression, with Jenny Bunn conscious of pre-marital stress and Bill Mor the victim of extra-marital pressure, the pair of them children of their nonconformist breeding.

Finally, both leading characters are out-manoeuvred by their opponent: Patrick takes carnal advantage of Jenny while she is practically comatose and, ruefully, she accepts the *fait accompli*: Nan makes a public announcement of Bill's political candidature, which he had decided to forego and which she had hitherto opposed, and Rain flees back to France. Both endings are fudged resumptions of normal service - 'you're still the same girl', encourages Patrick, 'what people do doesn't change their nature'; Felicity sobs, 'Everything was alright now. It was alright. It was alright.' There hangs over both conclusions no more than a tempered optimism. Bill Mor is awarded the second prize of realisation of his parliamentary ambition but domestic harmony will be flawed by the corrosive presence of the vinegary Nan. As for Jenny, whilst accepting the inevitable, she 'can't help feeling it's rather a pity', and, in the TV adaptation in 2000, a smug voice-over, as the serial ended, spoke of separations and new partnerships in the sweet by-and-by. One feels that neither of these sandcastles is likely to hold together for long.

Most relevant of all, both authors, about half way through their respective tale, introduce a quite prolonged piece of cricketing action and, in either case, it is the annual highlight game of a private school fixture list. Furthermore, each cricket match is employed with the same aim. Whereas E.M.Forster, in *Maurice*, and L.P.Hartley, in *The Go-between*, each used his cricket match to mirror the main plot, the one in recall, the other as prelude, Kingsley Amis and Iris Murdoch are more direct. The cricket match in these two novels brings a step-change in the development of the story. It carries the plot forward and upward. Both authors are comfortable with cricket, its values and its flavours. Kingsley Amis pursues the theme beyond the school match to embrace MCC and the Tourists at Lord's and cricket broadcasting. The polymathic Iris Murdoch appears to be as much at home with the fast bowling action as she undoubtedly is with the oriental rugs and the theory of portrait artistry that are other attributes of *The Sandcastle*.

Patrick Standish captains the Masters in their annual tussle with the College First XI and Jenny Bunn, summer-like in her pink check gingham, arrives as his guest. He is already out, not before striking Horace, the unappetising son of Patrick's arch-foe, F.B.Charlton, the College's supercilious administrator, for two fours through mid-off - 'as good as sex', he says, 'Sorry. And

it wasn't really.' Jenny is in teasing mode, wondering whether he has to borrow pads from the juniors for his 'funny little stumpy legs', comparing them
with her 'lovely long racehorse legs.' They embrace and tell of their
unbounded love for each other; they whisper of holidaying together: 'The
smell of cut grass mingled with his breath and the sun beat down on the
nape of her neck.' The seasonal climate and the relaxed yet structured atmosphere stimulates them. The temperature of their passion is heightened.
Jenny feels more convinced of his seriousness and Patrick more persuaded of
her readiness. She murmurs, "Darling..." She forgot about auntie and the
curate.'

There are distractions. Sheila Torkington, the headmaster's daughter, some
kind of voracious schoolgirl-harridan with whom Patrick has been entan-
gled, makes a move, but Jenny is swept into tea, where she chats haltingly
with Graham McClintoch, another master, of decidedly inhibited mien,
who nervously desires her. Even a precocious sixth-former propositions her.
The school orchestra plays, reminiscent of the brass band at the Scarborough
Festival. The Masters score a paltry 88, but make early inroads into the
school batting, with Graham coping valiantly with the wicket-keeping
duties. The 'short, cruel-looking' Skinner, the College biffer, smites about
him, but then Dick Thompson, guesting for the Masters, is introduced by
Patrick, principally, as is his wont, to expose Dick to ridicule. In a farcical
scene, that A.G.Macdonell might have invented, Dick Thompson contrives
to take 3 for 4 in one over and the Masters win by three runs, with Skinner
helplessly stranded at the bowler's end. The tiny moral is expressed that
those who do well at cricket - Graham and Dick - do not necessarily receive
the blissful rewards of heaven. It is in the pleasant after-glow of the match,
and, for all the motion of boys and adults around her, Jenny 'paid no attention to any of them. She was with Patrick.' It is precisely at this point that
she agrees to yield to his impassioned pleas. The plot changes gear quickly.

Of course there are further comic barriers to this ecstatic togetherness and
cricket continues to be engaged. There have been cricketing hints beforehand. Even the roadhouse, where Patrick drinks with his older, louche
friend, Julian Ormerod, has tables with 'bas-reliefs of W.G.Grace's face all
over the supporting framework', while, in one of Patrick's supplications to
Jenny, he claims she makes him feel as if he could 'score a century before
lunch for the Gentlemen.' Again, 'it often seemed to Patrick that sex was just
something that happened in his own mind, no more relevant to anybody

else's bedroom habits than a passion for ballistics would be to a man playing cricket.'

There is also the suggestion from Julian, that may surprise some of its *habitués*, to the effect that Lord's is absolutely the finest locale 'to run into girls in London', especially during the Varsity match or the Tourists' fixture with MCC. Surrey members will be intrigued to learn that Julian totally rules out the Oval on that romantic score. Later Patrick recalls this advice when wanting to rid his accommodation of his flat-mate, the sober-sided Graham, ready for his crucial tryst with Jenny. There is a passage devoted to persuading Graham that 'to miss the first day's play in the impending match between the MCC and the touring team would rank as a crippling deprivation.' These discussions of the tourists' new fast bowler and the MCC spinners is capped with the suggestion that Lord's cricket ground will be packed with 'decent girls, seeing what's available.' However, Patrick's efforts are haunted by the prospects of bad weather and, even after he has bustled Graham off to London, and as he waits for Jenny's arrival, there is the fear that he might return. There is an affectionate *pastiche* of television commentators optimistically talking viewers through the ritual of umpires' inspections. In the event, Jenny funks her chance of attaining womanhood; Sheila Charlton arrives instead; and Patrick does not return: 'Still at Lord's making sure of a decent seat for Monday or sitting in the Savoy cocktail lounge with some animate pin-up who has asked him to share her umbrella on the mid-wicket boundary?'

High jinks are decidedly not part of the more sedate and more compact chapter in *The Sandcastle* devoted to the House Match, the final of the knock-out competition between Prewett's House and Bill Mor's House. It follows immediately after Bill and Rain, with a pulsating embrace, have wordlessly revealed their love, the one for the other. The day is cloudless and unbearably hot and Bill Mor is trying, on this major festival - a two day match and a headmaster's dinner - in the school calendar, 'to walk and talk as if everything was perfectly ordinary.' Dazed and uncertain, Mor, in the midst of the clapping and excited throng of boys and visitors, is 'astonished that he could be so moved and softened merely by putting to himself the idea that he was in love.'

'Rain's arrival caused a stir' - the invasive nature of her characterisation, as with Jenny's, is suddenly focused with her appearance at the cricket match, in her light blue cotton dress and carrying 'a frilly white parasol.' Even some of the fielders were disturbed: "Over!' shouted the umpire, waking up to his duties', as the deck-chairs tipple and the consternation is also inwardly experienced by Bill, who 'felt as if an enormous vehicle had been driven through him.' As in the Amis novel, the tea interval provides an ideal opportunity for the characters to mingle and, in consequence, Bill goes to view Rain's portrait of Demoyte. The plot elevates itself on to a higher terrace; he invites her to visit him at home; 'he knew that he had done wrong'; the evening brings scudding black cloud and 'a lurid premature darkness'; and early morning finds Nan, hastening back from her Dorset holiday to deal with what is afoot.

Nan has inadvertently discovered something of the incipient affair from her two children who have also stumbled on the liaison by accident. The cricket match encompasses a tiny cameo that indicates not only this but that rumours are flying wider. Donald Mor is a competent bat who plays for Prewett's House against his father's House, for whom Donald's best chum, Jimmy Carde, is a quick bowler. Their relationship might remind the older listener of the Beryl Reid characterisation in the BBC 1950s programme 'Educating Archie', with the ventroloquilist, Peter Brough and his dummy, Archie Andrews. 'She's my best friend', Beryl Reid's schoolgirl, Monica, would confide, 'and I *hate* her.' Donald is playing 'with style and force' and a couple of boundaries win 'prolonged applause.' At 23, not out, from a total of 52 for 1, 'it looked as if he was settling in.' Jimmy Carde comes on to bowl. He is 'a rather ostentatious bowler, with a long run and a good deal of flourishing and bounding', but his 'thunderbolt' deliveries are sometimes off target. It is the classic contest of modest capability and self-assured *bravura*, something close to introversion and extroversion. Donald cover drives him tidily for four.

Then Rain appears. Carde passes near Donald. 'Your pappa's poppet!' he said - and he went away down the pitch dancing and whistling, 'A nice girl, a decent girl, but one of the rakish kind', a borrowing, one supposes, from the old Guy Mitchell standard. Donald 'coloured violently' and lowered his head. Jimmy Carde 'bounded up to the wicket like a performing panther. The ball left his hand like a bullet. Donald poked at it ineffectually; and turned to find that his middle stump was lying neatly on the ground. There was a burst of applause. Donald turned at once and walked rapidly toward the pavilion. He did not look at Carde.' Rather as Leo Colston 'catches out' Ted Burgess in *The Go-between*, Jimmy Carde now 'bowls over' Donald Mor, both with his express delivery and with his taunting jibe that warns

Donald that his father's secret is broadly known. It emboldens Donald to be ever more ruthless in the struggle against the female invader of his family hearth. The cricket match serves to intensify the course of love between Bill and Rain, but it also marks out the gathering strategy of his family's determination to thwart its path.

Thus might two novels, so different in foundation, be compared in this skilled deployment of a school cricket match to lever the plot-line up a notch. And yet the perceptive Amis burlesque and the thoughtful Murdoch drama alike end with a curious tentativeness. Jenny and Patrick and Nan and Bill face an uneasy prospect in their respective marriages. They might have paused to contemplate the words of Gerald Brodribb's 'dissenter', Robert Louis Stevenson, introduced at the head of this chapter, in his 1881 collection of short stories and essays, *Virginibus Puerisque*. Having pronounced that, at its lowest, matrimony is 'a sort of friendship recognised by the police', he expound the opinion that 'marriage is a step so grave and decisive that it attracts light-headed, variable men by its very awfulness.'

Chapter 15

SCREEN TEST: CRICKET AND THE CINEMA

Charles Laughton as W.G.Grace; Robert Donat as Jack Hobbs; Stewart Granger as Denis Compton...not films coming to a cinema near you shortly, or ever. Indeed, there does not seem to be one film dedicated to the life of a famous cricketer. That does seem odd, especially given the close affinity of literature and film.

First of all, the lives of famous sportsmen and sportswomen have, in fact, provided the *motif* of many films. Baseball has offered a fruitful strand. William Bendix played the eponymous hero of *The Babe Ruth Story*, while, more recently, Roseanne's telly-husband, John Goodman, emulated him in *Babe*; Gary Cooper was cast as Lou Gehrig in *The Pride of the Yankees*; Anthony Perkins was Jim Piersal in *Four Strikes Out*; James Stewart was Monty Stratton in *The Stratton Story*, whilst even Ronald Reagan strode to the plate as Grover Cleveland Alexander in *The Winning Team*. Boxing has enjoyed its cinematic successes, notably with Errol Flynn as Jim Corbett in *Gentleman Jim* and Grew McClure as John L.Sullivan in *The Great John L*. The film critics also liked *Fat City* (1972), John Huston's sombre tale of a boxing has-been, played by Stacy Keach, and Martin Scorsese's *Raging Bull* (1980), the compelling yarn based on the life of middle weight champion, Jake La Motta, with Robert DeNiro in the lead. American football has been represented, among others, by Burt Lancaster in the title-role of *Jim Thorpe All-American*; golf found movie glory with Glenn Ford as Ben Hogan in *Follow the Sun*, and Esther Williams donned the swim-suit of Annette Kellerman in *Million Dollar Mermaid.*

Hollywood has dealt methodically with sport over the years. Beginning with *Casey at the Bat* in 1899, there had, by the end of 1992, been 818 USA sports films, with 197 having boxing, 138 horse racing and 110 American football themes. Very much the world game, soccer has spread its cinematic wings, with some hundred films produced by no less than 28 different countries. English cinema has responded rather poorly to this, to coin a phrase, fine track record. Football gave us, in 1939, *The Arsenal Stadium Mystery*, which featured the then splendid Highbury and the then triumphant Arsenal team in a weary murder plot, while the 1981 Scottish *Gregory's Girl* used soccer in a commendably whimsical manner. In 1981, much more potently, *Chariots of Fire*, sang a hymn to the feats of Harold Abrahams and

Eric Liddell in the Paris Olympics of 1924. One of a score of Olympic-oriented movies, it is possibly the best British film with real-life sport as its theme. Its nearest rival is probably Lindsay Anderson's *This Sporting Life* (1963), the rough, dismal tale of a miner turned rugby league star, with Richard Harris doggedly mixing it on-field with friend and foe alike and with the earthy Rachel Roberts off-field.

Cricketers, however, have not been fondly served by the cinema. Which is, in the second place, peculiar, because of the enormous literary and artistic merit to be discovered in the cricketing cult, far more extensive as it is than in practically any other sport. One problem may be the difficulties of portraying technique genuinely in team-oriented field-games. The Australian tele-series of the late 1980s, *Bodyline*, featuring the clash of the *nonpareil* Don Bradman - Gary Sweet was the actor charged with the privileged task of portraying the secular saint - with the patrician Jardine and the plebeian Larwood, showed just how difficult it is to picture cricket authentically. It is perhaps no coincidence that many of the more watchable sports films concentrate on games where the focus is smallscale and the locus tight. Boxing is a good example of this, as is pool: remember the haunting performance of Paul Newman as the pool room champion in *The Hustler* (1961) with Jackie Gleason and George C.Scott in vibrant support. The claustrophobic atmosphere was oppressive 'and the air of spiritual decadence', wrote critic David Robinson, 'has rarely been conveyed so vividly.'

Although there seems to have been no actual portrait of a famed cricketer on the screen, cricket has appeared in glimpses. Those two cricket buffs, playwright and screen-play writer Harold Pinter and director Joseph Losey, collaborated in a couple of films in which a cricket match just had to be included. In *The Go-between* (1970) based on L.P.Hartley's elegiac novel, there is a well-known pastoral cricket scene where young Leo Colston (Dominic Guard) catches out the tenant farmer Ted Burgess (Alan Bates) in the hall and village match, as chapter 13 analysed as per the book of the film. Rather more gratuitously, in *Accident* (1967) based on Nicholas Mosley's ascetic novel, Pinter and Losey have Stanley Baxter demonstrating his donnish arrogance, the counterpoint to Dirk Bogarde's donnish wistfulness, with some brisk batting.

There are other cricket glances. E.M.Hornung's Raffles was referred to, in both literary and cinematic guise, in chapter 10. You will find Richard Attenborough taking a net in that somewhat patronising film, *The Guinea-*

pig (1949), based on Warren Chetham Strode's play. As a lower-class oik, blessed with a public school place, his new-found smoothness is exemplified by his straight bat. You will find Ian Carmichael, in *Happy is the Bride* (1957) allowing his prospective father-in-law, Cecil Parker, to bowl him out in a village green encounter, so that he might be more susceptible to allowing his daughter, Janette Scott, to become engaged.

There are cricketing moments in *My Brother Jonathan,* the 1947 film based on a doctor's life in the Black Country, already discussed in the preceding chapter; it starred Michael Denison and Dulcie Gray, while R.C.Sheriff's 1930 play *Badger's Green,* with its 'rustic comedy' of rival village teams and predatory developers, was filmed twice. Valerie Hobson and Wally Patch were in the 1934 version and Garry Marsh, Barbara Murray and Kynaston Reeves were cast in the 1949 re-make. There is a minute or so of junior cricket in the evocative study of childhood in the blitz, *Hope and Glory* (1987).

The Common Touch was a grainy 1941 British film, based, in part, on the MGM 1932 talkie, *Dosshouse,* about a young tycoon, Peter Henderson, played by Geoffrey Hibbert. He goes slumming to an Orwellian-style cockney dosshouse to discover why his company nefariously plans to demolish it. While the sophisticated fleshpots of the Hotel Majestic are utilised to act in social juxtaposition to 'Charlies', this cheap but cheerful shelter, there is also a cricketing dualism. The disguised Peter plays a scratch game in a factory yard with a rusty piece of iron for a wicket, whereas he visits Lord's, and we catch a glimpse of a 1930s Test match, as he conveys a message to Sylvia Meadows (the glamorous Greta Gynt), fiancee of Stewart Gordon (John Longden), the promising middle order England batsman. Peter and his girlfriend, the willing Mary, played by Joyce Howard, save 'Charlies' with a dashing piece of social action that pre-dated Blairite stakeholding by half a century.

However, it was Peter's cricket shots, more Eton than East End, that enabled 'Lincoln' Inns (Harry Welchman), a pauper lawyer, to pierce his hobo mask and lead both toffs and tramps in a combined op. that saves the day and the dosshouse. Apart from the cricket, there are doughty down-and-outs in the persons of Bransby Williams, Edward Rigby and Wally Patch, together with the youngsters, Bernard Miles, Bill Fraser and Alfie Bass. There are also cameo variety performances, not only from Greta Gynt, but from dance band leader Carroll Gibbons, Sandy Macpherson at the organ, the musically adept Scott Sanders, and Mark Hambourg, famously belting out *The Warsaw Concerto* on the stained ivories of a busker's piano. Although popular in its day, the critics have damned this early exercise in social conscience with faint praise. Rather after the manner of cricket journalists judging some English Test displays, they said it was 'naive' but 'a brave try.'

Probably the best remembered allusion to cricket in the cinema is in *The Lady Vanishes*, of which the critic, Frank S.Nugent, said, 'if it were not so brilliant a melodrama, we should class it as a brilliant comedy.' Suspensefully produced by Alfred Hitchcock in 1938, it has Michael Redgrave and Margaret Lockwood in search of a disappearing old lady aboard a speeding train in a 1930s Europe beset by war's alarums. Basil Radford (who turned out for the stage eleven, the Thespids) and Naunton Wayne supply a patriotic cameo of English phlegm as Chambers and Chaldicott, obsessed with what might be happening in the Test match at home, but resolute under fire when the situation demands it. This was a nicely judged representation of up-kept left elbow and stiff upper lip. A pity about the 1979 remake, which not even Arthur Lowe and Ian Carmichael, reciting almost a word-for-word duplication, could save from a banal shapelessness.

A late news item tells of a screen debut for Sourav Ganguly, the Indian cricketer. Anjaan Chaudhury, the Bengali film-maker, cast Sourav's wife, Donna, as a dancer in his film, *Chandramallike*, but Sourav Ganguly refused to allow a male actor to play opposite his wife. Anjaan Chaudhury cut through this matrimonial red-tape with a single slash and cast the husband in the role.

Yes, you will find many such sketches of cricket and cricketers, and others will recall examples from their own movie-going memories, but there is no 'biopic' and possibly only one film that is entirely founded on first-class cricket. This is *The Final Test*, made by Rank in 1953, nearly fifty years ago, and inspired, it has been said, by Don Bradman's duck in his final Test five years previously. It starred Jack Warner as the batsman in <u>his</u> last match at the Oval, with George Relph in support. Jack Warner, from an act devoted, in part, to impersonations of Maurice Chevalier, first came to fame as the private soldier in *Garrison Theatre* on wartime 'wireless', with his persuasive catch-phrase, 'mind my bike'. He then enjoyed great success on radio and film in the varied tales of the Huggetts, before rising from his death in the 1949 film *The Blue Lamp* to become TV's *Dixon of Dock Green* for twenty years and etch the image of the London bobby - 'Evenin' all' - on the minds of a generation.

However, he is, despite some off-screen coaching from Alf Gover, as uncomfortable as the veteran bat as are the genuine English players, such as Len Hutton, Denis Compton, Alec Bedser and Cyril Washbrook, who add unsubtle verisimilitude to the rather laboured proceedings. Everyone, be he actor or cricketer, is uneasy in the other's role. The 1981 movie, *Escape to Victory*, where a POW football team seeks to escape from German captivity, suffers in the same fashion, as Michael Caine and Sylvester Stallone attempt to pass as footballers and Pele and Bobby Moore endeavour to pass as Thespians. Jack Warner's best friend, the umpire, gives him 'out' LBW first ball after a lengthy pause that might have had today's audience wondering whether the third umpire should have been consulted. But stay the starting tear, for Jack Warner gets the girl, the pleasing Adrianne Allen, snatching her from the arms of the conceited tyro playing in his first Test. What's more, his cricket-loathing, would-be poet son is restored to a more sensible appraisal of life's priorities by his guru, a cricket-loving poet played by Robert Morley.

It was written by that excellent theatre craftsman, Terence Rattigan (1911-77). His carefully plotted plays, although they tended to be sidelined when, with the onset of John Osborne and *Look back in Anger* in 1956, the French windows were closed and room had to be found for the kitchen sink. Nonetheless, plays like *French without Tears* (1936), *The Winslow Boy* (1946), *The Browning Version* (1948) and *The Deep Blue Sea* (1952) remain deservedly popular and some have found their way satisfactorily on to the screen. Terence Rattigan, who was knighted in 1971, opened the batting for Harrow against Eton in 1929, but he could not manage to animate *The Final Test*. With a Rattigan screenplay and directed by Anthony Asquith, one might have expected better, but it tended to receive the thumbs down - or maybe the forefinger up - from the critics. Bolton's own omniscient cinema umpire, Leslie Halliwell, judged that it was 'a flat character study some way below the author's best style' and he suggested it was 'cluttered up with real cricketers and stymied by lack of action'. Since then, very little. It seems we must wait a little longer for the showing at our multiplex cinemas of Sean Bean as Freddie Trueman or Hugh Grant as David Gower.

Such are the limitations of the stage that it could not readily compete with the screen, in respect of cricket, in any realistic way. *Badger's Green* (mentioned above in its filmic interpretation) is one exception, although the critics did not find R.C.Sherriff's rural venture as convincing as his 1928 drama of World War I angst, *Journey's End*, for which his service in the East Surrey

Regiment - he was wounded at Ypres - supplied much of the background. Robert Cedric Sherriff (1896-1975) went on to make more of a living producing screen-plays, among them *The Invisible Man, Goodbye Mr Chips, Odd Man Out*, quite a tasty set of credits. Sherriff had been captain of cricket at Kingston School; he played good club cricket, mainly for Hampton Wick, while he was also a successful schoolboy athlete and skilled oarsman.

The eminent cricket historian and biographer, Gerald Howat, has, in his superb collection of essays, *Village Medley* (1993) examined *Badger's Green* with his usual clarity and insight. *Sherriff of Badger's Green*, first published in *The Journal of the Cricket Society* in 1990, must rank as one the most illustrious analyses of the deployment of cricket in any art-form. Gerald Howat tells us how the play was being performed at London's Prince of Wales theatre even as Bradman and company were thrashing England in the 1930 Lord's Test. In Act I the rivalries and squabbles of the village cricket club officers must be shelved as Mr Butler, from forbidding London, threatens that his Development Syndicate will cover the cricket ground with bungalows. In Act II Mr Butler, played by Felix Aylmer, tenders the bribes of a cottage hospital and a club-house for the golfers and the debate continues, until chance provides for Mr Butler being invited to play for the village team. In Act III the match is observed from the tea tent and the would-be entrepreneur, having scored the winning run off his capitalist knuckles, leaves Badger's Green in peace. As Gerald Howat comments, 'Some other village will be developed and that is not our concern'; or as the modern acronym has it - NIMBY.

While admitting the slenderness of plot and characterisation, Gerald Howat points up the manner in which the play complements *Journey's End* in its celebration of normality and the enjoyment of unheroic living, as expressed through the friendly virtues of village cricket. He reminds how post-1918 Idealism was swiftly dispelled by Disillusion and how books, films and theatre offered nostalgic escape. The pacifism of *Journey's End*, daring in its day, and the more placid sentiment of *Badger's Green* was part of this. The inter-wars years found a place for anti-war dramatists and novelists, like the German, Erich Maria Remarque, whose *All Quiet on the Western Front* became a landmark film in 1930, the year *Badger's Green* was staged.

Other stagings of cricket have been rare. Alan Ayckbourn has engaged cricket as an off-stage presence, as in his 1972 comedy, *Time and Time Again*, starring Tom Courtenay, while the greater scope of television has allowed the occasional play or even series touching on cricket. *Outside Edge*, a play directly founded on cricket, written by Richard Harris, was staged in 1980 and modern technical apparatus, such as improved sound-efects, gave it useful credence. It became a television vehicle for the dry humours of Maureen Lipman and then was transposed into a series in 1994. This rather thinned out its attractions, although the irked frustrations of club captain, Robert Daws, and the resigned patience of his wife, Brenda Blethyn, were ever entertaining. Peter Gibb, the Oxford blue and Derbyshire opening bat, has written a number of radio and television plays with cricket themes. He played 145 matches for Derbyshire from 1967 to 1972 and scored a thousand runs in each of five seasons, making him something of a crack among cricketing-dramatists.

Cricket does appear in television drama periodically. A kindly correspondent, Rev. Ian W.Thomas, reminds that even the ne'er-do-well Rigsby, played by the incorrigible Leonard Rossiter in the Yorkshire Television series, *Rising Damp*, could not entirely escape the noble game. There was an episode about the exorcism of the grey lady and, when the humdrum truth emerged and there was no such apparition, a curate, garbed in cricket clothing, cried, 'you've been clean bowled, Mr Rigsby'. The same correspondent also tells of an episode in the James Herriot series, *All Creatures Great and Small*, based on his north Yorkshire veterinary practice and set in the early 1950s. The vets, Siegfried Farnon, played by Robert Hardy, and James Herriot, played by Christopher Timothy, represent the village against a Yorkshire XI starring a youthful Fred Trueman. There must be a hundred more samples of cricket turning up on the telly in fictional form, but the game has still not grown as televisually big as, say, police-work or medicine.

According to an interview in *The Journal of the Cricket Society*, vol.8, no.3, Autumn 1977, *Dad's Army*, that richly comic 1960s spoof of the home guard, was replete with cricket-lovers. This Poujadiste collection of Warmington-on-Sea shop-keepers was practically a cricket eleven. The late Don Rowan, most enthusiastic of amateur tape-recordists of cricketers and those interested in cricket, tracked down Ian Lavender, the immature Pike, bank clerk and 'stupid boy', and found that, in what passes for real life, he was a wicket-keeper of near-county standard. The blustering bank manager, Captain Mainwaring, otherwise that fine character actor, Arthur Lowe, was a generous supporter of the village team of Hayfield, Derbyshire, his birthplace and the club where his father had been chairman for over twenty years. His minion, the assistant bank manager and ageing charmer, Sergeant

Wilson, played some high-class cricket in Suffolk; the incontinent, dotty Godfrey, ex-Army and Navy Stores, was also a cricket buff, and Bill Pertwee, the rough-hewn greengrocer and chief ARP warden, had played as an all-rounder in and around Essex. It would only have needed that valiant butcher, Corporal Jones, to encourage - 'they don't like it up 'em' - the extravagant use of bouncers, and another episode, MCC v Warmington Home Guard, possibly - might have been born.

What perhaps is truly remarkable is that, aside from its paucity of theatrical incidence, there are countless numbers of playwrights who are devoted to cricket. Writing in *The Journal of the Cricket Society* (vol 16, no 3, Autumn 1993) Michael Billington, the experienced theatre critic of *The Guardian*, maintained that 'almost every single first-rate dramatist of the past eighty years has been passionate about the game.' He reels off an astonishing roster. Apart from Terence Rattigan, Alan Ayckbourn and R.C.Sherriff and, inevitably, J.M.Barrie, whose cricketing adventures were addressed in an earlier chapter, he lists Ben Travers, Harold Pinter, Tom Stoppard, Simon Gray, David Hare, Tim Rice and others, some of them belying, as he demonstrates, the falseness of Kenneth Tynan's claim that 'cricket attracts artists who are either conservative or non-political.' Michael Billington urges that 'cricket specifically attracts dramatists who are wedded to form and ritual...Cricket, at its very best, is a codified, aesthetically pleasing ritual in which two forces are battling for supremacy. So too is drama...you will always find a murmur of playwrights behind the Lord's Pavilion.'

Harold Pinter's wandering side, the Gaieties, seems to be in line of descent from the Allahakbarries and the Invalids. Indeed, pursuing the Michael Billington thesis, John Fowles, author of *The French Lieutenant's* woman, a schoolboy bowler at Bedford School in the early 1940s and an Essex trialist to boot, claims that the secret key to Harold Pinter's work (which includes the 1981 screenplay of that intriguing Fowles novel) is 'his intense and evident love of cricket.' Sam Mendes, the director of such Hollywood films as *American Beauty*, currently director at London's Donmar Warehouse Theatre and an outstanding all-round cricketer at Magdalene College School in the early 1980s, is one of the Gaieties.

All other theatrical examples pale in to wan insignificance, however, compared with the exploits of the playwright, Samuel Beckett, for his record of being the only first-class cricketer to win the Nobel Prize for Literature, which he did in 1969, may be some little while in emulation. Samuel

Barclay Beckett was born in 1906 in Dublin but moved to Paris in 1927, where he usually wrote his material in French and then translated it into English. It was not really until the 1950s that his very individual voice, bleak, objective and concerned with dogged human travails, began to bemuse but fascinate theatre audiences. In particular, in *Waiting for Godot* (1955, the English version) *Endgame* (1958 in English) and *Happy Days* (1961), Beckett, a one-time associate of James Joyce, carved out a reputation as a most distinctive presence in world theatre in the second half of the 20th century. He died in 1989.

It must be confessed that his cricketing laurels blossomed less fulsomely. Nonetheless, while at Trinity College, Dublin, he played two first-class matches for the University in 1925 and 1926, both against Northants. A left-hander, he scored 35 first-class runs and took two first-class catches, but his medium pace proved innocuous and he took no first-class wickets for 64 first-class runs. Michael Billington's anecdote of Samuel Beckett's visit to a Lord's Test match in beautiful weather is worthy of repetition. His companion exclaimed that it was the sort of morning that makes you glad to be alive. 'Well', said the dramatist, 'I wouldn't go so far as to say that.' Thus did the hardy pessimism of the dour cricketer meet the sober barrenness of the Theatre of the Absurd.

Incidentally, that same issue of *The Journal of the Cricket Society* includes a complementary article by Philip Scowcroft, the connoisseur of cricket-associated detective fiction, on cricket and music. This detailed and comprehensive account argues that no other sport has 'inspired such a wealth of varied music', such is 'the measure of the significance which cricket has acquired in English life and social attitudes', precisely the overarching point pressed by this scrutiny of literature and cricket. Because lyrics play so large a part in this musical *genre* - and Philip Scowcroft rightly commends David Rayvern Allen's 1981 collection, *a Song for Cricket* - it is tangential to literature and the examples are profuse, from the choruses of Hambledon to the calypsos of the West Indies. Even Sir Donald Bradman, we are told, composed a cricket song. In 1959 a one-act operetta, *The Batsman's Bride*, by two teachers, Percy Heywood and Donald Hughes, was entirely devoted to cricket and moulded after the fashion of Gilbert and Sullivan.

The variety stage, too, has known its cricketing adherents, including George Robey, 'the Prime Minister of Mirth', who was an MCC member from 1905, who practised occasionally in the nets at Lord's and who claimed to have played against W.G.Grace. That veritable craftsman among wicket-keepers, Warwickshire's 'Tiger' Smith, bowled to George Robey in the Lord's nets when he was on the MCC ground staff around the mid-1900s. How valuable George Robey's polished orotundities might have been had he been appointed match referee: 'Desist', he would order mirthful audiences, 'kindly temper your hilarity with a modicum of reserve.'

Amid the welter of comedians and other variety artists who have played for the Lord's Taverners or in like charitable fixtures, the name of Joseph George O'Gorman ranks prominently. He actually played three first-class matches for Surrey in 1927, scoring 106 runs and taking four wickets. His appearances were curtailed by his theatrical engagements, for, with his brother, Dave, also a useful cricketer who played for Surrey second XI, he formed a well-known comedy duo. One of a host of cross-talk acts in the 1920s and 1930s, Joe died in 1964 and Dave in 1974; their father, Joe, had been a partner in the Tennyson and O'Gorman double-act, noted for its rendition of the lively, if repetitious, ditty, *The Wild Man of Poplar*. A member of a later generation, T.J.G.O'Gorman, played some matches for Derbyshire. J.A.Cutmore, the Essex professional and opening bat, scorer of 15,937 runs in 342 matches, was also known as a music hall performer. Brian Heald, the diligent Essex CCC statistician, has found that Jimmy Cutmore certainly made use of his commanding tenor voice in pantomime at the Dominion Theatre, Tottenham Court Road, in variety, with cricket bat in hand, at the Walthamstow Palace, and that he made a record in 1930, featuring *The Things we Want most are Hard to Get* and, on the flip side, *Those Smiling Irish eyes*.

The radio, of course, became a natural outlet for variety artists and singers, as it also provided, with now imperishable voices such as Howard Marshall and John Arlott, another dimension to cricketing communication. Obviously, cricket, in fictitious action, was not for the 'wireless', except through the prose, poetry and song that makes up the game's cultural inheritance. This could make itself manifest at a popular level. Another helpful correspondent, Anthony G.Townsend, tells how he listened to his parents' 1930s record, 'No-one believes I'm a mermaid', which included the emotional declaration:

> Sutcliffe and Hammond and Jardine
> Insisted I must be a sardine.
> No-one believes I'm a mermaid at all;
> But honest and truly I am.

It is of passing interest to note one or two radio personalities who were crick-eters. Two names familiar to those who remember the 'wireless' are Freddie Grisewood, recollected, for instance, for his *Home Front* recipes and for his hosting of many other programmes, including *Any Questions?*; and Francis Worsley, the producer of the unforgettable ITMA, with Tommy Handley the Maypole around which a hundred linguistic ribbons were woven, bring-ing morale-boosting laughter to the nation in war and leaving a heritage of catch-phrases. Freddie Grisewood played for Radley and for Worcestershire in one first-class match in 1908, while Francis Worsley played a couple of matches for Glamorgan in 1922 and 1923.

Another broadcaster and variety star, Webster Booth, on such occasions not in tandem with Anne Ziegler, with whom he formed so glamorously pre-sented - 'Only a Rose' - a singing act, played for the Thespids. Another Thespid was Oscar Asche, whose theatrical skills are most remembered for his writing the book and lyrics for, directing and, along side his wife, Lily Brayton, starring in *Chu Chin Chow*, with its record 2238 performances from 1916 to 1921. The writer, S.P.B.Mais himself an enthusiastic cricketer who claims to have been called upon by Lord Hawke to field substitute for Wilfred Rhodes at the Parks (see the enjoyable article by Timothy J.McCann, 'S.P.B.Mais, 1885-1975 - a Champion of Cricket, *The Journal of the Cricket Society*, vol.19, no.4, Spring 2000) drew attention to the exploits of Christopher Stone. Quite simply, Christopher Stone created the profes-sion of disc jockey as early as 1927 and held gramophonic court for three decades. It is said that he had hit W.G.Grace for a six and he proved to be a stylish hitter for S.P.B.Mais' President's XI at Southwick in West Sussex.

A final illustration draws together stage, radio, writing, cricket and everyday life, the very premise for this brief study of cricket and literature:

"Now it's the last wicket, you fellows; our backs are right up to the wall,
And we're facing some very fast bowling; but this wicket's not going to fall.
We've got all our pads and our gloves on, and there's one thing that can't be denied,
We'll crack every ball through the covers...if we Play Up For The Side."

Those of a certain age will find the next few lines redundant, in that they will recall the superb radio and stage act, the Western Brothers. George, lan-guid at the piano, Kenneth, in reality his cousin, nonchalantly leaning against it, as fastidiously evening-jacketed and be-monocled, they warbled and drawled their bang-up-to-the-moment lays on current happenings in mock-public schoolboy tones. 'Play the game, you cads' was their catch-phrase, as they poked needling fun in those pre-satirical years at politicians and pundits. While never eschewing the amusing - picking up on the wartime travel slogan, they commented, 'as the doctor said to Hitler on the day that he was born, 'Is Your Journey Really Necessary?'' - they often included a more serious offering during World War II. Others, such as the monologist Nosmo King, also sought the chance to brace their audiences for the awesome task, and, while seemingly banal when coldly read sixty years later, such direct sentiments did then have an appeal.

A BBC cassette collection, *The Comedy Greats*, includes the Western Brothers performing their morale-boosting recitation to piano accompaniment, *Play Up For The Side*, recorded early during the war on the BBC Light Programme's *Top of the Bill.* All cricket's clichés are deployed, from the straight bat to knocking for six, an allusion also beloved of Montgomery in relation to his tussle with Rommel in the Western Desert. Walter Hammond and Herbert Sutcliffe are included for good measure, and there is a mention of Bodyline, with the Luftwaffe standing in for Larwood...

> No invader has passed our defences; no umpire has lifted his hand...
> But now all the Empire is fighting and Churchill is there at the crease.

George, born in 1895, was pianist for the well-known Roosters' concert party until, in 1925, he joined his cousin, Kenneth, born in 1899, to form the 'Old School Tie' double-act in 1925, entertaining with such offerings as:

> Sing a song of Britain that will make your bosom swell,
> Of Britain and the Empire - and the Hippodrome as well;
> Play the game, you cads, play the game.

From one angle they were music hall's version of the cinema's Charters and Chaldicott. Both stage and radio audiences enjoyed their sometimes sharp, topical critique of the establishment, but, according to Roy Hudd, 'when there were no nobs left to send up they retired.' One suspects we could still find them a few targets. Kenneth had a tobacco kiosk for several years at Weybridge Station. He died in 1963, and George passed on in 1969.

We might wonder whether cricket is still sufficiently populist today to warrant such a common usage. It is likely that football, soap opera or pop music

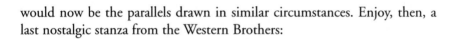

would now be the parallels drawn in similar circumstances. Enjoy, then, a last nostalgic stanza from the Western Brothers:

So open your shoulders, you fellows, and let's take what comes in our stride,
And we'll win; they can't take this wicket...if we Play Up For The Side.

Footnote: some of the information about cricket on film was included in an article in *The Cricketer*, May 1999, entitled 'Screen Test.'

Chapter 16

PAVILION'D IN SPLENDOUR; CRICKET IN POETRY

William Wordsworth (1770-1850) took the familiar intellectual journey from stripling radicalism to crusty conservatism. A friend of one of the few aristocratic revolutionaries, Michel de Beaupuy, he was passionately committed to the values of the French Revolution and, as if marking his devotion in personal currency, he had an ardent love-affair with a native of Blois and a fellow-adherent to the tricolour, Annette Vallon, by whom he had a daughter, Caroline. The involvement of Britain and France in war and the deterioration of the Revolution into terror and cruelty grieved him sorely. After years of uncertainty and mental stress, he eventually settled down with his sister, Dorothy, and, later, his wife, Mary Hutchinson, to an uneventful existence, writing Romantic poetry of compelling power and canvassing for the local Conservative candidate.

It was a sorrowful voyage from:

> Bliss was it in that dawn to be alive,
> But to be young was very heaven.

To:

> I recoil and droop and seek repose
> In listlessness from vain perplexity,
> Unprofitably travelling toward the grave.

During the Peace of Amiens, that brief respite in the European wars, the Wordsworths left the cosiness of Dove Cottage, Grasmere, for a continental trip in 1802 just before his marriage, in part to visit Anne and Caroline. On his return, he composed the sonnet, *Dear Fellow Traveller*, comparing the serenity and freedom of England to what he now saw as the tyranny of Napoleonic France. He addresses his 'dear fellow traveller', Dorothy Wordsworth, thus:

> Dear fellow Traveller! here we are once more,
> The cock that crows, the smoke that curls, that sound
> Of Bells, those boys that in yon meadow ground
> In white-sleev'd shirts are playing by the score...

> Thou are free,
> My country! and 'tis joy enough and pride
> For one hour's perfect bliss, to tread the grass
> Of England once again, and hear and see,
> With such a dear Companion by my side.

William Wordsworth was immediately doing what several novelists would later do: he was utilising cricket as a piece of lyrical shorthand for tranquil peace and contented liberty. Five years later, in 1807, George Gordon, the young Lord Byron (1788-1824) subscribed to this trend. It may scarcely be argued that the importunately passionate son of the profligate 'Mad Jack' Byron was himself the soul of placidity. The scribe of such Romantic and heroic lore as *Childe Harold* and *Don Juan* married Annabelle Milbanke in 1815 with catastrophic results. It was the fall-out from this unhappy match that found the English public in what Lord Macaulay called, in a phrase much-cited since, 'one of its periodical fits of morality.' Byron fled the country and joined Percy and Mary Shelley. A Byronic champion in practice, he adopted liberty's cause and, during his campaigning for Greek independence from Turkish rule, he succumbed to rheumatic fever.

Nonetheless, whilst at Harrow, and in spite of a maimed limb, he had enjoyed his cricket. In 1805 he played for Harrow against Eton at Lord's, 'very badly', according to his captain, John Arthur Lloyd, who, in another long-standing cricket convention, had been opposed to his selection. Harrow were, in Byron's own words, 'most confoundedly beat.' He scored 7 and 2, although in a letter he claimed he had made 11 and 7, a pardonable instance of poetic license. Two years later, when at Trinity College, Cambridge, where he contrived to combine a rake's progress with some sonorous poesy, he wrote *Hours of Idleness*, a wonderfully mature collection of lyrical verses for a nineteen year old undergraduate. One of the poems was *Childish Recollections*, in which he captured the essence, as he felt it, of Harrovian life:

> Flush'd with his rays, beneath the noontide sun,
> In rival bands, between the wickets runs,
> Drive o'er the sward the ball with active force,
> Or chase with nimble feet its rapid course...

> Together we impell'd the flying ball;
> Together we waited in our tutor's hall;

Together join'd in cricket's manly toil.

As a postscript to these accounts of cricket in countryside and school, the adventures of Charles Wordsworth, the poet's nephew - his father, William's younger brother Christopher, became Master of Trinty College, Cambridge - should be added. Aged but fifteen, Charles had played a principal role in Harrow's defeat of Eton in 1822 and befriended the skilled Harrovian, Herbert Jenner. Once at Oxford, he battled against dull authority, one of his tactics being a counterfeit visit to a London dentist, to organise the first University match in 1827, Herbert Jenner now being a Cambridge student. As the old rhyme rang:

> Oxford, round a Wordsworth clustered,
> Cambridge, under Jenner mustered,
> Met in friendly quarrel.

Charles Wordsworth's off-breaks again did the trick and Oxford returned home the initial victors; he also had a say in the choice of dark blue colours, borrowed from Christ Church, for Oxford - and in 1829 he was busily helping to arrange the first Boat Race. As a private tutor at Oxford, he taught Gladstone, famously a lumberjack on his Hawarden estate but no batsman, and H.E.Manning, who converted to Catholicism in 1851 and was appointed Cardinal in 1875. Manning played for Harrow in 1825 and at Oxford he responded in rhyme to a gift of a bat, complete with apt verses, from his tutor:

> The bat that you were kind enough to send
> Seems (for as yet I have not tried it) good;
> And if there's anything on earth can mend
> My wretched play, it is that piece of wood.

Charles Wordsworth had an equally successful career within the Anglican community. He was made Bishop of St. Andrew's in 1852 and died in 1892. Another Oxonian, A.E.Housman shifted theologically in another direction. For Alfred Edward Housman (1859-1936), classical scholar, conscious pagan and poet, there was a despairing poignancy in the vanishing substance of the countryside and the emotional and physical mortality of humanity. His pessimism, and its cause, was like unto that of his contemporary, Thomas Hardy. His editor has explained how public indifference to his major work, *The Shropshire Lad*, was replaced during and after World War I by immense popularity, as his themes of lost youth, broken love, parted friends and futile death 'struck a powerful chord with a nation that was losing an entire generation of young men in the trenches.' Somehow the unrelenting rigour of his balladry heightens the bleakness of his content.

> To skies that knit their heartstrings right,
> To fields that bred them brave,
> The saviours come home not tonight:
> Themselves they could not save.

Village sports figure amid these sobering losses and, once more, cricket must be the ensign of rustic, if doleful, sentiment. Stanza XVII of *The Shropshire Lad* reads:

> Twice a week the winter through
> Here stood I to keep the goal:
> Football then was fighting sorrow
> For a young man's soul.
> Now in Maytime to the wicket
> Out I march with pad and bat:
> See the son of grief at cricket
> Trying to be glad.
> Try I will; no harm in trying:
> Wonder 'tis how little mirth
> Keeps the bones of man from lying
> On the bed of earth.

Dudley Carew made a prudent choice of 'the son of grief' for the title of his melancholy cricket novel, published in 1936. A.E.Housman's is truly 'a land of lost content.' *The Shropshire Lad* ends on downbeat, despondent note: speaking of flowers, he prophesies:

> And fields will yearly bear them
> As light-hearted spring comes on,
> And luckless lads will wear them
> When I am dead and gone

A.E.Housman found no comfort in cricket, although apparently he favoured a cricket cap for head-gear. Leonard Jenkinson tells how, in his preface to a book of essays by Arthur Platt, a Greek scholar, published in

1927, Housman lists among the mock-vices of the author the fact that 'he would squander long summer days watching the game of cricket.' As school-boy, student and academic, Housman proved to be something of a lone and reserved person with few athletic interests.

Much more engaged in cricket, Edmund Blunden (1896-1974), no mean poet himself and an excellent critic of the poetic form, reviewed the linkages of cricket and poetry in his 1944 book, *Cricket Country*. He touches on the facts that William Cowper (1731-1800), that exceedingly mentally disturbed poet, was 'once the pride of Westminster cricket' and that John Keats (1795-1821) was an 'occasional cricketer' and 'neat long-stop': it is recorded elsewhere that, whilst at Clarke's School, Enfield, round about the 1805-10 period, 'he was noted more for his love of cricket and boxing than for any studiousness until his final two years.' John Keats' encouraging friend and son of his head master, the critic Charles Cowden Clarke (1787-1877) apparently recalled in older age 'the cricketing speed' of his own youth. He is, of course, happily recalled for his editorial work on and written contributions to the Hambledon classics, *The Young Cricketer's Tutor* and *The Cricketers of my Time*, both published in 1833, after the recollections and writings of John Nyren, son of Richard, the Hambledon captain in the 1770s. As for William Cowper, his most famous line - 'God moves in a mysterious way' - has certainly been oft-echoed by frustrated cricketers over the generations.

Cricket Country amounts to a most civilised undertaking; a learned yet deftly-handled exploration of cricket and poetry. In his musing, humane fashion, Edmund Blunden goes so far as selecting a Poet's XI, under the captaincy of Siegfried Sassoon, whose cricket poems include *The Blues at Lord's and the Extra Inch*. He selects Robert Bridges (1844-1930), of Eton and Corpus Christi College, Oxford, 'in exquisite flannels - one of our main hopes with the bat', and also George Crabbe (1755-1832), who, as a parson, at Muston in Leicestershire and Trowbridge in Wiltshire, would seek out 'a bit of smooth grass' for cricket with the local boys. There is later even a mention of Rabelais' grotesque character, Gargantua, for among the 214 games he played is listed cricket, while Thomas Gray (1716-1771), immortalised by his *Elegy written in a Country Churchyard*, published in 1751, speaks scornfully of the cricketing peers, the Lords Halifax and Sandwich: 'do you remember them dirty boys playing at cricket?' He presumably recalled them from his Etonian schooldays and he is further quoted from his earlier *Ode on a Distant Prospect of Eton College*.

What ideal progeny feed
To chase the rolling circle's speed,
Or urge the flying ball?

Wisden mourned the passing of Rupert Brooke, more officiously, Sub-Lieut. Rupert C.Brooke, who died, somewhat prosaically for a revered war poet, of sunstroke in 1915 at Lemnos, on the way to the Dardenelles. His 'corner of a foreign field that is forever England' is at Scyros and later sources cite blood-poisoning as the cause of death. He was born, in 1887, and educated at Rugby, where, despite little success in the annual Marlborough encounter, he topped the school bowling averages in 1906 with 19 wickets at 14.05 each. 'He had', added *Wisden* as an incidental afterthought, 'gained considerable reputation as a poet.' Possibly his obituarist was a Cantabrigian, for, although himself a King's College *alumnus*, Robert Brooke pronounced the well-remembered verdict:

For Cambridge people rarely smile,
Being urban, squat and full of guile.

Those quick glimpses of Wordsworth, Byron, Housman and one or two others apart, the classical English poets have usually fought shy of the game. That said, there is a vast quantity of cricket poetry per se. Indeed, the first inklings that cricket, as the modern eye might discern it, was taking shape are to be gleaned from poetry. In 1706 William Goldwin published a set of Latin poems, *Musae Juveniles*, one of which was titled *In Certamen Pilae*, 'on a game of ball.' This 95 line description of a cricket match was thankfully, and to the relief of the rusty classicist, translated in 1923 and again in 1926. It begins:

Springtime anew, with mild and limpid air
Smiling, with kindness coaxes earth to bear,
And active feet to sport where fields spread wide:
A team of youths, with crooken bats supplied.

If one excepts the persuasive view that, across Europe, folk-games were legion and localised, forming a kind of primeval swamp of 'game-ness', then this poem becomes very significant. As late as the early 19th century, England was sub-divided into no less than 15,000 parishes, atoms of mainly self-subsisting agricultural character, with their individual sporting frolics, as determined by the terrain, the implements and the forceful personality, playing out a thousand variations on the theme of club and ball and target. Although William Goldwin's account differs in detail from some other early descriptions and although his translators may have been a trifle retrospective in applying modern jargon to his classical wordage, etymology and practice do coincide for about the first time. In short, until this point it is difficult to accept that the word 'cricket' always applies to the same activity or that the activity now known as 'cricket' did not previously have different labels. The controversies rage over the places where cricket was started and what cricket meant - did, for example, the word 'cricket' derive from the target or the club, the butt or the bat? - whereas probably the simple answer is that lots of people, in parochial mode, were enjoying themselves at their own diversion, unconcerned that later generations of antiquarians would be bemused by this multifarious manifestation of 'play.'

However, William Goldwin was a student of Eton and King's College, Cambridge, and subsequently headmaster of Bristol Grammar School and vicar of St Nicholas Church, Bristol. School; varsity; church: he embodied the three establishments destined to advance the fortunes of cricket on a national stage. His poem serves not only to demonstrate that cricket was reaching maturity as a readily identifiable game, but that it was being acknowledged as such by the educated and moneyed classes. A further poem, *Cricket: an Heroic Poem*, of some 300 lines, was composed by James Love, originally Dance, but he changed his surname in honour of his wife whose maiden name was Lamour. This was in 1744 and it describes in exhilarating, mock-heroic Augustan couplets the game in that year between Kent and All-England, the first 'great match' for which the full scores are available. In stately accents, James Love, a graduate of St John's College, Oxford, describes the metropolitan hegemony of cricket by mid-18th century, as well as underlining how cricket is approaching its modern construct. Once more, the emphasis is on the very English nature of the sport:

> Hail Cricket! glorious, manly, British game!
> First of all sports! be first alike in fame!...
>
> O parent Britain! Minion of renown!
> Whose far-extended Fame all Nations own;
> Nurs'd on thy Plains, first Cricket learn'd to please,
> And taught thy Sons to slight inglorious Ease;

James Love dedicated his brash couplets to the 4th Earl of Sandwich, gambler and cricketer, the peer who gave his name to the Isles and who may well be regarded as the patron saint of the cricket tea.

A long continuum of English verse is dedicated to cricket, normally with the nostalgic sentiment uppermost. Little of it meets Wordsworthian or Byronic criteria and much of it falls into the second rank of English poetic composition. That may sound a trifle unkind, but it is meant generously: perhaps it would be helpful to aver that it is certainly not third-rate. John Arlott, in, among others, *Cricket at Worcester*, 1938; Alan Ross's *Cricket at Brighton* or his a *Photograph of Hammond;* Edmund Blunden's *Pride of the Village;* Gerald Bullett's *Flowing together by devious channels*, a fetching little concept of village cricket as a microcosm of civilisation; Gavin Ewart's *Valediction: To the Cricket Season* ('We count up that final inescapable total, remember huge sixes by maverick sloggers - compensating, like love, for the field that's deserted, the padlocked pavilion.'): these are examples, among many, that achieve a gracious reflection of the feelings evoked by cricket.

Warfare intensified these emotions. Arnold Wall, a Cambridge graduate of the early 1890s and later Professor of English Literature at the University of Canterbury, New Zealand, wrote a *Time will Come*, a wistful lay of hope amidst the carnage of the first world war, during which the *Wisdens* of those tragic years logged the deaths of over 2000 ex-schoolboy or varsity crick-eters. It ends with a line that was to become very familiar:

> Dream of the boys who never were here,
> Born in the days of evil chance.
> Who never knew sport or easy days,
> But played their game in the fields of France.

When, for a second mournful time, first-class cricket in England was peremptorily halted by baleful hostilities, it gave rise to similar expressions. In 1952 R.W.Moore, one-time headmaster of Harrow, published his anthology, 'Trophy for an Unknown Soldier.' It included the ode, *The Air is Hushed,*

> And all the players - where are they?
> Earthwide they wander quick and slain,
> And those who shall return to play
> Shall scan the scorebook all in vain.

John Masefield, whose maritime poems, like *Cargoes and Sea-fever*, were once the staple fare of many a junior classroom, is one Poet Laureate who made a serious and substantial contribution to cricket poesy. A lonely child and a sea-going youth, he was not himself much of a cricketer, as an admiring article by A.C.McKay on the centenary of his birth makes clear ('John Masefield, OM (1878-1967)', *The Journal of the Cricket Society*, vol.9, no.1, Autumn 1978). Nonetheless, as an infant he was enthralled by the legendary 1882 Test match at the Oval, from which the rite of the Ashes derived, and he subsequently composed a narrative account, *Eighty-five to win*, first published in *The Times* in 1956 and then in John Masefield's own anthology, *The Bluebells and other verse*, in 1961. It is an estimable try, in spite of some occasional lapses into triteness, at what has perplexed many a poet - producing a Homeric description of a sporting event. F.R.Spofforth, who so confounded W.G.Grace and his English *confreres*, is strongly characterised:

> Then, when he bowled, he seemed a thing of Hell,
> Writhing, grimacing; batsmen, catching breath,
> Thought him no mortal man but very death.

> Then, with England narrowly beaten by seven runs:
> Quickly the crowd dispersed to life's routine
> Of Life and Death and wonder what they mean.
> A thunder muttered and a shower fell
> As twilight came with star and Vesper-bell.

Among poet-cricketers might be mentioned D.L.A.Jephson (1871-1926), Oxford blue, Surrey all-rounder and composer of a book of verse entitled *A Few Overs*. He played for the Gentlemen and, overall, he made nearly 8000 runs and took almost 300 wickets in 207 matches. R.P.Keigwin (1883-1972), one of three athletic brothers, was a sportsman of wide-ranging talent, representing Cambridge University at hockey - he was a hockey international - soccer and rackets as well as cricket. He played a handful of games for Gloucestershire and Essex and, apart from being an acknowledged authority on and translator of the tales of Hans Christian Andersen, he wrote light verse. A rarity is the poet from the professional ranks, but Arnold Rylott (1839-1914), the quick left-arm bowler, not only took 456 wickets in his 85 first-class matches, chiefly for MCC, but published a collection of non-cricketing poetry under the title, *Our Bobby Rykitt when a Boy*. Thomas Moult (1885-1974) was a cricket reporter and author: he edited Jack Hobbs' autobiography in 1931, but he was also for many years President of the

Poetry Society and published two volumes of cricket verse, *Bat and Ball* and *Willow Pattern*.

A word in season about Alfred Cochrane: he was a first-class cricketer as well as a poet, and the erudite Hampshire archivist, Neil Jenkinson, has written of him in both contexts. A.H.J.Cochrane (1865-1948) played for Repton and was an Oxford blue who played four matches for Derbyshire and once for the Gentlemen. Business commitments reduced his first-class appearances to 28, in which his left-hand steadiness earned him the creditable figures of 103 wickets at an average just a shade under 19. He played for MCC and the Harlequins and leavened his career in shipbuilding and armaments with a deal of writing, much of it on cricket. He published four or five collections of verse, some of it of a cricketing connotation, as in:

> But for an hour to watch them play,
> Those heroes dead and gone,
> And pit our batsmen of today
> With those of Hambledon!

Even misanthropic Philip Larkin ('Give me your arm, old toad;/Help me down Cemetery Road') turned to cricket for occasional escape. Perhaps Britain's most critically acclaimed post-war poet, one of the high-spots of his fairly insular life was to attend the Lord's Test each June. He did so in the company of his long-term lover and companion, Monica Jones, who became a literary footnote in that she was caricatured in two of the most popular novels of university life since 1945, Kingsley Amis' *Lucky Jim* and Malcolm Bradbury's *Eating People is Wrong*.

Aside from this heritage of poetic sentiment and nostalgia, a second proclivity has developed of humorous cricketing verse, much of it reliant on a sometimes heavy irony or on a sometimes ponderous hyperbole. Exceptions, such as the shining brilliance of P.G.Wodehouse have already been noted in this respect, while A.P.Herbert (1890-1971) is another light-hearted and felicitous versifier, best known probably for his libretto for *Bless the Bride*, first staged in 1947, or his 1930 novel, *The Water Gipsies*, who also turned his adept pen to cricket. *His Ninth Wicket*, with its cheerless refrain, 'I can't imagine why I play this game', is guaranteed to find a sympathetic ear among the majority of recreational cricketers. Honourable mention, too, for Norman Gale's jaunty *The Church Cricketant here on Turf* ('I bowled three curates once with three consecutive balls!') from his 1896 collection 'Cricket

Songs'; for G.F.Bradby's *The Black Sheep*, a terrible warning about infringe-
ment of stern protocol in the Lord's pavilion, and for R.C.Robertson-
Glasgow's *The One-way Critic*, poking gentle fun at the cricket buff for
whom the past is always better - a harsh lesson for us all.

Among all of this versifying there is only one poem that does what Hugh de
Selincourt's *The Cricket Match* achieves in prose; namely, it surpasses
dependence on its subject-matter and enters the list of classically great
poems.

In 1878 a Roman Catholic teenager from Preston went to Old Trafford to
watch Lancashire play the mighty W.G.Grace's Gloucestershire side. The
Gloucestershire eleven, and the amiable reader will pardon the indulgence,
included William Evans Midwinter, cricket's first global commuter and the
only man to have played for England *versus* Australia and Australia *versus*
England. It was one of the first great provincial cricket occasions, with over
30,000 attending over the three days, sometimes in such disorderly swarms
that improvements to the primitive facilities were prompted. That youth
knew a life of destitution, ill-health and drug-addiction, in between whiles
writing usually mystical religious poetry, such as *The Hound of Heaven*. He
was Francis Thompson. The literary critic and Gloucestershire supporter,
Gilbert Phelps, has described how, just before his death in 1907, 'he was
invited to Lord's to see his beloved Lancashire play.' Such was his emotional stress at the remembrance of that match nearly thirty years before, he
could not bring himself to accept, but rather 'wrote a poem about it, and
entitled it *At Lord's* as a token of gratitude to those who had invited him.' *At
Lord's* manages to be both the finest and the most memorable of cricket
poems, with its haunting refrains:

> For the field is full of shades as I near the shadowy coast,
> And a ghostly batsman plays to the bowling of a ghost,
> And I look through my tears on a soundless-clapping host
> As the run-stealers flicker to and fro,
> To and fro:-
> O my Hornby and my Barlow long ago!

Fortunately for posterity, Francis Thompson altered his original draft of 'my
Monkey and Stonewaller' and used the formal surnames of the legendary
Lancashire opening pair rather than their sobriquets. Almost all would
accept Edmund Blunden's opinion that *At Lord's* is the 'only one piece' that

'travels on its own power as poetry into a general anthology.' A lone voice suggests that the verses 'do not bear too much analysis', but that caustic assessment dripped from Yorkist lips and may so be explained, if not condoned. And in answer to the unspoken question, W.E.Midwinter scored 22 and 25 in a low-scoring drawn match, during which W.G.Grace and 'Monkey' Hornby had a typically heated row over a duplicitous run out.

Chapter 17

A BUMPING PITCH AND A BLINDING LIGHT: SCHOOL STORIES AND CRICKET

Could reading all those schoolboy comics and books, full of stirring cricketing yarns, help one, in an educationalist mode, to answer the pertinent question: why did Britain never contrive to construct an effective and satisfactory secondary schools system in the twentieth century? The vast array of schoolboy literature pumped out between about 1860 and 1950 seemed to create a cultural miasma which floated over the nation. It is arguable that it persuaded both adults and children that the boarding school story model, with its crucial cricketing element, should be deployed when secondary education for all was evolved. The consequence - a system disastrously alien and off-putting for many young adults, trying to make sense of a rapidly changing society - has caused immeasurable damage of a social and economic kind, as well as offering to thousands a misleading version of the value of cricket.

For what cannot be gainsaid is the major part that cricket played in those stories. Four or five generations of cricket-watchers and -players found some introduction, at a tenderly formative age, to the delights of cricket through these stories. The effects of that major transmission of cricketing habits, whilst difficult to measure, must have been profound and it may be of interest to examine both the quantity and the quality of that enduring shared experience. This barrage of cricketing yarns was fired through two calibres. At one level - what might be called the heavy artillery - was a sequence of schoolboy novels with cricket either the sole or a major *motif*. At another level - the light artillery, so to speak - was the periodic magazine, often a weekly, which came generically to be listed as a 'comic'. Naturally enough, the weeklies attracted many more readers than the actual books, and thus it was through these periodicals that the cricketing prowess of dozens of school -boy champions was conveyed to a wide and willing public. However, it was the books which laid down a set of unwritten laws about how cricket should be woven into the plots and about the characterisation of such stories.

Just as the 1939 western film *Stagecoach* came to be described by the film critic, John Baxter, as 'the basic western, a template for everything that followed', so did *Tom Brown's Schooldays*, first published in 1857, originate the schoolboy story and the place of cricket therein. Tom Brown, as Gerald Howat, scholarly as ever, has explained ('Cricket and the Victorian Church, Part III', *The Journal of the Cricket Society*, vol.9, no.4, Spring 1980) was based on Augustus Orlebar, vicar of the Bedfordshire parish of Willington for over fifty years. His opponent in the fictional fight, Slogger Williams, was, in the authorised version of that scrap, Bulkeley Owen Jones, destined also for the cloth; indeed, Thomas Hughes viewed both of them, suitably enough, as 'Muscular Christians.' Augustus Orlebar played in the 1841 Rugby and MCC match, which Thomas Hughes utilised for the finale of his book, bar an epilogue mourning the death of the head of Rugby School, Thomas Arnold, who, truth to tell, what not quite the lover of organised games we are sometimes led to believe. Tom Hughes, like Tom Brown, was cricket captain, and the fictional game reaches the statutory exciting climax of nine to make and two wickets to fall, very similar to the genuine match, with Johnson - his original was Arthur, the Third Baron Wrottesley, born 1824, died 1910 - taking most of the wickets for Rugby.

Gerald Howat, in yet another of his masterly essays ('Thomas Hughes' Two Rugbys', *The Journal of the Cricket Society*, vol.17, no.4, Spring 1996) has written perceptively of the life, 1822-1896, of Tom Brown's energetic origi-nator. Berkshire born and an Oxford cricket blue, he joined the ranks of the Christian Socialists, led by Charles Kingsley and F.D.Maurice, did much earnest work, both in the UK and the USA, and probably played for a Christian Socialist cricket team.

The young master says to Tom and Arthur, 'What a noble game it is too'. 'Isn't it?' answers Tom, 'but it's more than a game. It's an institution'. Arthur joins in with a statement which suggests, given formal cricket's relatively modern origins, that the history teaching at Rugby is below par. 'Yes', said Arthur, 'the birthright of British boys, old and young, as *habeas corpus* and trial by jury are of English men'. 'The discipline and reliance on one anoth-er it teaches is so valuable', affirms the master, apostrophising cricket as 'an unselfish game. It merges the individual in the eleven; he doesn't play that he may win, but that his side may.' All of a sudden, and in a Tom Brown nutshell, the lesson of school cricket was encompassed. It was all present and morally correct. Cricket as excitement and good fellowship; cricket as a manifestation of a swathe of fine virtues; cricket as a builder of character; cricket as a tutor of discipline and dependability; cricket as an expression of team-work; and cricket as an outlet for leadership.

The books which followed inexorably in the Tom Brown canon adhered rigidly to the formula, many of them developing more of a story than the rather episodic *Tom Brown's Schooldays*, and employing the set-piece cricket match as a twist, often enough, the final twist, the unraveller, of the plot. There might have been an untoward occurrence, with the school rotter to blame, to threaten our hero's appearance on the satiny sward, but, bang on time, rightly and salubriously, goodness would prevail. With a rippling cover drive off the last ball of a sun-dappled evening, all's well that ends well.

Recall a few of those instances. P.G.Wodehouse told Malcolm Muggeridge (and George Orwell, another firm admirer of Wodehouse, and the scribe of a compelling essay, *Boys' Weeklies*, in 1961, agreed) that *Mike* was his best book. P.G.Wodehouse felt that Mike recaptured 'the ring of a ball on a cricket bat, the green of a pitch, the white of flannels and the sound of schoolboy cheers'. *Mike*, published in 1909, tells the tale of Mike Jackson, destined to captain the Wrykyn eleven but finding himself transferred to the unathletic Sedleigh School, where he contrives to create a cricketing ambience and eventually lead Sedleigh to triumph against - no prizes for guessing - Wrykyn.

Arthur Conan Doyle, who procured his best-ever bowling figures of 7 for 61 for MCC against Cambridgeshire in 1899, the same year P.G.Wodehouse took his 7 for 50 for Dulwich College, felt that his brother-in-law, E.W.Hornung, produced better work in his school story, *Fathers of Men*, than in his more celebrated series on Raffles, a character examined in chapter 10. In *Fathers of Men*, published in 1912, the mandatory cricket match is with the Old Boys, and the plot, Raffles-style, involves Evan Devereux and his friend, Jan Rutter, the skipper of the eleven and the book's main protagonist. Having disposed of the Old Boys with his fiery bowling - a modest return of 9 for 26 - he then joins the miscreant but brilliant Devereux in a late order stand of intense thrills. Devereux scores a century; there is a near run out; and the match is won.

David Blaize was written by E.F.Benson. Edward Frederic Benson (1867-1940) was the son of Archbishop Benson and the younger brother of the *litterateur*, Arthur Christopher Benson (1862-1925), best known for penning the words to *Land of Hope and Glory*, Elgar's first Pomp and Circumstance march, originally used as part of the Coronation Ode for Edward VII. E.F.Benson is remembered for his amusing stories of Lucia and Dodo, such as *Dodo Wonder* and *Queen Lucia*. *David Blaize* was published in 1915 and it includes a house match at the fictional Marchester school, Adam's versus Tovey's, as its obligatory curtsey to cricket. David, like Rutter, having done the damage with the ball, then joins his bosom companion, Frank Maddox, *aka* Devereux, and they swing the match for Adam's. It is another of those standard incidents, redolent of Tom Brown, where close pals win the day; there is nothing better than a batting partnership to epitomise friendship. At the end, 'Maddox paused. 'Best of all the days I've had at school, David,' he said. 'Same here,' said David'.

A couple of years later, in 1917, Alec Waugh wrote *The Loom of Youth*. This precocious novel was mentioned in chapter 12, when the Waugh brothers were more fully discussed. The cricketing element finds A-K Senior facing the much-favoured Buller's side in the house trophy final at Fernhurst, based on Sherborne, but, inevitably, the underdogs, with the book's hero, Gordon, and his friends, Collins and Foster, in the van, emerge victorious. 'The umpire's hand rose. A wild shriek rose from the crowd. Gordon's last game at Fernhurst was over; his last triumph had come; at last 'Samson had quit himself like Samson'.' Every book seem to make the cricket match the centre-piece, more frequently, the end-piece, of the plot. Even Dean Farrar's benighted hero, *Eric, or Little by Little*, a decidedly anti-athletic story, first published in 1861, but re-published again and again (thus bringing a wide usage of a very beautiful forename, almost forgotten since Viking times, right into the 1920s and 1930s), yes, even Eric played cricket for Roslyn School, as he sinfully descended the primrose path.

This prototype school story, with the cricket match central to it, was religiously adopted by the more widespread and more commonplace display of school boy literature. This more popular brand of literature, purveyed on a periodical basis, had three main incarnations, although each overlapped with the others. These might be labelled the BOP phase, the Magnet phase, and the Hotspur phase.

The Boy's Own Paper, or *BOP*, was launched by the Religious Tract Society in 1879 and holds the record for the longest-running juvenile periodical ever. By the 1890s its print run was 665,000 weekly, giving an estimated readership of nearly two millions. It was created, it has been said, for those who wanted their children to have something 'manly' to read, the specific occasion for its launch being the felt need to challenge the penny-dreadfuls which were flooding the market, and which, rather in the manner of violent television today, were held responsible for juvenile crime. It was to face stiff competition from *Chums*, first produced in 1892 by Cassell's, and by the Newnes magazine launched in 1899, *The Captain*, in which P.G. Wodehouse's *Mike* was serialised. *BOP* was forced to go monthly in 1913, but it struggled on until as late as 1967.

Although not all its tales and articles were about schools, it has been authoritatively said that *BOP* 'became a prime vehicle for the popularisation of the public school ethos', and the seminal influence in that regard was the writing of Talbot Baines Reed and, in particular, his famous story, *The Fifth Form at St. Dominic's*. Whilst *Tom Brown's Schooldays* was its inspiration, most commentators agree that *St. Dominic's* is the true begetter of the school story, replete as it is with all the sub-plots - the stolen exam paper, for instance - the 'what rot' slang and the bevy of stereotyped characters which were to be endlessly reproduced in thousands of tales over the next fifty or sixty years. It was serialised in *BOP* in 1881/82; published in book form in 1887; and reprinted as late as 1971. It describes in full the Sixth versus the School cricket match, the School represented entirely by members of the fifth form. Among them are Oliver Greenfield and Horace Wraysford, whose friendship forms a chief element of the plot, and whose cricketing prowess enables the School to fight out an enthralling tie with the Sixth.

The *BOP* concept was overtaken by the more purely commercial activities of the Amalgamated Press and Fleetway Publications. *The Gem*, in 1907, and *The Magnet*, in 1908, were the opening and most successful shots in this publishing campaign, which brought school stories, usually with a modicum of cricketing and, of course, footballing interest in most of them. They were cheap and aimed at the widest possible audience; around the time of the first world war *The Magnet* sold 200,000 copies weekly, but that would have to be multiplied several times to compute the actual readership, given the swappping and second-hand sales which the magazine generated.

Charles Hamilton was far and away the most abundant writer of these yarns, the huge majority of which involved boarding school-life. Frank Richards was the most famous of his twenty-five pseudonyms; he is reputed to be the most prolific writer there has ever been, weighing in with 60/70 million words, the equivalent of a thousand full-length novels; and he created 105 fictional schools, of which Greyfriars, St Jim's and Rookwood were the best known. There can be little doubt that the stories transfixed whole generations of youth and inculcated into them a code of ethics and behaviour. 'Sportsmanship' - a rather hearty, bluff credo of giving and taking knocks without complaint or telling tales - conveys the gist of it. Among hundreds of endorsements of the appeal and spread of the doctrine perhaps the most telling and poignant is that of Robert Roberts in his evocative account of his Edwardian childhood in the Salford slums: '..with nothing in our own school that called for love and allegiance, Greyfriars became for some of us our true Alma Mater, to whom we felt bound by a dreamlike loyalty'.

Friendship was once more the predominant theme, but Frank Richards enlarged the concept to embrace the group rather than the older convention of the pairing. The Greyfriars Famous Five, led by Harry Wharton, all of them useful cricketers, personified the notion of the individual within the team. In sharp contrast with them stands the selfish, cowardly, bumptious anti-hero, Billy Bunter, and, not for the first time in literary annals, it is the villain of the piece - think of Long John Silver or Fagin - who grabs all the laurels. An articulate writer of sprightly pace, he modelled himself on Charles Dickens and W.S.Gilbert, not least in permitting the characters to rise and dominate over the story-line.

Cricket is the perfect canvas to paint that portrait of good and bad values. When boastful Billy Bunter inveigles himself into batting against a village team, he faces Parker, who, in a sly class-ridden aside, is dismissed as an 'estate-office young man' who 'rather fancied himself as a bowler' but who 'would not have been very useful against the average man in Harry Wharton's team at Greyfriars'. To the sound of many spluttered 'ha ha ha's', Bunter is castled first ball. Once again, his egotism is severely punctured, although many of us might echo his final grumbling comment: 'what a game this is for flukes'. Those seeking further news of such matters are invited to consult the excellent article, *Cricket at Greyfriars*, by J.F.Burrell, in *The Journal of the Cricket Society*, vol.1, no.2, Spring 1983, in which they will discover that, among Frank Richards' sometimes slightly vague cricketing allusions, Bunter's initials were W.G.; that Mr Lascelles was the cricket master, and that popular Bob Cherry once scored a fast 124.

As *BOP* was overtaken by *The Magnet* and *The Gem*, so were they, in turn, emulated by the products of D.C.Thompson and Co. Ltd. That company, like Greyfriars, boasted a famous five. *The Adventure* (started in 1921), *The Rover* and *The Wizard* (both 1922), *The Skipper* (1930) and *The Hotspur* (1933). By the beginning of World War II, the huge majority of boys, certainly as many as 75%, were reading one or more of these 'comics', as they were perhaps, with their lots of competent prose and comparatively few illustrations, misleadingly called. They did not include, as many will recall, just school stories, for they encompassed the other threads in the skein of boys' yarns of those sixty or so years, notably Empire-building adventures and detective thrillers. For instance, *The Adventure* offered its readers the escapades of Bill Simpson, the Wolf of Kabul. His militant associate, Chung, was armed with 'clicky-ba', which cricketing implement pressed home the link between the laws of cricket and Imperial rule.

From the present viewpoint, however, it was *The Hotspur'* which must take precedence, for it was billed as 'a school story paper'. From its origin in 1933, until 1958, when it was superseded by *The New Hotspur* which was, in fact, produced in the contemporary mode of pictorial strips, it narrated the doings of Red Circle School. With R.G.Thomas and A.R.Linden the chief early editors and scribes, it was planned carefully over four stages, encompassing in all no less than 1155 stories. Unlike *The Magnet* and *The Gem*, the boys actually grew up and left, and, for example, Dead-wide Dick Doyle became school captain and later Cripple Dick Archer held that coveted post, both of them excellent cricketers. It was a new school, built as a circle of three red sandstone 'houses', with Mr Smugg, the abrasive master, the *alter ego* of Mr Quelch of Greyfriars, and the value-system, not least the esteem proffered cricket and those pupils who excelled in it, was exactly the same.

Thus it was that, for the best part of a hundred years, the reading of British boyhood was inundated with school stories, almost all of them deploying cricket as a key ingredient, as a medium for expressing the values of what Thomas Hughes would have called 'manliness'. What was the overall effect of this enduring exercise in brain-washing, one of the most profound and lengthy examples of cultural indoctrination ever practised on generation after generation of youngsters?

First of all, it was, in the main, deliberate and conscious. Thomas Hughes averred that 'my sole object in writing was to preach to boys' about self-reliance. Tom Brown's 'young master' was modelled on G.E.L.Cotton, who became head of Marlborough in 1852, despite his broken engagement with Thomas Arnold's daughter, Jane, on the grounds of his mother's suspected heavy drinking. Jane married instead William Forster, Gladstone's minister responsible for education at the time of the passage of the seminal 1870 Education Act, a major stage in the development of state schooling. George Cotton really started the games mania, and what one commentator has termed 'the hysterical adulation of the good athlete'. A 'great-souled' Muscular Christian, Thomas Hughes' evangelical torch was grasped in turn by Talbot Baines Reed who was very much his disciple. He gave all his royalties to the Religious Tract Society and lived off the income from his family's printing business. His creed has been defined as 'cheerful Puritanism'. It brooks no argument that the *Boy's Own Newspaper* was for youthful Muscular Christianity in late Victorian and Edwardian England what *Pravda* was for the USSR Communist party of old.

Frank Richards, in his turn, was an unabashed admirer of Talbot Baines Reed, and he took his task very seriously indeed, hopeful of inculcating the virtues of good form and English gentlemanliness into his myriad readers. The D.C.Thompson editors were more than happy to adopt this dogma wholeheartedly, and, whilst watchful of their commercial requirements, to make it salient to their publications. For each of these authors, cricket was the outward and physical sign of that inward and spiritual grace. Fighting, albeit fairly and with fists, in defence of the bullied, was permitted, but it was cricket which truthfully betokened the nobility of physical striving.

The location of the cricket match in the story is significant. It is often, as with *Tom Brown's Schooldays*, the final defining act of the play. *In the Loom of Youth*, Foster says to his friend after their last cricket match together, 'well, if we stopped on here for a hundred years...we shouldn't find a better time to leave'. There was a poignant dimension to this. The 'happiest days of your life' was no idle hyperbole, for, in the very preparation for what was agreed would be a tough existence of uncomplaining duty in regiment, colonial outpost or socially deprived parish, was to be found the blissful heights of school-life. It is a rum paradox. Heaven precedes the vale of tears. In the cabined intensity of school-life, not least in the emotional fervour of a close friendship, was to be enjoyed the serene calm before the storm of adult life. The last rite of the cricket match symbolised this, its strict ritual celebrating, like a form of holy mass, the communion of white-garbed knights, preparatory to the battle royal.

This tendency gave rise to the concept of *puer aeternus*, the 'eternal boy', most lucidly discussed by Cyril Connolly in his 1938 book, *Enemies of Promise*. This theory suggested that, because of the concentrated density of the school experience, emotional, intellectual and even physical development became arrested at the point of what was called 'permanent adolescence'. In adult life, this was sometimes confused with homosexuality and, on occasion, paedeophilia or even sado-masochism, but it was more subtle than that. It was, if anything, asexual. Several of the authors under review might be characterised in such terms, including Thomas Hughes, Talbot Baines Reed, Frank Richards, and P.G.Wodehouse. E.F.Benson, author of the cited *David Blaize*, and a Marlborough pupil, claimed that 'in many ways boys are a sex quite apart from male and female', and, as we have noted, batting partnerships were constantly used by Benson and others to encapsulate these chaste but deeply-felt friendships, with the writers often invoking the love of David and Jonathan, 'wonderful, passing the love of women'.

Certainly the middle part of the era was an age of boy-men, and it is no coincidence that the two seminal texts on a refusal to grow up were both published at the very centre-point of this period. In 1904, James Barrie, something of a permanent child himself, after the fashion of Lewis Carroll, with his quaint, if relatively innocuous, delight in children, wrote *Peter Pan*, and, in 1908, Sir Robert Baden-Powell published the ambivalently-titled *Scouting for Boys*. One of his biographers tags him 'a perennial singing schoolboy'; he called his closest friend 'the boy'; and named his only son after Peter Pan. Baden-Powell, like J.M.Barrie, was a keen cricketer - asked for a truce for cricket during his resolute command of Mafeking when besieged by the Boers, he refused, on the grounds that the British were 200 days, not out, and enjoying the game...shades of Montgomery knocking Rommel for six in World War II...the Montgomery who played for St.Paul's School in 1905 and 1906.

It is uncanny how many famed Englishmen of that era might be tagged *puer aeternus*. As the revisionist biographies swell, the school might wriggle uncomfortably that had, say, Gordon of Khartoum, Kitchener, Cecil Rhodes, T.E.Lawrence and Captain Scott as Empire heroes to identify their 'houses'. Each had flaws of character, often indicative of something of fixated adolescence. Nigel Hamilton, Field Marshal Montgomery's authoritative biographer, has updated his previous three volumes study with *The Full Monty* (2001) in which he supplies evidence that the World War II hero was a 'repressed gay', but the consistent pattern of the soldier's loving afffection for young men and boys and the 'aberrration' of his marriage might also suggest that the phenomenon of 'eternal boyhood' survived deep into the 20th century.

Then there is the test-case of W.G.Grace. Clifford Bax, who published a memoir of W.G.Grace in 1952, wrote bluntly that he was 'a case of arrested development and remained, intellectually, always at the age of sixteen'. A.A.Thomson judged that he was 'very boylike' and Bernard Darwin wrote that 'he had all the schoolboy's love for elementary and boisterous jokes; his distaste for learning; his desperate and undisguised keenness; his guileless-ness and his guile; his occasional pettishness and pettiness; his endless power of recovering his good spirits.' Contemporaries thought him immature: 'just a great big schoolboy in everything he did', said one old acquaintance; 'a great big baby', commented Philip Trevor, a family friend and writer of *The Lighter Side of Cricket, Cricket and Cricketers* and other cricket pieces; 'he was a big grown-up boy', wrote Arthur Porritt, the amanuensis for Grace's 1899 book, *W.G.; Cricketing Reminiscences and Personal Recollections.* W.G.Grace was but one of many English notables of the age who appear to have been ossified, in terms of intellectual competence and moral assessment, at ado-lescence.

Whatever the case, when secondary education was expanded, after the Education Acts of 1902 and 1918, and through such devices as the Secondary School Memorandum of 1904, the fictional school type of struc-ture was largely adopted, together sometimes with its mandatory compo-nent of cricket. Unluckily, only about 3% or 4% of the population, albeit an influential minority, had any direct knowledge of such institutions, while the vast majority of local councillors, education officers, teachers, parents, and, of course, children, only really knew of such places through reading about them. Thus St Dominic's, Greyfriars and Red Circle designed the blueprint for English secondary schooling, and, with it, the significant role allocated to cricket. It mattered little that it was a bastardised image, and that, the more populist the literature became, the more inaccurate it grew; it is an interesting fact that Frank Richards, inventor of over a hundred schools, never in his life actually set foot inside a real-life boarding school.

The stories were assailed on all fronts for inaccuracy, both by public school attackers and defenders. However, this was scarcely germane, for, so power-ful was the image, that a highly successful music hall character comedian, Will Hay, could, on stage, screen and wireless, particularly in the 1930s, por-tray a beleaguered and faltering boarding school teacher, and every single person understood every last *nuance* of dress, content and *patois* at his Narkover school. Novels and films with public school backgrounds, like *Good-bye, Mr Chips*, James Hilton's 1934 book, screened in 1939, with Robert Donat, were easily assimilated by a public well versed in the ethos of such institutions. H.E.Bates, who, with *The Darling Buds of May* (1958) launched his saga of the hedonistic Larkins' clan, has described how he knew exactly what to expect at Kettering Grammar School - including 'a new kind of English in which words like 'cads' and 'rotters' and expressions like 'bally bounders' and 'beastly fellows' played a large part.'

Oddly enough, the majority of child purchasers of *BOP, Magnet and Hotspur'* were younger than the youngest boys at the schools about which they so avidly read. Until after the first world war, most boys had left school before, at thirteen, public schools boys had started. Assessing by birthdays, Jack Hobbs and Herbert Sutcliffe had left school - incidentally, along with most of their peers, without ever playing organised cricket there - before the likes of Archie MacLaren or F.S.Jackson had gone to share in Blaize/Maddox-type partnerships at Harrow. There are many myths about the place of cricket in schools over the decades: in fact, it was the 1950s and 1960s when more boys were playing school cricket than at any time before or since.

Nonetheless, the model held up well, and a significant aspect of the translation of the boarding school argot and curriculum was the cult of Athleticism, with cricket the major, often the exclusive, summer term game. This was especially true of the grammar schools. The grammar school had enjoyed a startling success in Elizabethan England, but later fell into a pitiable desuetude. Then it enjoyed an extremely brief resuscitation, chiefly between the two world wars. What had been a hundred grammar schools in the 1830s became 1300 by 1944, before, again, they collapsed - once more, there are now barely a hundred - in favour of the less divisive and more efficient extension of common schooling from the primary to the secondary sector.

This relatively transient recovery of the grammar school in mid-20th century chimed in with the boarding-school story as reflective of the inter-wars years' mood. One slightly risible example was the wellnigh universal use of the 'house' system in completely non-residential institutions. What must be pressed is that almost all of schoolboy literature was reasonably well and often elegantly written, with strong characterisation, juicy plots and clean-cut prose. Until the advent of the cruder pictorial strip comics for older children of the late 1950s, a meaty standard of decent accessible reading was wholesomely sustained. The attraction of the boarding school is evident enough. It is a closed community, and authors delight in the cohesion afforded by such secluded formats as the Agatha Christie country house, cut

off by heavy snow from the outside world, and stuffed full of murder suspects. The boarding school provides for just such an exercise in social claus-
trophobia. The residential basis and the self-regulating canon of an enclosed
commune is just what the author ordered.

In a film like Lindsay Anderson's *If* (1968) and in a play-cum-pageant like
Alan Bennett's *Forty Years On* (also 1968), the boarding school - 'Albion
House' - becomes the metaphor for society. Especially in the 1920s and
1930s, when Britain was gripped by what the historian, David Thompson,
called 'the incorrigible *immobilisme*' of that period, there was perhaps an
unconscious acceptance, which the grammar school epitomised, of the
nation as one big boarding school, a safe and insular haven for the chosen
few, cut off from the rest of the nasty world, with George V the aloof chairman of governors and Stanley Baldwin the benign headmaster.

All this imagery and ideology conspired to grant cricket a special place in
English secondary education, and the foregoing testimony amounts to an
explanation of why it occurred. Come harsh government cuts in grants and
the resultant damage to the maintenance of cricket facilities; come a leftist
mini-crusade against the team ethic, largely confined to a few London bor-
oughs but loudly proclaimed in the right-wing press; come the less well-pub-
licised racketeering sale of school playing fields for expensive building development, some schools have valiantly tried to keep the left elbow of cricket
instruction well up, and, for example, the saintly work of the English
Schools' Cricket Association deserves much credit.

However, a more basic question is whether education and cricket should go
together as such 'David and Jonathan' bosom pals. It is extraordinary how
often one hears the schools, and even the universities, blamed for England's
impoverished cricket performances. In fact, there is little connection. With
14,000 cricket clubs and with over 500,000 players, and with highly sophisticated schemes for children and youth, there is, as several commentators,
including Micky Stewart, have urged, no problem about the proportion of
people, including young people, playing official cricket. The problem lies
perhaps more in the standards in the higher reaches of the game, where we
have no equivalent of the upper crust 'state' or 'province' preparation for Test
cricket which stands so many other international squads in such good stead.

More graphically, sagacious John Arlott spotted the answer as long ago as
1977: 'when it is asked, where is the former cricket talent, the answer is all

too obvious. It lies in the young men who are playing soccer for far more money than is paid to cricketers', a dramatic reversal in such fortunes from the previous generations. An intriguing cameo was played out a year or two back in the worthy township of Stretford. At precisely the same time at the two Old Traffords, two stars were requesting big rises: the cricketer, Andy Flintoff, wanted, and did not obtain, something approaching £50,000 a year; the footballer, Roy Keane was awarded more than £50,000 a week.

The point is rather to analyse the creation of a climate, through the assault on our senses over a critical hundred-year period of schoolboy tales, with cricket dauntlessly in the van, which makes it possible even for that question about schools' cricket and Test results to be posed by reasonable people. Is it really the task of the £10bn plus education industry, with its 10,000 places of business, over a million employees, and some 9 million customers, to invest time and money in finding eleven young men to play cricket for England? A more rational physical education regime would, and now, in many places, does, offer a wide gamut of activities - dare one entitle it a 'comprehensive' range of sports? - so that, for present health and future leisure pursuit, a large majority of children might find something of value.

As is well-known, there had been a close association of Muscular Christianity and cricket. Sermons and school hymns - 'God give us bases to guard and beleaguer' or 'And be faithful to the willow as your fathers were of yore' - were once awash with cricketing simile and homily. Around cricket's Golden Age, in the twenty years before the outbreak of war in 1914, it appears that Christianity is more often used as a metaphor for cricket than *vice versa*. Because of this, cricket was believed to be character-building, a worthy and necessary preparation for the game of life. This idea is famously embodied in Henry Newbolt's poem *Vitai Lampada*, where the schoolboy rallies the ranks when 'the Gatling's jammed and the colonel's dead', just as he had responded to the cry 'play up, play up and play the game', when, 'with ten to win and the last man in' and on 'a bumpy pitch and a blinding light', that same rallying call had worked the oracle and now is faithfully inscribed on the wall surrounding Lord's.

Unfortunately, this was and is not fully tenable as a psychological device, for character-building is a much more complex and cyclic process. The theory of the transfer of training - the idea, for instance, that by becoming a good school cricket captain, a schoolboy might become a good subaltern - has been shown to be somewhat fallacious. Cricket, like any other game or activity, is a vehicle by and upon which characteristics are exhibited and, for better or for worse, maybe reinforced. Thus the youth whose background and make-up include qualities of leadership will make them manifest both as cricket captain and army officer. The one does not produce the other.

It has to be said that, at all levels of cricket, there have been cheats, and the gambling scandals of the last years are but further evidence of this. Cricket does not cure fraudsters of cheating by appealing to hidden finer instincts; it merely provides them with another opportunity to practise their chiselling skills. In a phrase, cricket can build bad as well as good character. A reverse analogue might help to clarify the point. Many people have observed that lots of musicians wear glasses, and it was commonly believed that this was the consequence of them straining their eyes through staring at minuscule musical scores, often in the twilight zone of an orchestra pit. The opposite, in fact, is nearer the truth. Musicians are frequently the people who, because they have weak eyes, opt for a skill or pastime in which sharp eyesight is not crucial, often turning their backs on games like cricket, where it is. Cricket, like music, is a channel for, rather than a moulder of, qualities and character. Indeed, the most up to date research, a recent New Zealand report, concluded: 'our study does not support the view that involvement in sporting activity is a panacea for delinquent behaviour; if anything it indicates it may exacerbate the problem'.

Of all the connections considered in this study of literature and cricket, there can be little doubt that the main field where there has been significant social effect has been where schoolboy stories, with cricket an important component, has had great influence on the national mind-set. The chief thrust of this involved argument has been to scrutinise the cultural ambience, primarily evoked by schoolboy literature, in which cricket came to be granted such a high ethical profile in our schooling system, and to raise a question or two about whether that has been justified. The educationist, P.W.Musgrove, in his 1986 study, *From Brown to Bunter; the life and death of the school story*, urges the notion that this literature embraced 'a wonderful myth (that) had immense implications for the new state secondary schools...no other kind of school has had the benefit of such propaganda.'

Where surely an educational service was required that was wedded to openness, in terms of community involvement, and plurality, in terms of the differing needs of so many youngsters, the nation has had to struggle with its opposite: a traditional system founded in seclusion of style and singularity of content. Such may have been the confusion of the illusion of Greyfriars with the reality of the downtown secondary modern school that school cricket may have been, in the words of a famous definition of education, one of the artificial pearls thrown before real swine.

Footnote: some of the material in this chapter was used in a talk given by the author to the Cricket Society in London, 19 November, 1996, and on a subsequent article, *A Bumping Pitch and a Blinding Light; the influence of schoolboy literature on education and cricket in Cricket Lore* vol.2 no.10, 1997)

Chapter 18

EXTRAS AND SUNDRIES

If one pursues the topic of cricket and schoolboy literature, intriguing odd-ities may be revealed. For instance, Patsy Hendren, hitherto noted more for his bat than his pen, wrote at least three schoolboy stories, in the *Boys' Friend Library* and the *Popular* and *Chums* comics. Closer scrutiny suggests that all were 'ghosted' by one Alfred Edgar, hitherto noted more for his pen than his bat. During a fifteen year period, from about 1921 onwards, he wrote a huge amount of juvenile literature, including many Sexton Blake stories, before moving on, under the pen-name of Barry Lyndon, to become a playwright and screen-play writer (for instance, *The Amazing Dr Clitterhouse*, *The Man from Half-Moon Street* and the film version of Mrs Belloc Lowndes' *The Lodger*).

Wally Hammond was another. He wrote, ostensibly, for *Modern Boy*, but he, too, had a literary phantom, in the ethereal shape of F.T.Bolton, a promi-nent Fleet Street operator, who concentrated on acting as the shadow scribe for sporting stars, including, it is believed, Gilbert Jessop, in respect of his tales in *The Boys' Friend Weekly*. In that same dimension of spectral author-ship, made manifest to the physical world, like all these facts, through the medium of W.O.G.Lofts and D.J.Ardley, in their book, *The Men behind Boy's Fiction* (1970), Jack Hobbs supposedly wrote a story for Chums. It was, however, Sydney Horler, whose serial 'Goal' in *The Football Weekly* was pub-lished as a novel, proving that, in such cases, the pen is mightier than the bat.

Another famous cricketer to float before the eyes of the schoolboy story researcher is Archie MacLaren, and, although there are no claims that he actually wrote any such tales, there is a slim and curious link between that noble batsman and Billy Bunterdom. The story begins with MacLaren entering into partnership with John Nix Pentelow who, under no less than eight pen-names, wrote hundreds of ripping yarns. Unlike many of A.C.MacLaren's cricketing alliances, this one was doomed to failure. All would agree that the signs were not propitious. In his enjoyable biography of A.C.MacLaren, *Archie*, published in 1981, Michael Down lists among MacLaren's ventures: journalism, broadcasting, advertising, hotel ownership, bloodstock agency, banking, cricket equipment (including pneumatic pads, and bats made from imported Spanish willow) whisky sales, motor cars sales,

Hollywood film extra, secretaryships (to Ranji and as assistant secretary at Old Trafford), school-teaching and lecturing, cricket film hire, cricket coaching and management, as well as cricket magazine ownership. He concludes, 'it can be honestly said that not one of these ventures was ever remotely successful'.

Michael Down records how, among the lengthy list of Archie MacLaren's hapless business schemes, was the notion of a cricketing magazine, *The World of Cricket*, in line of descent from the long-running, but fading, *Cricket: a Weekly Record of the Game*. Founded in 1882, with the celebrated sports administrator, Charles Alcock, as editor, it had been acquired by J.N.Pentelow, a regular contributor to the magazine, just prior to the first world war. Pentelow himself took over the editorship, and, in 1914, he formed his liaison with Archie MacLaren in an attempt to boost sales. When he acquired the paper, its sales were about half the required break-even point of 5000, and, although there were occasional good times, circulation slipped towards the 2000 mark. The cricketer was described in the first issue as editor, with Pentelow the assistant, but, unsurprisingly, most of the work, both editorial and production, fell upon the assistant, and the plan foundered after a year. No great shakes as a businessman, Pentelow was left with a mountain of debts, and, in Michael Down's phrase, 'MacLaren's characteristic unreliability with money - the details of the affair have even been described as 'sordid' - left Pentelow very much in the lurch'. According to the unfortunate Pentelow, 'I ran it at a heavy loss, and MacLaren let me down so badly that the loss was doubled'. Elsewhere he wrote 'I have put £1000 into the paper...the continual disappointments sour me'.

One element that scarcely helped was MacLaren's suggestion that the publication of the magazine be halted, despite the fact that subscriptions had been paid, because of the onset of the 1914/18 War. Many will recall that MacLaren adopted a most jingoistic attitude to the war, and, initially in concert with Captain Gilbert Jessop, Lieutenant MacLaren of the Royal Army Service Corps proved to be a most vigorous recruiting officer, especially in the Manchester area. Everything had to stop for war. MacLaren also used *The World of Cricket* to advance his staunchly chauvinist opinions. Readers seeking a little sporting solace were startled to find the Kaiser described in one issue as 'that crowned madman' guilty of 'insane lust for dominion', and, in the next issue, as 'the hog in armour'. Until his death during the next war, aged 72 in 1944, Archie MacLaren was never really to enjoy decent financial solidity.

The fiasco bore onerously on John Pentelow, so much so that he aged prematurely, exhibiting the classic symptoms of white hair, bowed posture and wrinkled face within weeks of his disappointment. His deafness, and his refusal to acknowledge the disability, contributed. Softly spoken himself, he would often break into another's conversation, usually with a cricketing anecdote, and the offices where he worked are said to have echoed with the shouts of frustrated colleagues unable to communicate with their chain-smoking companion.

J.N.Pentelow, a true expert on cricket, was the subject of a devotedly researched and sympathetically drawn essay by the redoubtable Irving Rosenwater, one of the great personalities of the world of cricketing research ('J.N.Pentelow; a Biographical Inquiry' in *The Journal of the Cricket Society*, vol.4, no.2, Spring 1969, and also published privately as a discrete essay) Born in St Ives, Huntingdonshire, in 1872, J.N.Pentelow began writing at the early age of fifteen, and thus wrote for and was influenced by the rather more piously inclined Victorian breed of schoolboy yarn authors. He had written, *inter alia, for the Captain and Pluck* before World War I, as well as occasional pieces in the cricketing press, a mixture that served him reasonably well until the dissolution of the MacLaren partnership, at which point he really had to toil as a writer to keep the creditors at bay.

While Archie MacLaren harangued the nation's youth and called them to glory, in 1916 J.N.Pentelow took on the war-time editorship of *The Magnet* and *The Gem*, thereby ensuring that the boys of Greyfriars and St. Jim's kept up their quota of spiffing adventures. He also acted as what was known as a 'substitute' writer, filling in with stories under the by-line of the usual author, quite a usual convention for those times. He did this for two reasons. One was because the stories were sometimes in short supply, and there were even examples of tales being scribbled in the trenches of Flanders: the other was because he desperately needed the cash to pay off the MacLaren-oriented debts. After the war, he edited Marvel, until it vanished, *Boy's Realm* and *Sport and Adventure*, as well as the *Boy's Realm Football and Sport*, the *Robin Hood* and the *Prairie* 'Libraries', that is, special series of magazine-type stories. As Madge North, he wrote for *Schoolgirls' Weekly*, the *Schoolgirls' Own Annual* and - Judy Gray of Newcombe House School - *Schoolfriend*. He was truly a unisex author. He died, still with financial anxieties, aged 59, in Carshalton, Surrey, in 1931.

The judicious Padwick, the essential cricketing bibliography, lists twenty-

one entries for J.N.Pentelow, although his overall output, some of it anony-
mously published, was enormous. These twenty-one items consist of about
half non-fictional publications, like the *Marvel* 1921 supplements, *Who's
Who in the Cricketing World* and *Australian Cricket Teams in England*, and
half fiction. Most of these latter are stories published by the *Boys' Friend
Library* under the pseudonym of Richard Randolph, and their titles are
redolent of the genre - for instance, *Smith of Rocklandshire, For Carden and
the County, Good Enough for England.* Cardenshire, along with
Rocklandshire, add further shires to the fictional geography of the county
championship; and, in June 1927, J.C.Squire, founder of the Invalids, wrote
a fond and amusing review of *Good Enough for England* in *The Observer*
newspaper. Yet again, hearty thanks are due to Peter Wynne-Thomas, who
kindly provided a copy of that piece. Jack Squire came across the fourpenny
book on the book-stall of Godalming Station, where 'curiosity was violently aroused' by the 'lurid cover' showing a young cricketer reeling, as he
approached the pavilion from the wicket, whilst 'over the window-still there
leaned a sombreroed and red-beared man blazing a revolver (held in the left
hand) at him.' J.C.Squire chose for his review the not inapt headline
'Brighter Cricket.'

For J.N.Pentelow, a gentlemanly figure, compared by his colleagues, in that
somewhat in-bred world, as akin to Dr. Locke, the fatherly if firm headmaster of Greyfriars, there were two people with whom Carden's creator
failed to form a solid relationship. One was Archie MacLaren; the other was
Charles Hamilton, the legendary founder of Greyfriars and its paternalistic
head, although there is some evidence that their disputes have been exag-
gerated.

The tale, which has some of the flavour of the petty squabbles of their own
fictional pieces, is well told by W.O.G.Lofts and D.J.Adley in *The World of
Frank Richards* (1975). There is some controversy about whether the impoverished Pentelow wrote 'substitute' stories, for which he was paid on top of
his editorial salary, when he had no need, which was Charles Hamilton's version, or whether, John Pentelow's interpretation, Hamilton was asked to do
too much by the bosses of Amalgamated Press, and reserves had to be mustered.

What is certain is that Hamilton, master of the breezy Edwardian argot of
jolly japes, thought all 'substitute' writers were 'duds', and, in particular, he
despised the more insipid and sentimental tones of Pentelow, especially

when the wordage appeared under his own by-line. Moreover, it has been precisely calculated that, for all the 'substitute' writing, Hamilton actually composed 1380 of the 1683 Greyfriars stories published under his pen-name of Frank Richards. On the other hand, it is said that Pentelow, who wrote some 69 of the *Magnet/Gem* stories during the war years, had to add a flavour of authenticity to Hamilton's cricketing dialogue, for Bunter's artistic parent was a little unsure on the finer points, whereas Pentelow wrote with enormous authority on cricket. What is more, his minor characters sometimes scored runs and took wickets, while his heroes were dismissed occasionally for ducks, as happens in the cruel arena of reality.

The final indignity for Charles Hamilton arrived with *Magnet* no.520 in 1918. In a Greyfriars story, written by Pentelow under the name of Frank Richards, he killed off Courtenay of the Sixth in a fire. Readers had been confusing this Courtenay with Frank Courtenay of Highcliffe, another school featured in *The Magnet*, and higher authority had decreed the name-sake's demise forthwith - but nobody thought to consult his creator, who inhabited the world of his characters in much the same way as Charles Dickens had done. He was livid and unforgiving, with poor John Pentelow receiving all the blame.

J.N.Pentelow's career serves as a rather salutary portrayal of the few ups and the many downs of the dozens who committed themselves to boy's fiction, much of it with a statutorily prescribed dosage of cricket The much-burdened Pentelow happened to find himself in close contact and conflict with two of the most famous and, in their own fields, the most self-opinionated and egotistical men of the age, Archie MacLaren and Charles Hamilton. The guilty story of Courtney's consumption by flames was entitled *A Very Gallant Gentleman*, and one may ponder on that title's aptness as an epitaph for Pentelow, the cricket buff, forced to scribble juvenile tales by the hundred to keep the wolf from the door, and of whom it was written by a colleague that his only fault was that he was 'overloaded with good nature'.

If C.B.Fry may justly claim to be the most renowned cricketer amongst occasional writers and Samuel Beckett the most celebrated writer among occasional cricketers, then the cold comfort for J.N.Pentelow may be that he was the most knowledgeable cricket scholar among full-time scribes. Turning from his rather remote and bleakly harassed existence to the glittering world of the screen, there are few rivals for the title of most well-known cricketer among the film-stars. That honour rests with

C.Aubrey Smith.

Cricket and entertainment have enjoyed a lengthy and convivial togetherness, as chapter 15, which included references to cricket in connection with
the cinema, broadcasting and the variety stage, bore plentiful witness.
Nicholas Wanostrocht, the immortal Felix, who lived from 1804 to 1876,
fell into penury and he was stricken by paralysis, or, as he put it with typical good cheer, 'most kindly admonished by God.' As well as being a pioneer
batsman of extraordinary gracefulness, he was inventor, classicist, linguist,
painter and musician - he would conduct the band and play his violin at the
theatrical productions which were the convivial aftermath of the Canterbury
Festival. From 1842 the Canterbury Cricket Week pursued its enthusiastic
career, with the Old Stagers a constituent part.

Among those who in the early decades of the Festival toed the crease by day
and trod the boards by night might be mentioned William Yardley, not least
because of the polished gem of his biography by Grenville Simons, published in 1997. He played cricket as an amateur with W.G.Grace and was a
professional colleague of W.S.Gilbert in the light theatre, thus contriving to
share his two preoccupations with each of their Victorian masters. Closer to
the present day, we find the dapper Basil Foster (1882-1959), one of the
famed Foster brothers of Worcestershire lore, who played seven first-class
matches for Worcestershire and twelve for Middlesex, as well as being an
actor of a rather lightweight charm on the London stage. He made his cricketing debut for Worcestershire in 1902 and his theatrical debut in *Mr Popple
of Ippleton* in 1906 at the Marlborough Theatre. His life is pleasingly recalled
in Jeremy Malies' *Great Characters from Cricket's Golden Age*. We find him
playing for the Actors against the Authors, with some of whom we made
acquaintance in chapters 11 and 12. In one such game, Basil Foster is, by
proxy, caught Winnie-the-Pooh off the bowling of Bertie Wooster.

Basil Foster played for the Thespids, the stage equivalent of J.C.Squire's lit-
erary Invalids. Among the same Thespid ranks were numbered Sir Gerald du
Maurier; Basil Rathbone; Nigel Bruce; the *farceur*, Sir Arthur Pinero (*The
Second Mrs Tanqueray, The Magistrate*); George Robey; George Edwardes
(the king of musical comedy at London's Gaiety Theatre) and Sir Frank
Benson. Lawrence Olivier, Donald Wolfit and Rex Harrison, sons of a later
generation of Thespians, also appeared in the role of cricketer. Arthur Conan
Doyle would have been delighted to learn, perhaps through one of his spir-
itualist contacts, that the classic screen Holmes and Watson duo, Basil

Rathbone and Nigel Bruce - they made their first of several such films in 1939, when they tracked down *The Hound of the Baskervilles* - were actor-cricketers. Stanley Holloway, Alfred Doolittle in *My Fair Lady* on stage and screen, was a Thespid and an MCC member, doubtless acknowledging dubious umpiring decisions with the stoicism shown by Albert's father, when that intrepid child was swallowed by the lion - 'Yon lion's 'et Albert, and 'im in his Sunday clothes, too.'

Although the combined line-up of cricketing actors reads like the sparkling attendance at some gala night or awards ceremony, the cricketing Oscar must still go to C.Aubrey Smith, fortunate in his civilised and fluent biographer, David Rayvern Allen, writer of *Sir Aubrey* in 1982. For Sir Charles Aubrey Smith, born in the City of London in 1863 and dying in Beverley Hills, California in 1948, managed both to captain England at cricket and secure a place in Hollywood history. Successful as a schoolboy at Charterhouse and as a student at Cambridge, he played for Sussex and England. All told, he played 143 first-class matches, as well as hundreds more for Actors' elevens, including the captaincy of the Thespids. He made 2986 first-class runs and took 345 first-class wickets, and skippered England in his sole Test match on the 1888-89 South African tour. He went on the stage on 1892 - 'My God', cried Mrs Patrick Campbell, objecting to playing opposite him, 'I can't possibly act with a cricket bat.' - and later found a bountiful *niche* as an English gent in Hollywood films. Cinema-goers will perhaps remember him - 'He was born to smell of tobacco and Harris tweeds and to wave portentous eyebrows', pronounced *Theatre World* - in such films as *Lives of a Bengal Lancer* (1935), *The Prisoner of Zenda* (1937) and *Rebecca* (1940).

However, cricket fans recollect how he was a founder-member of the Hollywood cricket Club, constructing a tiny morsel of Englishness, a very literary conceit, in the middle of the vigorous American film industry, just when it was at the acme of its tinselly might. Moreover, he was eager, after the manner of the 18th century estate owners finding employment for useful cricketers, to encourage the casting in films of actors with a cricketing pedigree. Desmond Roberts was one example of a cricketer for whom Sir Aubrey found 'bit' parts as a dignified butler or diplomat. Rather better known was H.B.Warner, of whom one critic said he brought 'dignity to a wildly disparate collection of films', including *Lost Horizon* (1937), *The Corsican Brothers* (1941) and *The Ten Commandments* (1956) - Hollywood must have seemed a far cry from his outings with Middlesex 2nd XI.

William Henry Pratt (1887-1969) was another of those Hollywood cricketers. He may have been entered as Boris Karloff on the team-sheet, that
being his screen-name. Although he won lasting and iconic fame as the
Monster in the 1931 film *Frankenstein*, he was a gentle soul at heart, with a
pet pig called Violet. The producer of *Frankenstein*, Carl Laemmle, Jnr., said
Boris Karloff was chosen for the part because 'his eyes mirrored the suffering we needed', a common condition in a cricket lover.

A batting partnership between Colonel Sapt of Ruritania and Mary Shelley's
Monster might bring a gleam to the eye of the comic novelist, Peter
Tinniswood, whose dry, mordant style has made him probably the funniest
story-teller of his generation. This genuine tribute comes with the health
warning of he and I being old school-mates and, in consequence, of sharing
that same resigned view of life that prevails in the east Mersey valley and in
the environs of Manchester. The alarm bell is seriously sounded, for humour
is a highly subjective affair. One was chastened to read a review of Peter
Haining's entertaining anthology, *LBW - Laughter Before Wicket* (2000) by
Murray Hedgcock, a commentator of thoughtful excellence. He evinces little enthusiam for Peter Tinniswood's narratives, preferring the writings of
Eden Philpotts or Stacy Aumonier. Eden Philpotts (1862-1960) is better
known for his Dartmoor-based novels, like *Children of the Mist* (1898), but
he wrote some cricket pieces, such as an *Ethiopian Cricket Match* - my own
copy of this, politically speaking, not too comfortable tale is included in a
1933 anthology, *Cricket Stories*, collected by the early cricket broadcaster,
Howard Marshall. Stacy Aumonier, of slightly later vintage, wrote the perceptively amusing 'the Match', published in the 1929 *Miss Bracegirdle, and
Others*.

Pressing the case for Peter Tinniswood, he made his reputation with his stories of the Brandon family, beginning with a *Touch of Daniel* in 1968. They
were superbly transferred to television in the *I Didn't Know You Cared* series,
somehow linking the stoical Ramsbottoms of the Marriott Edgar mono-
logues, as lugubriously recited by Stanley Holloway, and the Royles,
Caroline Ahearne's row of couch-potatoes. Phlegmatism is all. Nothing must
be allowed to surprise or disconcert. Neither heady bliss nor uncontrolled
woe is permitted. If there is a paradise, it is something like Lancashire heading the county championship and Manchester United holding the
Premiership title, both in perpetuity, the former heavenly prospect, alas,
rather more distant than the latter. Faced with only six months to live, Uncle
Mort is encouraged by his brother-in-law, Les Brandon, 'Well, at least you'll

get a few weeks of the rugby season in before you snuff it'. 'Rugby?' said
Uncle Mort. 'I wouldn't be seen bloody dead on a rugby field.' In the television adaptation Uncle Mort was played by that consummate character
actor, Robin Bailey. And, when Peter Tinniswood's cricket stories were tele-
vised, Robin Bailey reappeared, with a fresh but equally adamantine set of
prejudices, as the Brigadier.

His half a dozen sets of cricket yarns, under such titles as *Tales from the Long
Room* (1981) and *More Tales from the Long Room* (1982), achieved deserved
popularity during the early 1980s. During this study one has had agreeable
cause to advert to the fact that, in effect, cricket is a funny game; from
Charles Dickens to A.G.Macdonnell there have been hilarious moments in
cricket's fiction. However, for sustained laughter, page after page, the
Tinniswood tales offer cricket literature's most entertainingly amusing
sequence. His loyal affection for comparatively unsung but durable cricketers - the Lancashire opening bat, the lugubrious Winston Place, is a special example - and his lovingly careful coinage of names - Cowdrey's Bottom;
the Blessed St. Tony Greig of the Sorrows; the village blacksmith, Gooch;
old Squire Brearley; His Holiness George Pope the First; E.W. 'Gloria'
Swanton; the Dexter Arms, Langridge-on-sea; Cardus-in-Tyldesleydale; the
Trough of Bolus - is reminiscent of Beachcomber, perhaps of Lewis Carroll.
All these inhabitants of and around the village of Witney Scrotum are the
delectable confections of an idiosyncratic, inventive mind, one as well-versed
in the detail of cricket as in the possibilities of language.

The puns are comical in themselves but, more often than not, they carry a
sometimes disturbing hint of truth. In *Surrey County Cricket Club; 150 years,
1845-1995; a Celebration* (1995) on the subject 'Storm in an Armpit', the
Brigadier showed massive disdain for over-arm bowling, the legalisation of
which followed events at the Oval in 1862 when Edgar Willsher was
famously no balled six times for so infringing. Appealing to the theological
tenet that God would not permit over-arm bowling in heaven, the Brigadier
pompously reminds us that 'on the first day He created the sight screen. On
the second and third and fourth he created Mr Raymond Illingworth. On
the fifth He wished he hadn't. And on the sixth he created the tea interval at
Worksop.'

Predictably enough, this imaginative word-spinning embraces literature. In
one of the Long Room tales, *The Boys of Summer*, Peter Tinniswood embarks
on a literary extravaganza of copious and mind-blowing extent. It includes

Brian Brain, author of *Room at the Top*; Denis Amiss and 'his hilarious rib-tickler' *Lucky Jim*; Samuel Beckett's *Waiting for Boycott* and *Crapp's Last Tape*; Edna O'Brien's chronicle of the Essex county team, *The Casualties of Pearce*; Evelyn Waugh's 'savagely satirical bowlers' coaching manual', *Put Out More Faggs*, to say nothing of 'his affectionate monograph on Mr Robin Marlar', *The Loved One*; Ernest Hemingway's sensitive Kentish tribute, *Farewell to Ames*; and 'the incidence of litotes in the collected works of Lord Henry Blofeld', plus, for good measure, extracts from a play, *The Umpire*, by Harold Pinter, brother of the former Burnley and England centre-forward, Ray, and from the Barbara Cartland novel, *Bowling the Maiden Over*.

Yet again may be witnessed the cultural overlap of cricket and literature. Edmund Blunden, in his *Cricket Country*, chose a team of poets, the Paladins, captained by Siegfried Sassoon and including Lord Byron, while, a little more realistically, Alec Waugh, writing in *The Cricketer*, selected a writers' eleven, with Arthur Conan Doyle batting at number four and Rupert Brooke last man in. Even Kingsley Amis, in his *Take a Girl Like You*, the cricket content of which was examined in chapter 14, picked an eccentric team. While Patrick Standish anxiously awaits the arrival of Jenny Bunn for what he hopes will prove an earth-moving occasion, he prepares a team-sheet inspired by a book, *Twelve Bad Men*: as well as characters in the novel he dislikes, he includes Sir Malcolm Sergeant, John Milton, Selwyn Lloyd and, at twelfth man, Beethoven.

It is an honoured tradition. Some years ago I compiled for *Drumbeat*, the magazine of the London Savage Club, and on behalf of the literature category of that exhilarating fraternity, the following eleven, later reprinted in *Cricket Lore*, that endeavoured to build a bridge between first-class cricket and first-rate literature:

Thomas (Jack) Hobb(e)s	Surrey and England
Matthew (John) Arnold	Hampshire
Frank (Viv) Richards	West Indies
Evelyn (Steve) Waugh	Australia
Sir Thomas (R.E.S) Wyatt (capt.)	Warwicks., Worcs. and England
Arthur (Keith) Miller	Australia
Ngaio (Rodney) Marsh (wkt.kpr.)	Australia
G.B. (Alfred) Shaw	Notts and England
H.G. ('Bomber') Wells	Gloucester and England
Samuel (Ian) Johnson	Australia
Samuel (Harold) Butler	Notts and England

Published initially under the questioning heading of 'is Henry Fielding?', answer came there from a Savage member in the arts category, the much-lamented Pat Adams, the authority on the sports cartoonist, Tom Webster, as well as an adept exponent in his own right. Entitled, 'No, but Phil May', he selected a strong team of cartoonists on that same principle. Choosing specialist teams has long been a time-passer for cricket buffs during long winter evenings when there is no cricket and long summer days when the same circumstance applies. It is heartily recommended, for it demonstrates the richness of both the cricket and the language. However, the rules of 'Theme-teams' are extremely strict. The cricketer must be first-class and the team must be properly constituted, that is, it must have responsible openers; two or three other batsmen; a recognised captain; if possible, an all-round-er, a rational spread of bowlers and, most difficult of all, an identifiable wick-et keeper.

Contributors to *Cricket Lore* have supplied several samples. Among person-al preferences might be cited the *Coronation Street XI* that has Ted 'Liz' McDonald bowling, Richard 'Ken' Barlow batting and George 'Vera' Duckworth keeping wicket; or the Presidents' XI versus the Prime Ministers' XI that has Sir Stanley 'Andrew' Jackson, G.S. 'Bill' Clinton and Fred 'Harry' Tru(e)man facing Downing Street's finest of Ian 'Lord' Salisbury and Jack 'Lord John' Russell. Laftershire, like many a genuine outfit, was no more than a bunch of comedians, with Norman 'Over the Garden Wall' Godfrey Evans keeping wicket; 'the Cheeky Chappie', Max/Keith Miller providing the all-round fireworks and with the opening bowlers being the Middlesex pair, (John) Flanagan and (Gubby) Allen. Drawing on the pretti-ness or the ugliness of the very names, there were Beauties - Grace, Virgin Darling, Mead, Love etc. - and the Beasts - Trumper, Crapp, Bastard, Belcher, Bottom, Woof *et al.*

For sheer ingenuity the late Derek Lodge, who was so civilised a man as well as a most erudite cricket statistician, takes the tea interval biscuit. He found an eleven in *Good King Wenceslas* - and then had the wit to call them the Bohemians. Finally, there was the pleasant accident of the Sylvestershire bat-ting-order. If numbers seven to eleven - Warwick (Louis) Armstrong, John (Sir Harry) Mortimer, Wes (Henry) Hall, Curtly (Bert) Ambrose, Malcolm (Jack) Hi(y)lton - bowled in that sequence for the band-leaders' team, their styles would be: Slow, Slow, Quick, Quick, Slow.

Enough. Surely that must be enough to persuade of the infinite possibilities of cricket, literature and language. Except that there is just one more curio. For a relatively brief period, from somewhere at the end of the 19th to somewhere part way through the 20th centuries, it became more of a habit for writers to be identified by their initials. It was H.G.Wells, H.E.Bates, T.S.Eliot, L.P.Hartley, A.E.Houseman, J.B.Priestley, R.C.Sherriff P.G.Wodehouse - readers scarcely knew their actual forenames - where it had not been C.J.H.Dickens or E.J.Bronte. Of course, the formula was not, in either usage, an exclusive one, but, for a spell, there does appear to have been a keenness for initials, which, latterly, with the extensive familiarity in the use of forenames, has faded.

The ranks of first-class cricketers have also been blessed with an abundance of initials, as a million almanacs and score-cards bear testimony. Whether the two practices encouraged each other is difficult to assess, although there is some additional evidence that, during the same period, this was also the protocol in some professions. The music halls boasted no less than three G.Hs; Messrs Chirgwin, MacDermott and Elliott, the last with his wildly politically incorrect bill-matter, 'the Chocolate-coloured Coon.' Whatever the parallels, it is a phenomenon that produced the closing story in these essays on the connections between cricket and literature.

Alan Alexander Milne, himself the proud owner of a brace of well-known initials, was born at Kilburn (in which district his father was head of Henley House School, where H.G.Wells was an assistant teacher for a time) in 1882; he went to Westminster School, where he played for the school eleven, and studied mathematics at Trinity College, Cambridge; he served as a signals officer with the Royal Warwickshire Regiment in the 1914-1918 war, and he embarked on a literary career. He wrote plays, like *The Dover Road* (1922), and stories, including cricket-oriented ones, like *The Day's Play*, a mildly diverting account of taking a team to play at Chartleigh and holding an impromptu selection committee meeting on the train. He also played cricket for various authors' elevens. He died at Hartfield in Sussex in 1956.

Despite all his efforts with *Punch* and with detective stories and so on, he only really found fame with his children's tales; even his most successful play was *Toad of Toad Hall*, first produced in 1929 but much-revived, based on Kenneth Grahame's 1908 children's classic, *The Wind in the Willows*. In five short years, between 1924 and 1928, he published *When we were Very Young, Winnie-the-Pooh, Now we are Six* and *The House at Pooh Corner*. This was a charming and enduring collection of tales and poems about animated nursery toys. Whether, given his cricketing interest, what a standard authority refers to as 'Pooh's greediness, Eeyore's misanthropy, Tigger's bounciness or Piglet's timidity' may be identified with any first-class cricketers is a matter for private conjecture. The illustrations of E.P.Shepard, who also provided some of the drawings for *The Wind in the Willows*, boosted Pooh and the others up the steps toward the plinths of immortality. A.A.Milne was influenced by J.M.Barrie, bringing to his writing what the critic, E.V.Knox, called 'the weighing of much laughter with a little pathos, and, if need be, a fairy wand.'

Like the comedian anxious to play Hamlet, A.A.Milne came to resent his own triumph, believing that it distracted from his work for adults. This may, in turn, have further undermined his tenuous relationship with his son, the original for Christopher Robin. All is revealed in *Beyond the World of Pooh, selections from the memoirs of Christopher Robin*, edited by A.R.Melrose in 2000 and embracing the testimony of Leslie Milne, A.A.Milne's daughter-in-law. Christopher Robin Milne died, aged 76, in 1996, having been for much of his adult life a book-seller in Devon, haunted to the end by that cherubic infant, who seemed forever to be either kneeling at the foot of the bed or visiting the Palace with Alice. A somewhat unemotional man, A.A.Milne gave little comfort to his son, in an era when, in upper middle-class homes, the nursery and then the boarding school institutionalised parent-child aloofness.

'My father's heart', said the son, 'remained buttoned up all through his life.' It was, says his wife, Leslie Milne, 'a curious relationship, as neither knew the other very well' and Christopher 'spent the rest of his life fighting for a separate identity.' There is the scrap of a letter from him, bravely biting the lip at preparatory school, anxious to please his distant father; 'I am playing cricket (net practice) nearly every day here.' Strange are the ways of parenting among some children's writers: it is understood that Enid Blyton left something to be desired in this regard, while Kenneth Grahame's son, Alistair, to whom the yarns of Mole and Ratty were first related, committed suicide aged 19.

Christopher Robin Milne was, indeed, the object of much cruel and insensitive amusement at school and, even as a bookseller, customers remained obsessed with his *alter ego*. The problem was magnified by his father's decision to insist on the regular use of two forenames. Either Christopher or Robin might have been bearable, but the two in harness proved insufferable, which leads to the reason why this section might be sub-titled, 'Now We Hit Six.'

We have all heard of the consciously designed M.C.C of Lord Cowdrey's birthright or the Neil Harvey of N.H.Fairbrother, the stalwart little Lancashire left-hander. We have all, that is, heard of the success stories, where doting parents have cherished ambitions for their prattling babes. We hear less of the failures, where, for instance, the child named Donald Bradman Bloggs grows up to be a serial killer, a Manchester City supporter or the treasurer of his local Conservative party. Something like that happened with Christopher Robin. A.A.Milne hoped that his son would play for England and speculated that, after the fashion of W.G.Grace or C.B.Fry or A.E.Stoddart or A.C.MacLaren or A.W.Carr or D.R.Jardine, two first names would be of assistance. As St. Matthew teacheth, 'for many are called but few are chosen.' He may have been called C.R.Milne, but he wasn't chosen.

The nicety of the famous author, who utilised the formula A.A.Milne, desperately wishing for his son to evolve into the famous cricketer, C.R.Milne, is just one last tiny example of the intermesh of literature and cricket. Unluckily, there was never to be that ultimate stanza:

> Hush, hush; silence the hordes;
> Christopher Robin is playing at Lord's.

Footnote: varied 'Theme-teams' are to be found in *Cricket Lore*, vol.2, nos.2, 7 and 8; and vol. 3, nos.3,4 and 7